Presented to:

_____

From:

_____

Date:

_____

❖

FATHERS OF
INFLUENCE

Inspiring Stories of Men Who Made a Difference
in Their Children and Their World

HONOR **B** BOOKS

Inspiration and Motivation for the Seasons of Life

COOK COMMUNICATIONS MINISTRIES
Colorado Springs, Colorado • Paris, Ontario
KINGSWAY COMMUNICATIONS LTD
Eastbourne, England

Honor Books® is an imprint of
Cook Communications Ministries, Colorado Springs, CO 80918
Cook Communications, Paris, Ontario
Kingsway Communications Ltd., Eastbourne, England

Fathers of Influence: Inspiring Stories of Men Who Made a Difference in Their Children and Their World © 2006 by BORDON BOOKS

First printing, 2006
Printed in the United States of America

1 2 3 4 5 6 7 8 9 10

Product developed by Bordon Books
Manuscript written and compiled by Matthew Kinne in association with Snapdragon Group℠ Editorial Services

ISBN 978-1-56292-883-4

Contents

Fathers of Influence from the Bible

Introduction

Our fathers, while they can be as nurturing and gentle as our mothers, have been entrusted by God with a far different task. Theirs is the responsibility to help us make something of ourselves, to teach us by word and example how to be strong, hardworking, trustworthy, responsible men and women of character. Even for those who succeed only in part, the results can be astonishing, influencing many generations.

The fathers included in this book, *Fathers of Influence*, are men who have changed their worlds, contributing significantly to the accomplishments of their children. Although some of these men had no biological children of their own, they led movements that had a dramatic impact upon their generation. None of these men is perfect, but each exemplifies a notable, timeless child-rearing principle. We hope that learning these principles will allow you to guide your own children as they strive to reach their full, God-given potential.

Be inspired as you read about these remarkable men. Then set out to be to your own children—a father of influence.

Nate Saint

1923–1956

Steve Saint. Though Steve Saint was only five when his missionary father, Nate Saint, was speared to death by the Waodani tribe of Ecuador, his father's sacrifice influenced him not only to return to live among them but also to forgive and love the man responsible.

Nathaniel Saint loved to fly. He took flying lessons in high school and then used his skills to serve his country during World War II. Following combat, he enrolled in Wheaton College, but the call of the air and the call of Christ were stronger than his desire for a degree. He joined Mission Aviation Fellowship, and in 1948, he and his wife, Marjorie, went to work in Ecuador, establishing an airbase at an abandoned oil exploration camp. From that simple post, they supplied local missionaries with medicines, mail, and other necessities.

In 1950, their son, Steve, was born in Ecuador. By the time Steve could walk, he'd go out to the bank of dirt that separated his house from the sand and gravel airstrip and watch his dad take off into the jungle. Then he'd wait for his father to return. Even as a small boy, Steve seemed to sense the dangers inherent in his father's mission.

In September of 1955, three teammates—Jim Elliot, Ed McCully, and Peter Fleming—joined Nate in his effort to reach the Waodani tribe (or Auca settlement) he had found deep in the jungles while searching in the air. Roger Youderian joined them a short time later. Nate knew the tribe was isolated from the modern world, but more important, he knew they didn't know about Jesus and His saving power. The group devised a slow, methodological plan to reach out to the tribe in friendship. First, Nate and the team lowered gifts, including machetes and clothing, to the Waodani in a bucket tied to the plane. The tribe showed excitement about receiving the gifts, and soon gave gifts of their own. After three months of this give and take, the missionaries decided it was time to meet the people on the ground.

> *[Jesus said,] "Love your enemies and pray for those who persecute you."*
>
> **MATTHEW 5:44** AB

On January 3, 1956, they set up camp four miles from the Waodani settlement, using a portion of a riverside beach as a landing strip. The initial personal contact was encouraging—deceptively so. Five days later, the entire team was killed on the beach when armed Waodani met them with thrusting spears and swinging machetes. When the news of the massacre reached base, Steve's mother had the impossible task of telling her son that his father would never return home again.

Steve's aunt Rachel was undeterred and unfazed by the murder of her little brother and the other members of the faithful group of missionaries. She continued to live among the Waodani, teaching them about the trail of *Waengongi* (God) and the saving love of *Itota,* His only Son. In fact, by 1964, most of the Waodani had become Christians.

From the time of his father's death, Steve's aunt felt spiritually bonded to the tribe and returned to Ecuador to continue evangelizing them. Steve witnessed his aunt's work among the tribe and was convinced of the authenticity and genuine nature of their faith. One amazing day, there in the river at the place where his father died, Kimo and Syawi, two of the warriors who participated in the murders, baptized Steve. Following the example set by his father, mother, and aunt, the fourteen-year-old boy never thought to hate them.

Soon after, Steve returned to America and didn't return to Ecuador until 1994 for the funeral of his beloved aunt Rachel, who had remained among the Waodani all her life. After Rachel died, the tribe asked Steve and his family to come and live with them. They wanted Steve to teach them how to interact with the encroaching outside world. Steve initially didn't want to do it. He had launched several successful businesses back home. Yet after prayer and consideration, he and his family moved to live in the Ecuadorian jungle for a year and a half. Steve's goal was to teach the tribe how to survive in the modern world, but he discovered it was he who needed to learn the most lessons.

Through living the simple Waodani lifestyle and receiving the unconditional love they offered as a result of their transformed hearts, Steve became more integrated than ever into the lives of the tribesmen. On this second visit, he befriended and found a father figure in Mincaye, the very tribesman who had killed his father.

In his book *End of the Spear*, Steve writes, "I can't imagine not loving Mincaye, a man who has adopted me as his own, and the other Waodani. What the Waodani meant for evil, God used for good. Given the chance to rewrite the story, I would not be willing to change it. I have personally paid a high price for what happened, but I have also had a front-row seat as the rest of the story has been unfolding for half a century. I believe only God could have fashioned such an incredible story from such a tragic event. Because those five men were willing to die, everyone else in the tribe had a chance to live."

Today, Steve and Mincaye travel around the world telling their amazing story of God's transforming love. Steve is the founder of I-TEC, an organization that develops new technologies to equip indigenous people as they strive to meet the needs of their own communities.

By reaching out to a dangerous group of people that didn't know Jesus, Nate Saint paid the ultimate price—his life. But through this and subsequent efforts, the Waodani tribe not only became followers of God, but also family to his son, Steve. By loving his enemy, Nate Saint taught his son and multitudes of others that there is no price too steep to pay in order to reach those who need the redeeming love of Christ.

A Father of Influence teaches his children to love and forgive their enemies.

George H. W. Bush

1924–

George W. Bush. By living a life of faith and modeling
professional excellence, George Herbert Walker Bush
became the first U.S. president since John Adams to raise a
son who would also fill the office of president.

D ays after four-year-old Robin Bush died from leukemia,
George H. W. Bush and his family struggled to put their
lives back together. One Friday night, they decided to
attend a local high school football game to take their minds off
their troubles. Seven-year-old George W. Bush stood on his tiptoes
in the bleachers to see the game and blurted out, "Dad, I wish I was
Robin."

Visibly disturbed, the elder Bush replied, "Why would you say
that, George?"

George explained, "Because Robin is in heaven. She can probably see the game better from up there than we can from down
here." As the elder Bush gave his son a smile and a hug, he must
have been relieved to realize that he and Barbara had been able to
effectively convey concepts to George W.—spiritual concepts like
heaven and the loving care of a heavenly Father—concepts that
allowed him to accept his sister's death with hope and serenity.

George H. W. decided not to attend college right after high
school, but instead, joined the navy to serve alongside his fellow
Americans during World War II. On his eighteenth birthday he
enlisted and ten months later became the youngest navy pilot com-
missioned in war.

After the war, H. W. enrolled at Yale University and excelled in every activity he undertook. He joined the Delta Kappa Epsilon fraternity and was elected president. He also captained the Yale baseball team, played first baseman, and participated in the first College World Series.

While still attending Yale, George Herbert Walker Bush and Barbara Pierce met and married in Connecticut. A year later on July 6, 1946, George Walker Bush was born. According to Barbara, her husband is the only man she ever kissed; and no matter where he traveled during his expansive political career, he always called his wife and they prayed together before going to sleep. In all, H. W. and Barbara raised six children.

As a young boy, George W.'s neighborhood buddies marveled at how H. W. could catch a baseball behind his back. They all tried to imitate the feat with varying degrees of success. Father and son would play catch, and George W. remembers a defining moment in his development when his father told him, "Son, you've arrived. I can throw it to you as hard as I want." As George W. grew, he would go on to share his father's love for baseball, and he eventually became co-owner of the major league team the Texas Rangers.

Following college, H. W. moved his family to Midland, Texas, where he ventured into the highly speculative Texas oil exploration business with considerable success. He created Zapata Oil in 1953 and secured a position with Dresser Industries.

In Midland, the Bush family attended the First Presbyterian Church, even though H. W. was reared Episcopalian. He felt it was important for the family to worship together, and that meant someone crossing denominational lines. He was quite willing to do the moving and did much more than settle into a pew. Perhaps inspired by his parents' habit of reading a Bible story at the kitchen table every night after dinner, H. W. became a regular Sunday school teacher.

In 1959, the Bush family moved to Houston so H. W. could be closer to his oil rigs. This saddened George W. and his siblings, but it broadened their horizons. New friends, sights, and challenges awaited them, not the least of which was a new school.

In the 1960s and 1970s, H. W. Bush devoted a great deal of his time to seeking public office and holding government-appointed positions. In 1964, he ventured into conventional politics by running for the U.S. Senate. After a difficult contest, he gained the Republican nominee for the office, running against the incumbent Democratic Senator Ralph Yarborough. H. W. lost in a Democratic landslide but ran considerably ahead of the GOP presidential nominee, Senator Barry Goldwater of Arizona. He didn't give up on elective politics, and was elected in 1966 and 1968 to the House of Representatives from the 7th District of Texas. In 1970, he relinquished his House seat to seek the Republican senatorial nomination, but lost the election. During this time of victory and defeat, H. W. taught his children a great deal about perseverance and the ability to bounce back from setbacks, insights that would prove invaluable to George W. in future years.

Train up a child in the way he should go: and when he is old, he will not depart from it.

Pʀᴏᴠᴇʀʙs 22:6 ᴋᴊᴠ

Throughout the seventies, H. W. Bush held a series of offices that led to his eligibility for the White House. His posts included United States Ambassador to the United Nations, Chairman of the Republican National Committee, Chief of the U.S. Liaison Office in the People's Republic of China, and Director of Central Intelligence. Bush has since commented that he did not particularly enjoy this string of jobs, saying he never wanted to be a "career bureaucrat." However, had Bush not received this succession of appointments after his Senate defeat in 1970, it is unlikely he would have risen to a level of national prominence in politics.

During this time, George W. was busy exploring his freedoms as a young adult. Like his father, he attended Yale, but was not the consummate achiever his father had been. Instead, he was known as a party boy and heavy drinker. He calls the early '70s his "nomadic" period. Still he was about to earn his M.B.S. from Harvard Business School in 1975.

Following in his father's footsteps, George W. then decided to try his hand in the oil business. He returned to Midland and formed an independent oil and gas exploration company that he called Arbusto (the Spanish word for "bush"). Then in 1977, George W. married Laura Welch, a former teacher and librarian. He sometimes says marrying her was the best decision he ever made. In 1981, Laura gave birth to twin daughters, Barbara and Jenna.

Throughout the years, H. W.'s love for his son never wavered. By the early '80s, George was still drinking, but knew he needed to change his life if he was going to be a good citizen, son, and father. One day on H. W.'s invitation, Billy Graham came to visit the family vacation home in Kennebunkport, Maine. Billy and George W. walked the beach and Graham pointedly asked if he was "right with God." George W. responded, "No, but I want to be." There on the beach, he rededicated his life to Christ.

Shortly after his fortieth birthday in July 1986, George W. quit drinking altogether and turned to his wife's Methodist faith. He also became noticeably more serious and driven professionally—in part to help in his father's run for president in 1988. Drawn by the challenge of national politics, George W. moved with his family to Washington DC in the fall of 1987 to work on H. W.'s successful campaign. Though George W. had no official title on the campaign staff, he was his father's most trusted confidant and a major point of contact for his colleagues. He also became known as a talented speaker with appeal for Christian conservatives.

H. W. returned his son's kindness and throughout his twelve years as vice president and president, H. W. was never too busy to take a call from George or write him lengthy letters.

This father-son respect continued right on through the years until George W. ran for president himself. At the start of the Republican convention in August 2000, in response to President Bill Clinton allegedly calling George W. a "daddy's boy," the younger George looked toward his father's seat and proclaimed before a national audience, "I am *proud* to be your son." And, at the dedication of his father's presidential library, George W. called H. W. "the world's greatest father."

In 2001, George H. W. Bush became the first president since John Adams to be father of another president, a fitting tribute to a man who lived an example before his children that emphasized hard work, determination, and faith. Prayers, Bible study, and love reigned throughout the Bush household. Even as George W. momentarily left faith in God as a young man, his father's instruction echoed inside his heart, challenging him to come back home to the faith. Because George H. W. Bush modeled Christ to George W. and his family, George W. returned to the faith of his father and went on to hold that faith and proclaim it boldly, even while serving in the highest office in the land.

**A Father of Influence leaves a legacy of faith
to his children.**

Martin Luther King Sr.

1897–1984

Martin Luther King Jr. Ebenezer Baptist Church pastor Martin Luther King Sr. firmly led his congregation and his children by example as he stood against racial inequality. So powerful was the dream he implanted in his son's heart that it literally changed a nation.

Martin Luther King Sr. never was one to mince the truth. One time, the elder King was stopped by a white traffic policeman who addressed him as "boy." He pointed to little Martin Jr. on the seat beside him and snapped, "That's a boy. I'm a man."

Another time father and son entered a shoe store where the shoe clerk insisted they move to the rear of the store to be served. Martin Sr. didn't move and said, "We either buy shoes sitting here or we won't buy any shoes at all." The younger Martin noted these strong character traits and in time they became part of his character and ministry as well.

While attending Crozer Theological Seminary, Martin Jr. wrote, as recorded in *A Testament of Hope: The Essential Writings and Speeches of Martin Luther King Jr.*, "The thing that I admire most about my dad is his genuine Christian character. He is a man of real integrity, deeply committed to moral and ethical principles. He is conscientious in all of his undertakings. Even the person who disagrees with his frankness has to admit that his motives and actions are sincere."

Raised a sharecropper's son in south Georgia, Martin Luther King Sr.—or Mike, as he was called then—was burly enough to stop his drunken father from beating his mother. This forceful, physical disposition so alarmed Mike's mother that she made him flee to Atlanta to escape his father. Arriving in the big city, Mike found work preaching at two country churches by the time he was twenty.

[Jesus said,] "I have given you an example to follow. Do as I have done to you."

JOHN 13:15 NLT

Eventually, Mike began attending Ebenezer Baptist Church and married the preacher's daughter, Alberta Williams. On January 15, 1929, Alberta gave birth to "Little Mike." When "Little Mike" turned five, the elder King changed both their names to the name of Protestant Reformation founder Martin Luther, foreshadowing the liberating, paradigm-altering role his young son would one day fulfill.

Martin Sr. reared Martin Jr. both in middle-class, comfortable accommodations and strict, authoritarian protectiveness. Atlanta knew both racial hostilities and black bourgeois gentility. Martin Sr. favored his eldest son, allowing him luxuries like piano lessons, abundant portions of soul food, opera, and strenuous bouts of wrestling. This favor included high expectations, and Martin Jr. quickly learned discipline and proper behavior.

Echoing the humiliation Rosa Parks must have endured before her defiant act, Martin Jr. and his black high school contemporaries had to stand on a ninety-mile bus trip back to Atlanta in deference to more white passengers who boarded demanding seating. These indignities compelled Martin Jr. to say, "I was determined to hate every white person."

Martin skipped grades in order to graduate from high school by age fifteen and entered Atlanta's Morehouse College, a campus that then served as a sort of gentlemen's finishing academy for the sons of Atlanta's black elect. Holding vague notions of escaping his father's ministerial occupation, he considered medicine but instead majored in sociology to prepare for a career in law.

Martin Jr.'s heart softened toward whites when he started working in several integrated campus groups during his college years. He wrote that his parents would always tell him he should not hate the white man, but that it was his duty as a Christian to love them. This Christian love contributed later to King's enduring, nonviolent response to white oppression.

A career in law never materialized for Martin Jr., but a position in the ministry seemed assured. He had grown up in the church. His only brother, uncle, father, grandfather, and great-grandfather were all preachers. Martin Jr. didn't seem to have much choice. He entered Crozer Theological Seminary in Pennsylvania and graduated at the top of his class in 1951.

At Crozer, Martin Jr. grappled with the idea of going into the ministry. Though the younger King differed theologically from his father, he held great admiration for the man. Martin Jr. felt his father set a noble example that he didn't mind following. In the end, that respect compelled him to do the Lord's work.

Martin Jr. went on to receive his PhD in systematic theology while serving as the pastor of Dexter Avenue Baptist Church in Montgomery, Alabama. He hoped he would become a scholar, teaching theology at the university level—but God had other plans.

Instead, Martin Luther King Jr. assumed a spokesperson, leadership role in the growing Civil Rights movement as blacks began to demand equal rights and equal protection under the law. He quickly became the eloquent voice of freedom to blacks everywhere. In 1957, he and 115 other black ministers formed the Southern Christian Leadership Conference. Boycotts, sit-ins, marches, speeches, and protests filled the rest of his days as his mantra for freedom and equality rang through public squares and city halls.

By 1963, Martin Luther King Jr. was married to Coretta Scott and had fathered two children, including Martin Luther King III. Articulating his hope for all of America's children, King emphasized freedom ringing out everywhere so that all of God's children of every race and creed could join hands and together sing songs of freedom.

On April 3, 1968, Martin Luther King Jr. gave his last speech at the Mason Temple in Memphis. Setting forth his vision of a just and free society for all peoples, he said, "I want you to know tonight that we as a people will get to the Promised Land." The next day, King was gunned down by an assassin's bullet. Though his voice fell silent, his prior words and courageous actions still echo today.

Martin Luther King Sr. held a strong, authoritative presence as pastor of Ebenezer Baptist Church and set a firm example of Christian love in the face of injustice for his three children. Martin Sr. laid a philosophical and religious foundation for Martin Jr. that would serve his son through difficult, though ultimately victorious, nonviolent protests against racial inequality. His father set a "noble example" and shaped a son who challenged and changed the face of America.

A Father of Influence sets a godly example for his children.

Caspar ten Boom

1860–1944

Corrie ten Boom. A kindly Dutch watchmaker
created a hiding place for Jews during World War II
while teaching compassion and forgiveness to his daughter
Corrie, one of the twentieth century's greatest traveling
evangelists and authors.

In January 1837, Caspar ten Boom's father, Willem, hung a small sign
in a shop window in Haarlem, Netherlands, reading "ten Boom,
Watches." There, the ten Boom family lived and worked. It was a
typical old-Haarlem structure: three stories high, two rooms deep, and
only one room wide. At some point in its history, its rear wall had been
removed to join it with the even thinner, steeper house in back of it,
which had only three rooms, one in back and two in front with one on
top of the other. A narrow corkscrew staircase squeezed between the two.

In this humble structure, watchmaker Caspar ten Boom would
raise three girls and a son, among them Corrie (short for Cornelia)
born April 15, 1892. As a watchmaker, Caspar valued beauty and pre-
cision. He would take the train to Amsterdam each week solely to
bring back the time from the Naval Observatory. He prided himself
that his clocks were never more than two seconds off. The city loved
Caspar, and residents called him "Haarlem's Grand Old Man." Indeed,
he was known for his gentle courtesy, disarming the foul moods of all
who would approach him.

The ten Boom home, known as the Beje, was always open to anyone in need. Through the years the ten Booms were active in social
work in Haarlem, and their Christian faith inspired them to serve the

religious community and society at large. In the 1920s, the home became a shelter and refuge for child victims of World War I.

The Beje was never without residents. Caspar loved children, and whenever he heard of a child in need of a home, a new face would appear at the table. Somehow, with the meager earnings from his watch shop, he fed and dressed and cared for eleven more children after his own four were grown.

With white hair and beard, Caspar ten Boom's disposition was as sunny as his face. Born right there in the Beje, Caspar was the first child of his parents to survive. For that very reason, he was always treasured and loved, and he was able to pass that sense of value on not only to his own family but to the downcast, poor, and neglected as well.

Caspar's love for others grew out of his Christian faith, and he held regular prayer and Bible-study sessions every day for everyone staying in the house, family or otherwise.

His daughter Corrie loved the Beje too. Never married, she filled her days working at the shop and running Haarlem Girls' Clubs, a task she worked at faithfully for almost twenty years. At one time, these clubs had thousands of members in Holland and Indonesia.

One night in early 1940, the ten Booms were listening to the radio. The Dutch prime minister was assuring the people of Holland they had nothing to fear. He had been given promises, he told them, that they would not be attacked by any of the countries engaged in the fighting around them. Caspar was not convinced. He turned off the radio and told the girls that unfortunately, the prime minister was mistaken. He rightly predicted that Holland would be attacked and defeated by the Germans.

Corrie and Betsie didn't want to believe it, but on May 10, 1940, Nazi German forces entered their homeland and began to persecute, mistreat, and round up the Jews. The ten Boom family loved their Jewish friends. They understood the Jewish people to be God's chosen people and recognized full well their Savior Jesus Christ was himself a Jew. Unable to watch this horror occur right in front of them, the ten Boom family began their underground work, helping Jews escape from the clutches of the oppressive Germans. Caspar would say, "In this household, God's people are always welcome."

Frightened Jews would knock continually on the Beje door, looking for temporary refuge and a kind face. Caspar never refused them. When at last it became too dangerous, Caspar would ask his son Willem, a pastor, to find places for them elsewhere in the country.

When it became apparent that drastic measures were needed, a place was prepared to hide Jews in the event the Gestapo tried to round them up and send them to concentration camps. Caspar, Corrie, Betsie, and their friend Mr. Smit inspected the Beje carefully. Finally, at the very top of the house where Corrie's room was located, they devised a way to create a secret room. Working quietly and furtively, a brick wall was constructed to enclose what became known as "the hiding place." While they continued to find locations outside their own home to hide their Jewish friends, they now had a safe place for up to four people. It was risky business, but they were determined not to let their friends down.

In February 1944, German soldiers entered the Beje, smashed open cupboards and flung open doors trying to find the secret room. But they could not, and after about half an hour, they gave up. The ten Boom family could only stand by, watch, and pray.

The officer in charge ordered that the family be taken to the police station. Then he set a guard outside the house, figuring that anyone hiding inside would eventually have to come out or starve to death.

After reluctantly emerging, Caspar, Corrie, Betsie, and Willem were taken to the police station where they spent the rest of the day sitting on the floor of a large room. Many other people had been arrested at the same time, including their friend Pickwick.

Though their situation looked bleak, Caspar took the opportunity to practice his nightly ritual: prayer. So, there in the police station, a group gathered around and Father ten Boom led them into the presence of God. They had no Bible, but Father ten Boom knew many prayers by heart anyway.

In his deep voice, he quoted some words from Psalm 119:114 and 117: "You are my hiding place and my shield; I hope in Your word....

Hold me up, and I shall be safe" (NKJV). His faith in God gave the others comfort and strength during that hour.

My dear children, let's not just talk about love; let's practice real love.

1 JOHN 3:18 MSG

The next day they were taken to a prison near the Hague, a town forty kilometers south of Haarlem. Each prisoner was placed in a different cell, and that was the last time they saw Father ten Boom. Ten days later, under the duress of imprisonment, the elder ten Boom died.

The death of the ten Boom patriarch might have broken the spirits of his children, but they knew of a hope greater than their circumstances. One day, a warden threw a parcel into Corrie's cell. She was thrilled to find that it contained some biscuits, a bright red towel, and a needle and thread. It had come from her married sister, Nollie, who lived in Haarlem. Corrie noticed there was something odd about the address. It was written at an angle, pointing to the stamp. According to Corrie's book *The Hiding Place*, Corrie peeled off the stamp and saw writing underneath: "All the watches left in the cupboard are safe." She knew this meant that all the Jews hiding in the ten Boom home had escaped. Corrie was elated.

One day in June 1944, all the prisoners packed their belongings, marched to the railway station, and were put on a train. Boarding the train, Corrie saw her sister Betsie, and managed to push her way through the crowd to reach her. Together again, the train took them to a labor camp in southern Holland. Here they lived in barracks and worked throughout the day. Corrie made radios for German aircraft at the Philips factory—making sure there were plenty of mistakes.

Though life was hard in the camps, Betsie encouraged her sister Corrie that after the war they would go around the world telling people about God's goodness. She reminded her sister that they were suffering to a degree that few others ever would. If they could testify to God's goodness then perhaps others could give up their hatred and bitterness.

Corrie gave Betsie and some of the other prisoners a few vitamin drops each day—miraculously the bottle never became empty. Nobody understood it until Betsie reminded them of the story in the Bible of the widow's jar of oil that did not run dry for many days.

Despite the vitamins, Betsie became weaker and weaker—eventually she died of disease and starvation, leaving Corrie alone.

Only a few days later, Corrie heard someone shouting her name. "Prisoner ten Boom, report after roll-call." She feared she was going to be punished. Or shot.

"Father in heaven, please help me now," she prayed.

Reporting to the guard, she was given a card stamped *Entlassen*, which means "Released." She was free! Corrie could hardly believe it. She was given back her few possessions, some new clothes, and a railway pass back to Holland. After a long, hard journey, she arrived in her own city and was greeted by friends.

Years later she learned that she had been released "by mistake." God had been watching out for her, because a week after her release all the women of her age in the camp were killed.

As soon as she was well enough, Corrie began to honor her sister's vision by telling others of her experiences. One woman gave Corrie a large house, hoping to establish a place where people who had suffered through the war could go to be healed and renewed.

Corrie's story so fascinated people that she was invited to speak in many churches in many countries, including America and England. Eventually, she also visited Germany, even with all its bitter memories. But God helped her love and forgive, even when she met some of the former guards from the concentration camp. Corrie also wrote several books about her experiences including *The Hiding Place, Tramp for the Lord,* and *Jesus Is Victor.*

Caspar ten Boom taught his children all about Christian love and compassion. Though he was never able to see his daughter Corrie valiantly endure suffering and go on to share God's message of love and forgiveness to the world, he instilled in her a legacy that continues to overcome hate and oppression to this day.

A Father of Influence teaches his children to treasure and protect the innocent.

Henry Churchill DeMille

1853–1893

Cecil B. DeMille. Theologian and playwright Henry Churchill DeMille passed his love for God and theatrics down to his son Cecil, who directed *The King of Kings*, *The Ten Commandments*, and many other classic films from the first half of twentieth-century cinema.

After Cecil B. DeMille's 1922 movie *Adam's Rib* came out, he decided to let the public choose the subject of his next film. To set up the contest, DeMille's publicist contacted the *Los Angeles Times*. First prize for best idea was a thousand dollars with lesser prizes making up another thousand. Other papers began picking up the story and what began as a local contest brought in thousands of letters from almost everywhere in the world. They ranged in subject matter from the most sacred to the most profane. DeMille was struck by the quantity suggesting a religious theme. One writer from Michigan started his answer with these words: "You cannot break the Ten Commandments—they will break you."

The letter amazed C. B. DeMille. It was an idea bigger than any he had previously attempted to put on screen. It was also a theme that reminded him of his father, who regularly read the Bible aloud to him. Henry DeMille had taught his son that God's laws are more than simple rules—they are the final word.

Eight contestants had suggested the Ten Commandments as a theme. Cecil awarded a thousand dollars to each of them and quickly moved ahead with the picture.

Late in his life, Cecil B. DeMille described his father in his autobiography as a Democrat, a good Christian, and a Southern gentleman, always reading, one of those rare minds that not only devoured but also retained information.

The famous film director wrote that religious quest runs through their family history. There were deMils who clung to the Old Church of Abbot Anthony, deMils who were priests and friars, deMils who carefully noted bequests to the church in their wills. Clearly, biblical and religious thoughts were never far from his mind.

Regarding his name, C. B. DeMille says that there are about a dozen different spellings in the family records. The oldest is deMil. DeMille with an *e* on the end appears for the first time in 1747, but DeMill, Demill, and various others kept cropping up until his father's time. Henry made it well known to the theater crowd that he had chosen DeMille.

Henry DeMille was happiest in 1866 when he made his first appearance on the stage in an amateur production of *Nan Good-for-Nothing*. Cecil was amused that the defeated South, though beaten and broken, still had the time and spirit for amateur theatrical presentations. Cecil admits he never read the play but would always think kindly of the old, and in his opinion, bad farce for it gave his father a love for the theater.

After traveling north to New York City to visit his grandfather, Henry Churchill DeMille entered the Adelphi Academy in Brooklyn. It was September of 1867, and the academy was conducted by John Lockwood, one of his uncle Richard's classmates. He was just fourteen.

Henry DeMille said John Lockwood taught about the welding of religion and learning and the brotherhood of humanity. He said it was a sane and balanced program that neglected neither body, mind, nor soul. It was under this instruction that Henry came to believe in an *all-merciful* God, perhaps the strongest single motivational force in the elder DeMille's life.

In 1871, Henry DeMille entered Columbia College, aided by a grant of $175 from the Society of New York for the Promotion of Religion and Learning. Cecil would think of the $175 gift to his father when signing contracts involving millions of dollars for motion pictures like *The King of Kings* or *The Ten Commandments*; or even more so, when he received letters from all over the world witnessing on the religious values of those pictures. Later Cecil tried to honor the Society for the investment it had made in his father's life, but it could not be found. Though never able to return that money, he has been able to give in other ways, in keeping with the Society's initial purpose.

Blessed is the man who does not walk in the counsel of the wicked or stand in the way of sinners or sit in the seat of mockers.
But his delight is in the law of the LORD, and on his law he meditates day and night.
PSALM 1:1–2

Henry DeMille didn't have a lot of money for expensive fun, but he managed to save enough pennies for the Saturday matinees at Barnum's Museum. He dreamed of being an actor, but it was apparently a hopeless dream. He thought boys from nice Southern families with strong religious leanings didn't go on the stage in the 1870s. He once asked his mother jokingly what she thought of him becoming an actor. She told him it would break her heart. That answer never left Henry though the hope of the stage always lingered in his heart.

Henry DeMille was greatly influenced by preacher and theologian Charles Kingsley. He purchased his works and studied them carefully. On May 27, 1878, the Standing Committee of the Episcopal Diocese of Long Island accepted Henry as a candidate for Holy Orders—but he was never ordained. By 1886, he was becoming a serious playwright, reaching far more people than he could from the pulpit.

Henry C. DeMille met actress Miss Tillie Samuel in November of 1872 backstage at a performance. He called her Beatrice, and they married in 1876. After the birth of their son William, Cecil was born in 1881. The family settled on Pompton Lake, near Oakland, New Jersey, where Cecil enjoyed his childhood, often listening to his father read from the Bible or from one of the classics. DeMille writes in his autobiography, "*The King of Kings* and *The Ten Commandments* were born in those evenings in Pompton, when father sat under the big lamp and read and a small boy sat near his chair and listened."

When Henry died of typhoid fever, Mrs. DeMille wrapped her
arms around her two sons and stood with them beside her husband's
casket. She then expressed her wish that her sons would be as fine
and noble, good and honest as their father had been. Her hope was
that they would follow in his footsteps, helping God and their fellow
man, never turning from the right path.

When Cecil decided to make a biblical picture, he had some concerns that his friends, executives in the motion picture business,
would fail to see the potential for the film. He convinced them that
his characters would be more than stiff stereotypes. He would portray
them as real, living, breathing men and women who had little idea of
the role they would play in history.

When his remake of *The Ten Commandments* opened in 1956, letters began to pour into DeMille's office. The director said people
always thought his movies made God real to them. Cecil credited his
parents' influence.

Henry DeMille didn't live long, but taught his sons a love of the
Bible, a love of theatrics, and a love of God's law. Famed motion picture director Cecil B. DeMille never forgot those lessons and made
continual conscious efforts to honor his father's memory and
mother's dedication. Television networks continue to broadcast *The
Ten Commandments*, and many Americans still consider it one of the
best, noblest motion pictures ever made.

**A Father of Influence gives his children an
appreciation for God's law.**

Alexander Maitland Stewart

1872–1961

Jimmy Stewart. A faithful Presbyterian, hardware-store owner, and longtime resident of Indiana, Pennsylvania, Alexander Stewart modeled courage and bravery for his son, acting great Jimmy Stewart.

E ducated, focused, and stubborn, Alexander Stewart attended the best schools that his family's ample income could provide. He studied at Chester and Kiskiminetas Springs School before obtaining his Bachelor of Science degree at Princeton University. In April 1898, only a few weeks after obtaining his degree, Alexander signed on with the Pennsylvania Volunteers and fought in the Spanish-American War. On returning, he worked in his father's hardware store, J. M. Stewart and Co., and saved enough money to buy a one-third interest in the company before marrying Bessie Jackson in December, 1906.

On May 20, 1908, Alexander and Elizabeth (Bessie) welcomed their one and only son, James, born in their home on Philadelphia Street in Indiana, Pennsylvania. In a biography of James Stewart by Dewey Donald, Alexander told the townspeople, "James is a fat little rascal. But you never saw a boy like him. Stop around and see him." It was an invitation Alexander also presented years later with regard to his son's screen appearances at the local movie theater.

The Stewart family took the Christian faith seriously and church attendance was compulsory. At every meal, they took hands and gave thanks. They regularly sang hymns at home. Each Sunday, they attended church. Mr. Stewart was in the choir and Mrs. Stewart was the organist. James would often dash down the aisles before sliding into the pew.

Young James was also able to observe his father's dedication to his position as a volunteer fireman. At the sound of the siren, Alex would immediately stand erect in the choir loft and then quickly move toward the exit. All the parishioners would look at him and the minister would flounder. The minister would try to keep the attention of the people, but they couldn't relax until Alex returned. Mr. Stewart would pretend that all eyes and ears were awaiting his sign, but once he had settled himself in he would turn to the congregation and solemnly nod his head, indicating that everything was under control. A sigh would go through the church and finally, attention would return to the minister.

When James was five, he developed a taste for theatrics, and sneaked a couple of hand puppets into church one Sunday. He spent the service performing his own show. For a period of time, Alexander didn't know what was going on because he was up in the choir loft, but as soon as he heard about it, he put a stop to James's shenanigans.

Indeed, Alexander initially didn't encourage James's creative impulses and expected him to continue the family business at the prosperous hardware store his father had passed along to him. James would say in interviews that even after he grew up and moved away, the store remained in his heart and memory. He realized that the store wasn't central to his life, but the man who resided in it—his father—was.

Under only mild protest from his wife and family, Alexander Stewart enlisted in the U.S. Army in 1917 at the age of forty-five years. Lending his mechanical skills in the ordnance department, he contributed to World War I efforts.

Just before Alexander left the European front, James asked his father if he could have a couple of boards from the store for building a theater in the basement of the house. Alexander agreed, and the result was several productions, usually involving war themes, including a

title called *Beat the Kaiser,* and another production called *The Slacker,* about a man who at first
refused to fight against Germany but then saw
the light and won the war all by himself.

> *The integrity of the honest keeps them on track.*
>
> PROVERBS 11:3 MSG

After an honorable discharge with the rank
of captain in May 1919, Alexander fought
another battle on the home front to erect a memorial to those killed
during the war. Without waiting for authorization from town or
county officials, Alexander laid a foundation and raised a marble pillar
in a neglected German Lutheran cemetery. Initially the Lutherans
objected, but Alexander didn't care. He told his employees to put it up.

A few years later, Alexander swallowed his own aspirations for his
son and helped thirteen-year-old James get a job at a local movie theater. Alexander wanted James to do his part over the summer to make
spending money, but he didn't insist that James had to be at the hardware store. So Sam Gallo hired James to work as a projectionist at the
Strand Theater.

James escaped Indiana and the store for good when he attended
Princeton University. Abandoning his dream of a career in aviation,
Stewart pursued architecture and was going to study it as a graduate
student until he became attracted to the school's drama and music
clubs. He was invited to be part of the University Players, a performing arts club comprised of Ivy League musicians and thespians. Taking
bit parts in the Players' productions over the summer of 1932, he
moved to New York City in the fall, where he shared an apartment
with rising actor Henry Fonda and director/playwright Joshua Logan.
James began accepting bit parts in Broadway shows, which led to even
more substantial stage roles. After several favorably reviewed performances on Broadway, he attracted the interest of MGM and signed a
contract in April of 1935.

From 1935 to 1939, he acted in twenty productions for MGM
before hitting it big with the Frank Capra classic, *Mr. Smith Goes to
Washington.* This role defined him as the strong-willed, classic
American everyman who fought the good fight and stood up against
corruption and greed—qualities his father modeled and taught him

years before. Stewart cemented his role as an American hero with his next role in the 1939 Western *Destry Rides Again.*

Nearly a year before Pearl Harbor, James looked into the United States Army Air Corps. Only five pounds under the minimum limit and wanting to serve, James was able to convince the draft board to accept him, and he successfully enlisted in the army in March of 1941. Since the United States had yet to declare war on Germany, and because of the army's unwillingness to put celebrities on the front, Stewart was held back from combat duty, although he did earn a commission as a second lieutenant and completed pilot training. After becoming an instructor pilot for the B-17 Flying Fortress and producing several training and instructional films, James finally saw combat flying more than twenty missions. By war's end, James was promoted from private to colonel and twice received the Distinguished Flying Cross. He continued to be an active member of the reserves and even flew a combat mission in the Vietnam conflict before finally retiring from service in 1968.

James further established himself as one of the greatest American screen actors of all time, acting in seventy-eight more projects over his career, including the classics *The Shop Around the Corner, Rear Window, Vertigo, The Greatest Show on Earth, Harvey, Anatomy of a Murder,* and the great Christmas perennial *It's a Wonderful Life.* He won two Oscars, his first for *The Philadelphia Story* acting opposite Cary Grant and Katherine Hepburn, and the second as a Lifetime Achievement Award.

In the late summer of 1961, James received the disturbing news that his father had been diagnosed with stomach cancer by doctors at the Cleveland Clinic. James and his two sisters were at their father's side at the end. At the funeral, James asked the pastor to read Psalm 91. According to the pastor, Jimmy shook in tears because that was the psalm his father had stuck in his pocket in Sioux City before going off to war in Europe.

After the funeral for his father, James took one final look at the hardware store he knew so well as a youth. He let himself in with a key that he hadn't touched in thirty years. The interior smelled of metal, leather, oil, and fertilizer—odors of his childhood. He saw his old scarred oak desk and pulled open the middle drawer. It had pencils, paper clips, bolts, and paint samples inside. Then James left the store, locked the door behind him, and decided that he couldn't endure the thought of any other man standing in the store, living his father's life. So, ignoring offers he had received for buying the business, he opted to close it and gave the proceeds from the sale of the merchandise to his sisters.

Alexander Stewart modeled strong, yet faithful, manhood for his son, and took every opportunity to serve his country in war. This bravery, courage, and American idealism became the trademark persona for one James "Jimmy" Stewart, one of America's best and most beloved screen stars.

When the James Stewart Museum opened in Indiana, Pennsylvania, in 1995, the town celebrated its most famous citizen, but not its most popular. Thirty-five years after his death, and twenty-five years after the closing of his longstanding hardware store, Alexander Stewart, the actor's father, remained a special guest at the inauguration proceedings, both in the heart of his son and within those of the residents who still remembered him fondly. Jimmy expressed devotion to his father for having been a model parent, storekeeper, eccentric, Presbyterian, dreamer, adventurer, child psychologist, film critic, and patriot. Those who knew Alexander had their own stories about "Alex," "Al" or "Eck," and most of them said there wouldn't have been an actor in Hollywood if there wasn't a character in the hardware store.

**A Father of Influence teaches his children
to be brave and show courage.**

Lee Petty

1914–2000

Richard Petty. A pioneer of NASCAR and one of its first superstars, Lee Petty became the family patriarch of a racing dynasty, fathering seven-time NASCAR champion Richard Petty.

NASCAR great Richard Petty remembers how his father, Lee, first gave him a taste for speed. In his autobiography, *King Richard I*, he writes, "I'll never forget that first race with Daddy and Uncle Julie. It was nothing but a little old track that had been scraped out of a pasture field with a road grader, leaving a red clay oval, but it just about thrilled the pants off of me. There were twenty-five or thirty racecars, maybe more. The racecars were just regular old cars with their fenders off and some bumpers made out of a pipe and welded right to the frame. When the guy waved the green flag for the start of the first head race, I couldn't believe it."

Thrilled, Richard asked his father if they could come back soon, but Lee assured his son that the fun wasn't over—there were four more races that night. Now ecstatic, Richard told his father that that place was the best place he had ever been.

Though Lee Petty loved to race, he didn't begin the practice professionally until he was thirty-five years old. He first started racing NASCAR at Charlotte Speedway and finished in the top five in season points in NASCAR's first eleven seasons. In 1959, he won the very first Daytona 500 and obtained the NASCAR Championship on three occasions.

Lee raised Richard in Level Cross, North Carolina, four miles north of Randleman, and ten miles south of Greensboro. Ironically, Richard never dreamed of or discussed becoming a racecar driver when he was young. He was content growing up and gave little thought to his future career. Racing was just something his family did.

> *Do you not know that those who run in a race all run, but only one receives the prize? Run in such a way that you may win.*
>
> 1 CORINTHIANS 9:24 NASB

The first competitions with cars started when Richard was very little, maybe even seven or eight years old. He and his friends would dig out elaborate racetracks in the dirt and push toy cars around them. As they got a little older, that kind of play eventually bored them. Wanting more excitement, Richard went one day to a shed and took a can of axle grease from the shelf, removed each wheel, and greased up the axles. Then he went back and asked his brothers to race again. Richard knew his cars were fast—he beat them both easily.

From wagons, Richard, his brother Maurice, and Dale Inman moved to racing bicycles. At first, Lee Petty wasn't amused with his son's antics. The bike-racing period lasted all summer and would have gone into the fall, but Lee thought somebody might get hurt. So he put a stop to it and eliminated a lot of their free time by giving them more chores.

Lee Petty had a passion for cars and racing. When asked why he was always working on a car, he would answer that he was improving it. When Richard went along for the ride in one of these cars with his father's care, he knew it was true. He could feel the improved power and performance.

As Lee's cars got better, his reputation grew. He would outrun just about everybody around Randleman. There wasn't anybody to race for a while. Lee's car sounded different from the others too. It shifted differently, and its engine cranked out more power. New racers came from as far away as Raleigh and Charlotte—and then Atlanta.

After the 1946 season, Lee Petty bought a 1937 Plymouth Coupe. He and his brother Julie put a Chrysler straight-eight engine into it— taken from a car out back behind the garage. They took the engine apart, completely rebuilding, reboring, restroking, and making it much more powerful. When they were finished, they had put a great deal of money into it.

They realized they were going to have to win every race just to break even. Yet, Lee knew he could win. To start, he won at Danville, Virginia. Young Richard was overjoyed, but Lee pretended it was nothing. Secretly, he knew it was a winner.

Three years later, in 1949, Lee entered the very first NASCAR race held at the Charlotte Speedway, thus beginning his famed career and spawning the Petty family racing dynasty.

Lee's racing all started back in 1928, at the age of sixteen, when he traded his bicycle for a Model T. According to Richard, bikes were more valuable than a lot of cars at that time, so a trade was advantageous. Bikes were a luxury, while most cars weren't. Lee stripped down the Model T and raced it everywhere he could. That car started Lee on a love affair with speed that has consumed every Petty who has come along since.

Lee Petty died on April 5, 2000, and is buried at the Level Cross United Methodist Church Cemetery in Randleman, North Carolina. Petty Enterprises continues to this day, and while Richard (who won 200 of 1,184 NASCAR races over more than 35 years) has also retired from the sport, his son Kyle continues to represent his family name, winning many awards and races on the NASCAR circuit.

Richard summarizes his family legacy in *King Richard I:* "I guess it's why my earliest memories include cars. There was always a car in the front yard, or wherever there was a shade tree to work under. And it was always apart, in one stage or the other, being modified to make it run faster. It didn't matter if it was a brand-new car or an old one. Daddy was never satisfied with how fast it would run. It must be in the Petty genes."

A Father of Influence teaches his children to follow their passions and race to win.

Charles Henry Cooper

1865–1946

Gary Cooper. The son of a Montana ranchman,
Gary Cooper has come to define rugged American
masculinity and heroism, and great acting skill.

In the summer of 1906, when Gary Cooper was only five years old, his father purchased the Seven-Bar-Nine, a failing, 600-acre cattle ranch five miles north of their home in Helena, Montana. (In interviews, Gary has said this move was the first and most vivid memory of his adventurous youth.) There at the ranch, away from the hustle and bustle of the city, Gary (or Frank as he was known back then) enjoyed the great American outdoors.

Though Alice, his mother, worried sick over his disappearances, Frank was only operating in the same spirit that caused his father, Charles, to leave his native England and travel west. Charles Cooper was born in Bedfordshire, England, of middle-class farming parents. An exemplary scholar, he attended public school and was encouraged to pursue a legal career. Charles, however, was enamored by the lore of America. He begged his parents to let him go to America with his older brother Walter, and the brothers arrived in Boston Harbor in 1885, when Charles was nineteen. Soon after, Charles separated from his brother and headed west.

A solitary character, Charles loved the open land. At first a wheat farmer in Nebraska, he then moved even further west to become a cattleman. The practice of law, however, followed him, and he took a clerical job with the Northern Pacific railroad where he "read the law" as a consultant. By 1893, he had become a law expert, and it was in that same year he met Alice Brazier, who came to him seeking legal advice. Alice saw a certain level of refinement and dignity in Charles that she didn't find in other young men of the time. They soon married. Though she always favored returning to England over residing in the Western landscape that Charles loved, Gary said he saw his parents as the supreme example of wedded happiness.

Frank James Cooper was born to Charles and Alice in Helena, Montana, during a freak heat wave on May 7, 1901. (Charles had become an American citizen only a few months prior to Frank's birth.) At that time, the Cooper's eldest son, Arthur, was six years old. Doctors feared the pregnancy might kill a fragile Alice. She certainly wouldn't have been able to bear more children after this birth. So she hoped her second and last child would be a girl. It was not to be.

Frank was an infant of especially pleasant disposition, and he was easily amused. He cried at times when his doting mother was around but refrained in the presence of his more reserved, taciturn father. As a small child, Frank's mother dressed him in frilly boy clothes in the manner of Little Lord Fauntleroy. But this feminization never stuck, and by the time he was old enough to explore on his own, he became all boy. He liked playing with his scruffy Indian friends who lived on settlements within the ranch, and he befriended the rough-and-tumble cowboys who worked there as well. Sometimes young Frank would disappear for hours at a time hiking in the high country looking for bears and eagles. The ranch encouraged independence and an adventurous spirit.

Despite the fun Frank had there, the ranch was only marginally successful for Charles, so he took a position as a judge back in Helena and purchased a prestigious brick home there. According to *The Last Hero: A Biography of Gary Cooper,* Gary said, "My father poured his heart and all his money into his ranch, but never got much of it back because he had no business sense."

Alice took advantage of this turn of events and insisted the boys receive a proper education in Helena. She convinced Charles to let her take the boys back to the city during the winter months to enroll them in a more formal school. She worried that the log cabin ranch school that Frank, Arthur, and the local Indian boys of the ranch attended was inadequate.

When Charles enrolled the boys at Helena for the 1909–1910 winter season, Frank was devastated. He disliked school in the big city and had a penchant for wandering away from the grounds during recess and not coming back. Frank certainly had the taste for adventure and exploration. He loved and missed the frontier life.

In the summer of 1910, Charles sent his wife and sons off to England for an extended vacation. There, Alice decided that Frank and Arthur should attend Dunstable School, where their father and grandfather had attended. Surprisingly, Charles agreed. So in 1911, the entire Cooper family went to England, and Charles and Alice returned to America alone. Frank and Arthur would study in England for two years before returning home.

When Frank was thirteen years old, he was injured in an automobile accident. He asked his father if he could recuperate at the ranch, and his father agreed. When he was well enough, the cowboy staff at the ranch taught him how to ride a horse, amusing Frank immensely.

Hoping to further his son's boyhood education, Charles tried to turn his son into a baseball fan. Charles and his fellow judges followed play in the Northwest League, which met on fields in Butte and Great Falls. Oftentimes, the judges would take their sons on trips to watch games there. Though Frank never took a liking to baseball (ironic given his outstanding performance in 1942's *Pride of the Yankees*), he became quite friendly with the teenage sons of his father's associates.

Instead of baseball, Frank preferred hunting and fishing (particularly on the ranch). Charles rarely engaged in his son's pastimes but encouraged Frank in his interests.

In 1924, Frank Cooper moved to Los Angeles hoping to become

Stop in your tracks! Take in God's miracle-wonders! Do you have any idea how God does it all, how he makes bright lightning from dark storms, how he piles up the cumulus clouds—all these miracle-wonders of a perfect Mind?

JOB 37:14–16 MSG

an artist for advertisements, but instead he became an extra in the motion-picture industry. A year after that, he had a chance at a real part in a two-reeler with actress Eileen Sedgewick as his leading lady. After the release of this short film, he was called to Paramount Studios and offered a long-term contract, which he accepted. In 1925, he changed his name to Gary because his agent felt it evoked the "rough, tough" nature of Gary, Indiana.

"Coop," as he was called by his friends and peers, appeared in more than a hundred films. In 1941, he won his first Academy Award for Best Actor for his role as the title character in *Sergeant York*, a pacifist soldier who captured an entire German troop in World War I. In 1952, Gary won his second Best Actor Academy Award for his performance as Marshal Will Kane in *High Noon*, often considered by film critics and historians to be his finest role.

After his death in 1961, Gary was inducted into the Hall of Great Western Performers of the National Cowboy and Western Heritage Museum. And he was named the eleventh greatest actor of all time on "The 50 Greatest Screen Legends" list by the American Film Institute.

Oftentimes reporters and fans asked Gary about his life before Hollywood. He would tell them he took after his father, who was a true westerner. Indeed, Gary Cooper has come to personify the quintessential Western screen hero: strong, independent, cool under pressure, gentle, kind, and good. Charles Cooper gave his son a ranch and freedom to explore it, which translated into an endearing and enduring American icon, still treasured and revered today.

**A Father of Influence encourages his children
to explore the world around them.**

Col. Rick D. Husband

1957–2003

Laura Husband. Though he died in the *Columbia* space-shuttle disaster, U.S. Air Force Colonel Rick Husband taught his daughter, Laura, how to prioritize her life—God's way.

S huttle Commander Rick Husband and six other STS-107 crewmembers had been in space for sixteen days aboard the space shuttle *Columbia*. According to *High Calling: The Courageous Life and Faith of Space Shuttle Columbia Commander Rick Husband* penned by his wife, Evelyn, Rick made recorded videotapes prior to launch for his daughter, Laura, and infant son, Matthew. He told his wife, Evelyn, "I want to make a videotape for Laura and one for Matthew that they can watch each day I'm in orbit. I want the children to know how much I love them and that I'll be thinking about them every day." Second to his faith, Rick prized quality family time.

Rick loved nothing more than telling his children about God. To Rick, God wasn't some vague concept, but a real, living person. Jesus wasn't some kind of storybook character with good morals, but the Lord, the Son of God. Rick literally believed that Jesus lived on earth, died, rose again, and wanted everyone on earth to have a real relationship with Him.

Rick Husband first mentioned becoming an astronaut after watching John Glenn orbit the earth. He was just four years old at the time, but he never lost his zeal. His father bought him a telescope and his mother gave him a toy space helmet. When he was thirteen, he asked his parents for flying lessons. He asked every year until they finally granted his wish at age seventeen. Although the cost of the lessons was between twelve and fifteen hundred dollars, Jane and Doug were happy to provide Rick with the money. He took to the air wonderfully and quickly obtained his pilot license.

In 1975, Rick graduated from Amarillo High School with honors and headed to Texas Tech in Lubbock to study mechanical engineering. There, he met Evelyn Neely, his future wife, and found the courage to ask her out. On their first date, he told her that he wanted to join the Air Force and pursue his lifelong dream of becoming an astronaut. After graduation Rick immediately joined the Air Force as a pilot and after Land Survival School and Fighter Lead-in School, he and Evelyn married in 1982.

While working as a test pilot for the Air Force and obtaining his master's degree in mechanical engineering at Cal State University, Rick applied to NASA for enrollment in the astronaut training program—three times! Each time, he was denied. Rick was disappointed that he hadn't made it into the space program, but he left the matter in God's hands.

Rick echoed this in his journal. "I've finally come to the point where I've put God's will ahead of my desire to become an astronaut. Don't get me wrong—I still want very badly to be an astronaut, but only if it is God's will. I wish I had come to this point earlier, but better late than never."

Rick was accepted by the British Royal Air Force on a program called the Aircraft and Armament Evaluation Establishment in Boscombe Down, Wiltshire, England. There, Rick's Christian faith blossomed. Prior to that time, Rick may have thought of God as a good and loving Sunday school character, but in England he wanted to do away with his former, childish way of seeing God and wanted to get to know Him at a heart level.

While he was in England, Rick's father, Doug, was diagnosed with terminal kidney cancer. Rick returned home with his family to Texas to see his dying father one last time. Confronted with the brevity of life, Rick felt an urgency to let his kids know that with God's help, they could achieve whatever they wanted to do. He believed in them, and he wanted them to know that.

Though he'd surrendered his dream to God, Rick continued to struggle with the desire to become an astronaut. He contemplated Psalm 37:4, "Delight yourself in the LORD and he will give you the desires of your heart." This verse cut to his heart. He knew what really mattered was being a good husband and father. If being an astronaut compromised that role, he would not only be hurting his family but also hurting himself. He knew the best he could do was represent Christ to those he loved the most. He wanted them to have every opportunity to know Jesus. The race for space was incidental.

> *Love GOD, your God, with your whole heart: love him with all that's in you, love him with all you've got!*
>
> **DEUTERONOMY 6:5 MSG**

Rick made a fourth application for Astronaut Training School and finally was accepted. In 1995, he began candidate school at Johnson Space Center. Upon completion, he was a representative for Advanced Projects, working on space-shuttle upgrades and the Crew Return Vehicle (CRV). He studied returns to the moon and Mars travel. Finally, in 1999, he flew as pilot on STS-96, better known as *Discovery*. He logged 235 hours in space, finally achieving his dream of space travel.

In February of 2003, he was assigned to command STS-107, the space shuttle *Columbia*. After a successful mission in space, the crew performed what they thought would be a dangerous but routine reentry into the earth's atmosphere. The *Columbia*, after all, was on its twenty-eighth mission. But damage to the protective foam panels on the underside of the ship sustained during launch caused excessive heat and friction during reentry. The *Columbia* disintegrated, killing all seven crewmembers on board. NASA, the space community, America, and the world mourned.

Rick Husband didn't live a long life, but he lived a full life, knowing his priorities and keeping them straight. Evelyn is often asked to speak about Rick's faith and career. His daughter, Laura, remembers him with these words published in her mother's book *High Calling*. "My dad was a loving father who told me very often that I was beautiful. He was a very strong Christian man. He helped me accept Jesus when I was four years old. I am glad that his priorities were straight by putting God first, his family second, and his work third. He was humble in everything he did. I was blessed to have such a great dad even though it was a shorter time than I would have liked it to be. I am so glad to know that he is safe in heaven and that I will see him again and this time we'll never have to say good-bye."

A Father of Influence teaches his children to keep their priorities in order with God first, family second, and work third.

Thomas Gibson Walton

1892–1984

Samuel Moore Walton. Thomas Gibson Walton taught his
son frugality, simple living, and how to work hard,
a philosophy that has made Sam Walton, founder of
Wal-Mart, the most successful retailer in
American history.

F rom an early age, Sam Walton always knew it was important to
help provide for the home, to be a contributor rather than just
a taker. At seven and eight years old, he sold magazine sub-
scriptions. From seventh grade through college, he sold newspapers
on paper routes. He also raised and sold rabbits and pigeons. With
these childhood jobs, Sam Walton learned the value of a dollar.
Depression-era life also taught him the value of conservation. Money
was for making and rarely for spending.

In *Sam Walton: Made in America*, Sam's brother, Bud, wrote,
"People can't understand why we're still so conservative. They make a
big deal about Sam being a billionaire and driving an old pickup truck
or buying his clothes at Wal-Mart or refusing to fly first class. It's just
the way we were brought up."

Sam Walton was born to Thomas Gibson Walton and Nancy Lee
Walton near Kingfisher, Oklahoma, on March 29, 1918. (Bud followed
in 1921.) Sam's father decided farming didn't generate enough
income to raise a family, so in 1923, they left the farm, and Thomas
became a mortgage man in Missouri.

Thomas Gibson Walton worked hard, an early riser who put in
long days. People remembered him as an honest man, known for his

integrity. A character, he loved to trade and make deals on anything from horses to mules, cattle, houses, farms, and cars. Once, he traded the family farm in Kingfisher for another in Omega, Oklahoma. He also once traded his wristwatch for a hog to put meat on the table. As a great negotiator, he knew how far he could go with someone to press a deal so that the other guy never felt angry or resentful. They always parted friends. Sometimes, however, he would embarrass Sam with insanely low offers.

Despite his wheeler-dealer attitude, Thomas didn't have the ambition or confidence to build his own business. He also didn't believe in building debt. As Sam grew up, Thomas had many jobs—a banker, a farmer, a farm-loan appraiser, and an agent for both insurance and real estate. For a few months during the Depression years, he was unemployed. Eventually, he went to work for Metropolitan Life Insurance, part of his brother's mortgage company. He serviced Metropolitan's old, defaulted farm loans. From 1929 to 1931, he repossessed hundreds of farms. Families owned these farms for years, so Thomas told the farmers the bad news in a way that left them with as much self-respect as possible. Sam often came along for the ride, and witnessing this left a big impression on the young Walton. By the time he got out into the real world, he already understood the value of a dollar.

As a child, Sam exercised ambition by becoming an Eagle Scout at the age of thirteen—the youngest Eagle Scout in the history of the state of Missouri at the time. He put his scouting skills to good use when, a year later, he pulled a drowning boy out of the Salt River.

At Columbia's Hickman High School, Sam excelled physically, playing basketball and starting as quarterback in football. Their team won the state title in 1935. At Hickman, Sam also served as vice president of the student body his junior year and as president his senior year. He performed well enough academically to become an honor student, and upon graduating, he was voted "Most Versatile Boy."

College years further refined Sam's work ethic and attitude toward money. He attended the University of Missouri-Columbia, majored in economics, and was an ROTC officer. In college, he waited tables in exchange for meals and joined the estimable Zeta Phi chapter of Beta Theta Pi fraternity. He was also tapped by QEBH, the well-known secret society on campus honoring top senior men. At graduation, he was voted "permanent president" of the class.

Three days after graduating from college, Sam joined JC Penney as a management trainee in Des Moines, Iowa, working for seventy-five dollars a month. He resigned from this position in 1942 in anticipation of being inducted into the military for service in World War II. In the meantime, he worked at a DuPont munitions plant near Tulsa, Oklahoma, where he met his future wife, Helen Robson, in April 1942. They married in February 1943.

> *It is a good thing to receive wealth from God and the good health to enjoy it. To enjoy your work and accept your lot in life—this is indeed a gift from God.*
>
> **ECCLESIASTES 5:19** NLT

After a brief stint in the military, Sam decided he wanted to own a department store but would settle for a variety store. With some help from his father-in-law plus money he had saved from his time in the army, Walton purchased a Ben Franklin variety store in Newport, Arkansas. It was here that he pioneered many concepts that would prove to be crucial to his success. For example, Sam consistently stocked shelves with a wide range of goods at low prices. His store also stayed open later than most other stores. He also pioneered discount merchandising by buying wholesale goods from the lowest priced supplier. This allowed him to pass on savings to his customers, which drove up his sales volume. One factor that made his store successful was its central location, making it accessible to a wide range of customers.

Forced out of business by his landlord in 1951 and unable to find a new location in Newport, Walton located a variety store in Bentonville, Arkansas. He opened it as another Ben Franklin franchise but called it "Walton Five and Dime." Sam also opened a variety store in Fayetteville, Arkansas—about twenty miles south of Bentonville. He gave it the same name as the store in Bentonville—though it was not a Ben Franklin franchise—and it became as successful as the first. Sam found a store manager to help him, and offered him a percentage of the store's profit—profit sharing ahead of its time.

Walton also introduced the concept of check-out counters near the exits. Customers could be rung up for all their purchases and pay for them at one time instead of paying at several locations. Walton also insisted that his stores be clean, well lit, and all his employees participate in sharing profits, increasing their loyalty.

As time went on, Sam opened more Ben Franklin stores with the help of his brother, father-in-law, and brother-in-law. By 1962, Sam and his brother, Bud, owned sixteen variety stores in Arkansas, Missouri, and Kansas (fifteen Ben Franklins and one independent Fayetteville store).

The first true Wal-Mart opened in 1962 in Rogers, Arkansas. Through implementing his proven practices with his previous stores, Sam opened 38 stores in 5 states by 1970, 330 stores in 11 states by 1980, and 859 stores in 22 states by 1985. Wal-Mart eventually became the world's largest retailer, and in 2004, more than 1.5 million people were employed by the Wal-Mart Corporation.

Maintaining the philosophy of its humble beginnings, Wal-Mart holds bake sales for local charities and offers scholarships to graduating seniors from local high schools.

Sam admits he's cheap when it comes to Wal-Mart. He never bought a jet until after the business was approaching $40 billion in sales. Sam and his team would stay in Holiday Inns, Ramada Inns, and Days Inns, and eat, when they had the time, at family restaurants.

Tough times and Thomas Gibson Walton taught Sam Walton the value of a dollar. Thomas taught Sam that simple living is nothing to be ashamed of. By teaching his son frugality, he instilled a philosophy and work ethic into his son that has saved Americans billions of dollars on normal, everyday necessities found in every Wal-Mart store.

A Father of Influence teaches his children how to be good managers of their resources.

Chuck Heaton

1918–

Patricia Heaton. Cleveland sportswriter Chuck Heaton opened doors for his five children, including two-time Emmy Award–winning actress Patricia Heaton, by relying on his network of friends and associates.

Actress Patricia Heaton wasn't always successful at her craft. Like many before her, she paid the bills while waiting tables in New York. Her concerned father, Cleveland sportswriter Chuck Heaton, used his contacts to help her find other employment. He was concerned about his daughter in the food-service business, so he called his old friend George Steinbrenner (owner of the New York Yankees), also a Cleveland native. Chuck told George that his daughter Patricia was in New York and asked him if there was anything he could do to give her work. Patricia headed out to Yankee Stadium to meet George, and there she told him she was an aspiring actress. He told her about James Nerlander, a big Broadway producer. A week later, she was having lunch at the Plaza with the two of them.

Heaton eventually appeared on Broadway in the musical *Don't Get God Started* after which she and fellow students created Stage Three, an off-Broadway acting troupe. She and her team brought one of their productions to Los Angeles, where she caught the eye of a casting director for the ABC drama *Thirtysomething*. Then it was only a matter of time before she landed the role of Debra Barone on *Everybody Loves Raymond*.

Chuck Heaton actually downplays his contributions to his daughter's success, which he wrote about in *Cleveland* magazine. "My daughter Patty certainly has gone on to do great things with her talent, and you can be sure I'm very proud of her. Not that I'm taking any credit. Perhaps the best thing I did—besides put food on the table, pay tuition and make her go to church on Sunday—was to stay out of her way. *Everybody Loves Raymond* is a big hit and no one is happier about Patty's success than the Heaton family. And no one in the Heaton family is prouder than Patty's old man."

A member of the World War II generation, Chuck Heaton wrote three stories a day (a beat story, a column, and notes) for *The Plain Dealer* for fifty-one years. A contributor to *Sports Illustrated* and *Pro Football Digest*, he now has a place in the Pro Football Hall of Fame in Canton, Ohio, as a recipient of the Dick McCann Memorial Award given to sportswriters with exceptional careers.

As a child, Patricia always felt a sense of privilege being the daughter of Chuck Heaton. She recognized that being one of his children had its perks. She would often overhear people whisper when they figured out who she was. As she got older, her father would take her to his newspaper office. There, she would happily explore while her father caught up on business. She even enjoyed the ride to the big city of Cleveland because not many kids from her suburb got to go downtown. He also took her to Cleveland Municipal Stadium. Large and majestic, the stadium was the arena where the greatest Cleveland sports action happened. Everyone there knew Chuck Heaton. Her father took her to his office there, but they also went to the Stadium Club, the press box, and even on occasion, the owner's box. She felt special and important.

Chuck Heaton's faith and commitment to Catholic charitable organizations was as great as his work ethic. He wrote checks out to Maryknoll Missions, Father Flanagan's Boys Town, and virtually every Catholic organization that approached him. Troubled people held a special place in his heart.

Faith and family above all were emphasized at Chuck Heaton's Bay Village home. They also loved reading, writing, and the arts. Chuck knows Patricia lives, practices, and is motivated by her faith, something in which he takes greater pride than in her fame or celebrity.

In her book *Motherhood and Hollywood*, Patricia writes on her Catholic-turned-Presbyterian Christian faith, "What I know is that we're not perfect. Apparently God knows it too, or He wouldn't have bothered to show up here Himself, and get strung up to straighten the whole mess out. So much of the world is all about distracting us from the reality of God, our Father.... He loves us. We need to love Him and each other. I just want to be staunch in my love of God and everybody else."

> *Every time we get the chance, let us work for the benefit of all, starting with the people closest to us.*
> **GALATIANS 6:10** MSG

After having moved out to L.A. from New York, Patricia continued to struggle to get regular, paying acting work. During some down time between jobs, she went with her church, Hollywood Presbyterian, on a mission trip to a Mexican orphanage. The actual journey into Mexico, the forced media deprivation, the physical labor, and the openness and simplicity of the Mexican children changed her. She no longer felt the urgency to become an actress. If necessary, she was willing to walk away. Upon her return, the stream of work began to flow in earnest, but she has never forgotten the lessons she learned in Mexico about connecting to others in work, play, or deliberate service to God.

After her brief stint on *Thirtysomething*, Patricia was featured on three unsuccessful sitcoms, *Room for Two* (1992) with Linda Lavin, *Someone Like Me* (1994), and *Women in the House* (1995) with Delta Burke, before landing the award-winning role of longsuffering wife, mother, and in-law Debra Barone on *Everybody Loves Raymond*. Since 1999, she's been nominated every year for Outstanding Lead Actress in a comedy series at the Emmy Awards, winning twice. And, she has also collected two Viewers for Quality Television awards and a Screen Actors Guild trophy for her work on the series.

Today, she and her husband, David Hunt, are raising four boys and run a production company called Four Boys Films. An outspoken Christian, she was influenced greatly by her father's work ethic, faith, and how he networked and spoke with successful sports players and managers.

A Father of Influence opens doors for his children.

Tom Cunningham

Unknown

Loren Cunningham. Tom Cunningham taught his son

Loren to listen to God. Loren listened and founded YWAM

(Youth with a Mission), one of the largest

mission-training and deployment organizations

in the world today.

In his early twenties, Loren Cunningham was plagued by a peculiar vision. He kept seeing wave upon wave of young people, missionaries in their late teens and early twenties, marching on the shores of all the continents of the world. He knew this vision was from God, and he had a pretty good idea what it meant.

When he was thirteen years old, Loren closed his eyes and prayed at the altar. When he opened his eyes, he saw before him the words of Mark 16:15, the Great Commission: "Go into all the world and preach the gospel" (NKJV). From that day forward, he knew he had a call to preach. He thought he might even be a missionary since the words said, "Go into all the world." As God spoke to Loren, the seeds of a great mission-training and commissioning organization germinated. Several events in Loren's life caused his vision for reaching the lost to snap ever clearer into focus.

This kind of call from God never seemed strange or out of the ordinary to Loren. His father and grandfather had also been called. Loren writes in his autobiography, *Is That Really You, God*, "My dad's father owned a successful laundry in Uvalde, Texas, and was living comfortably when he received what he termed a "call" to preach. He put his business up for sale. 'You're a fool, I'll say it outright,' said

Granddad's brother, to which Granddad replied, 'If I heard God right and didn't obey, that's when I'd be the fool.'"

Loren's grandfather obeyed the call in a part-time fashion, taking odd jobs in various towns in Texas and preaching on the weekends. Then tragedy struck. His wife contracted smallpox and lay dying. After an apparent recovery, Loren's grandfather prepared to take his sick wife home, but without warning she took a turn for the worse and died.

By your words I can see where I'm going; they throw a beam of light on my dark path. I've committed myself and I'll never turn back from living by your righteous order.

PSALM 119:105–106 MSG

On top of this loss, authorities insisted that her bed and clothes be burned to avoid contamination. Incredibly, Granddad Cunningham didn't reject God or blame Him. Instead, he started preaching full time. His five children stayed with relatives and farmer friends while he traveled and preached the Word. Though several of his siblings turned away from God, Tom did not. After spending time in prayer, he began traveling with his father to different revival meetings throughout the Southwest.

Tom's sister Arnette offered to pay his college tuition so he could get an engineering degree if he finished high school, but Tom refused. Instead, he endured hardship while preaching with his father. Finally he left the ministry and found a good job in Oklahoma City working on a construction crew. One day a crane carrying a load of lumber swerved and came right at Tom. He grabbed at the first thing he saw as the load hit him and found himself dangling out in space. His coworkers rescued him, but Tom saw the accident as a sign from God, gave his boss two weeks notice, and rejoined his father for ministry on the road. Given a second chance at life, Tom was determined to obey God's voice, regardless of the difficulties.

Out on the road, Tom met another young evangelist by the name of Jewell Nicholson. They soon married. In 1935, Loren was born. When Loren was nine, the family lived in Covina, California. Loren was given a five-dollar bill to make a purchase and sent down the street to the market. When he arrived, he couldn't find the bill.

Scared and angry at himself for losing the money, he returned home to admit his carelessness. His parents immediately suggested that they seek God and ask Him to show them where the money was. They prayed and felt God was telling them the money was under a bush. Loren retraced his steps looking under every bush, and finally, grabbing deep at the base of an evergreen shrub, he found the crumpled-up bill.

Loren further understood his call to missions just before his fifteenth birthday. He was daydreaming in church one morning about the '39 Chevy he wanted to buy, even though he was supposed to be listening to his father's sermon. He had saved up his paper-route money and was going to paint his car metallic blue as soon as he bought it. He was also planning to strip off the chrome and lower the rear end.

Then his dad's voice caught his attention. The tone changed. The elder Cunningham was talking about an Arab child he had met on his very first overseas trip to Israel. Trying to control his emotion, his usually booming bass voice was soft as he explained that the little ragged Arab girl was from a Palestinian refugee camp. About eight years old, she wore a shabby dress and had stringy hair. An even younger girl sat on her lap.

Tom described how she stuck out her dusty hand pleading for alms. Her face had left an indelible image in his mind. Loren noticed his father looked down at him from the wooden pulpit as he spoke.

Even though his hosts discouraged him from giving to beggars, Tom admitted that he simply couldn't turn her away. He hadn't cared if others like her were encouraged by his generosity. He took some coins out of his pocket and put them in her hand.

For a moment, Loren thought his father would cry. The entire congregation held their breath, and the room was very still. As Tom knelt to pray beside his bed that night in his hotel room, a vision of the dirty, tanned Palestinian child appeared before him. He blinked his eyes, but she was still there. Again she reached out her hand, and it seemed she wasn't just begging for change, she was reaching out for comfort, encouragement, love, and a future—in short, the gospel.

The church was moved that day to raise more money for foreign missions. Loren pledged his Chevy money toward the purchase of a jeep for an African missionary.

Missions were now in Loren's blood. He took a trip to Mexico and got even more excited. Then he took the Word of God to Nassau, Bahamas. After the waves of missionary visions, Loren led a small group of young people on a short mission trip. Other trips took shape, as well as some organizational ground rules. A name was applied to the group, and Youth with a Mission began in December 1960.

Today, YWAM continues to have a passion: to know God and to make Him known. YWAM bases operate in more than 1,000 locations in more than 149 countries. With evangelism, training, and relief services as its key purposes, YWAM remains one of the largest missionary organizations in the world. And its leader, Loren Cunningham, wouldn't have found it if he hadn't listened to God, a skill he learned from both his father and grandfather.

**A Father of Influence teaches his children
to listen to the voice of God.**

Sir Randolph Churchill

1849–1895

Winston Churchill. Following in his father's footsteps
with a career as a statesman, Winston Churchill led
England as prime minister through the dark days
of World War II.

Young Winston Churchill hated study, overspent his allowance, and did poorly in school. His father, Sir Randolph Churchill, a member of Parliament, thought his son only had an aptitude for military life. Winston didn't mind this assessment, as he wanted nothing more than to be a diplomat like his father and thought that an illustrious career in the military just might write a ticket to his own seat in Parliament. Winston often told his childhood friends that he would one day be a statesman just like his father.

Winston was studious in some regards. An astute people watcher, he gathered information and considered all sides of an issue. As a young soldier in India, he read history books and biographies of world leaders in preparation for the role he would later play.

Winston loved his parents deeply, though as active socialites they left him to spend most of his time with tutors, nannies, and aides. When Winston was seven years old, his parents sent him to St. George's, an elementary school designed to prepare young, upper-class boys for England's finer public schools (similar to America's private schools). Unfortunately, Winston was usually in some kind of trouble there and was often flogged by the headmaster. His parents took him out of the school and transferred him to one in Brighton, but his experience at St. George convinced him never to let anyone bully him again.

By 1886, Winston's father, Randolph, had become prominent as the secretary of state of India, which at that time was part of the British Empire. From there he rose to Chancellor of the Exchequer, in charge of the British economy. He was also leader of the House of Commons. Winston was so proud of his father he asked him to send autographs to his address at school so that he could distribute them to his classmates.

> *We have different gifts, according to the grace given us ... if it is serving, let him serve ... if it is leadership, let him govern diligently.*
>
> **Romans 12:6–8**

By 1888, Winston left the Brighton school to attend Harrow, where he concentrated on Latin, Greek, natural science, mathematics, and military strategies. There at Harrow, Winston flexed his wit and resolve during a disagreement with the headmaster. According to *Winston Churchill* by Judith Rogers, the headmaster snapped, "'Churchill, I have grave reason to be displeased with you.' Winston quickly responded, 'And I sir, have grave reason to be displeased with you.'"

Winston later planned to attend the Royal Military Academy at Sandhurst before joining a regiment in India. He once told the family doctor, whom he was seeing for a lisp, that he ultimately intended to become a statesman like his father and couldn't worry about making an important speech unable to say the letter *S*.

However, Winston's health was the least of his problems. He failed the entrance exam to Sandhurst *three* times before passing. Randolph was certain his son would end up in a clerk's job. Instead of the infantry, Winston's poor performance relegated him to the less prestigious cavalry, but he vowed to do better academically.

At Sandhurst, Winston knuckled down, applied himself, improved his manners, and even neatened up his appearance. Randolph finally believed his son could have a career in politics and began introducing him to political leaders and young men of note.

Soon after, however, Winston's father's health began to deteriorate. His doctors persuaded him to go on a long sea voyage to rest and improve his state of mind. Unfortunately, the trip ended badly—Randolph was too unwell to continue. Winston's parents returned to London, where Randolph died just a few days later.

Though saddened by his loss, Winston was more determined than ever to gain fame and prominence as an elected official. Winston wrote of his father in his book *My Early Life*, "All my dreams of comradeship with him, of entering Parliament at his side and in his support, were ended. There remained for me only to pursue his aims and vindicate his memory."

It seems all the events following his father's death would prepare Winston to assume the office of prime minister during World War II. First, Winston served in Kitchener's army in the Sudan and published his first book. Then he escaped from Pretoria after being taken prisoner while covering the Boer War for the *London Morning Post*. He was first elected to Parliament in 1900 and held several public offices in the early 1900s (during which time he married). After a disappointing defeat during World War I, he resigned from the Admiralty, but was reelected to Parliament and was one of Hitler's first and worst critics during the 1930s. On May 10, 1940, he was appointed prime minister.

Though the task set before him was truly formidable, Churchill saw it as an honor to lead his country during the hardships of wartime. Speaking before the House of Commons, he displayed his formidable linguistic skill as a master statesman. "I have nothing to offer but blood, toil, tears, and sweat. You ask, 'What is our aim?' I can answer in one word: victory—victory in spite of all terror; victory, however long and hard the road may be; for without victory there is no survival … if we fail, then the whole world, including the United States, including all that we have known and cared for, will sink into the abyss of a new dark age made more sinister, and perhaps more protracted, by the lights of perverted science. Let us therefore brace ourselves to our duties, and so bear ourselves that, if the British Empire and its Commonwealth last for a thousand years, men will still say, 'This was their finest hour.'" His words gained him his nation's unanimous support.

For the next five years, Churchill steered his country and his commanders to victory. He watched Hitler's Nazis like a hawk as they invaded neighboring France. When Hitler threatened an invasion of England, Churchill refused to capitulate or negotiate, and therefore, was able to keep the United Kingdom as a base from which the Allies could eventually attack Germany.

Though Churchill's critical role in World War II was undeniable, there were critics in his own country. Immediately following the close of the war in Europe, Churchill was defeated in the 1945 election by Clement Attlee and the Labor Party. British voters believed that the best man to lead the nation in time of war was not necessarily the best man to lead it in peace.

The United Kingdom, however, was not done with Churchill, who had grown restless and bored as leader of the conservative opposition in the immediate post-war years. In the general election of 1951, Churchill again became prime minister, where he served until his resignation in 1955. During this period, he renewed what he called the "special relationship" between Britain and the United States and engaged himself in the formation of the post-war order.

In 1953, he was awarded the Nobel Prize for Literature "for his mastery of historical and biographical description as well as for brilliant oratory in defending exalted human values." Later, in 1963, he became an honorary citizen of the United States of America. On his death at age ninety in 1965, (seventy years to the day after his father's death), his body lay in state in Westminster Hall for three days by decree of the Queen. A state funeral service was held at St. Paul's Cathedral, the first state funeral for a nonroyal family member since 1914. The pageantry involved a nineteen-gun salute by the Royal Artillery, and the RAF staged a fly-by of sixteen English Electric Lightning fighters. It was the largest gathering of dignitaries in Britain ever, attended by representatives from more than a hundred nations.

Winston Churchill succeeded and achieved all he saw in his father, and held the United Kingdom together during the worst days of the twentieth century.

A Father of Influence teaches his children to embrace leadership and serve with honor.

John Vine Milne

1845–Unknown

A. A. Milne. John V. Milne was not only a father to A. A. Milne, the author of the *Winnie-the-Pooh* books, but he was also his teacher. He instructed his son to have confidence and showed him how to value enthusiasm and wonder.

One day in 1884, John Milne decided it was time for his two eldest children—five-year-old David and four-year-old Kenneth—to learn how to read. Mr. Milne put a chart of words on the wall and waited as David and Kenneth stared silently at the chart, unable to make out the words. Mr. Milne pointed at one word and asked, "What's that?" but the boys were silent. Then, from the back of the room, two-and-a-half-year-old Alan replied, "Cat." Mr. Milne grinned. His youngest child, Alan Alexander, was right.

Initially, Alan Alexander was named Alexander Sydney Milne, but John decided to legally change his son's name. (Alexander being the name of John's brother.) Alan (or A. A. as he was later known) was born in Scotland but soon moved to London to Henley House, the Milne's home and school for boys where John was headmaster. When Alan was born, the school was home to thirteen boarders, the youngest six and the oldest sixteen. Forty to fifty other boys came just for the school day.

John V. Milne fancied Henley House more as a meeting place for friends than a shop where education was sold. Only three rules applied at Henley House: No lying, cheating, or bullying.

A. A. thought well of his father. According to the book *A. A. Milne: The Man Behind Winnie-the-Pooh*, A. A. said his father "was the best man I have ever known: by which I mean the most truly good, the most completely to be trusted, the most incapable of wrong.... As a child, I gave my heart to my father." Later A. A. described his father as having a sense of humor and courage.

> *Listen, my sons, to a father's instruction; pay attention and gain understanding.*
>
> **PROVERBS 4:1**

A. A. particularly enjoyed listening to his father read him stories, especially *Uncle Remus* and *Reynard the Fox*. On Sunday, the Lord's day, John would read *Pilgrim's Progress*. Later, when A. A. himself became a reader, he took to *Treasure Island*, *Masterman Ready*, and *The Swiss Family Robinson*.

Henley House could have been a difficult place to study with its cold interior. But with love, it became the next best place to home for its students. A. A. could hardly wait to be one. A. A. was reading far more complicated words than *cat* before he was four, and by the time he was five, he was writing legibly and beautifully. When A. A. turned six, he officially became an enthusiastic student and John his enthusiastic teacher.

As a student, he performed so well at school that his mother became anxious and wanted Alan stopped. She thought that ambitious children tire themselves to the point of becoming dull. Yet Alan could not be stopped. He didn't even want to set aside his reading and learning to go outside and play. When he was denied his studies for a time, he became listless, mopey, and bored. His health suffered, and finally his parents let him return to his full study cycle.

Though A. A. took to reading and writing, he later attended Cambridge on a mathematics scholarship. Words were always a part of his make-up, however, and at Cambridge he edited and wrote for *Granta*, a student magazine. A. A. and his brother Kenneth collaborated, and their articles appeared over the initials AKM.

A. A. finished Cambridge in the summer of 1903 and then went to London to see what he could do with his writing. A. A. wrote his friend and former teacher H. G. Wells and told him he was going to try journalism. The young Milne had made an arrangement with his father to keep him financially afloat for two years, even without earning a penny. But the ambitious writer was determined to make money at his craft. Eventually A. A.'s work came to the attention of the leading British humor magazine, *Punch*, where he first became a contributor and then later an editor.

In 1910, A. A. met Dorothy De Selincourt, the goddaughter of *Punch*'s editor-in-chief. She wanted the young writer to call her Daphne, and in 1913, they married. Though antiwar, A. A. eventually signed on to fight for England during World War I. Following the war, in 1920, A. A. and Daphne had a child whom they named Christopher Robin, and A. A. was on track as a playwright and author.

John found great pride and pleasure in watching his son rise to fame and fortune. A. A. returned the admiration with works dedicated to his father's interests. Noting his father's weakness for detective stories, A. A. dedicated his first novel, *The Red House Mystery,* to him. In the dedication, he proclaimed his great affection and gratitude to his father. He said that after all his father had done for him, writing a detective book for him was the least he could do.

A. A. loved to watch his son Christopher Robin play with his toys, especially a stuffed bear Christopher named Pooh. As Christopher splashed around puddles or played among the trees, he always carried his teddy bear with him. A. A. wrote several children's poems and even put Christopher Robin's name in some of them. An illustrator named Edward Shepard created pictures for the book, and in 1924, the book *When We Were Very Young* was published.

In 1925, A. A. wrote a children's story for the *Evening News* about Christopher Robin and his bear, now named Winnie-the-Pooh. The story was so successful that he wrote more stories about the twosome and even added other creatures to inhabit the Hundred-Acre Wood, modeled after a real place called Ashdown Forest. *Winnie-the-Pooh* hit bookstores in October 1926, and critics and fans loved it.

As the Pooh books' popularity soared, John relished every sales figure, every sign of their widespread fame. John V. would write his friends and brag about the success of Alan's books. A. A. was pleased that his father was so happy and excited. It was a remarkable time for father and son.

Thankfully, John V. Milne let his son jump fully into the academic world, and A. A. became the best student possible. By encouraging him to read, write, and explore his world, John gave his son a valuable gift—the art of observing, processing, and recording his thoughts on paper. When he was older and married, A. A. enjoyed watching his own son, Christopher Robin. Thankfully, the whole world can enjoy the fruits of A. A.'s labor through the wonderful, imaginative, and joyous *Winnie-the-Pooh* books.

**A Father of Influence gives his children
permission to explore their world.**

James Liddell

Unknown

Eric Liddell. The son of Scottish missionaries to China, Eric returned to China to serve the Lord there after refusing to run the 100-meter race final on a Sunday at the 1924 Olympic Games and winning the gold medal in the 400-meter race instead.

When Eric Henry Liddell was born in Tientsin, North China, his Scottish missionary parents were originally going to name him Henry Eric Liddell. When a friend pointed out that his initials spelled H. E. L., Eric's father, James, switched the names around. A faithful Christian, James wouldn't toy with anything so unholy.

Eric loved to play at the large London Missionary Society compound in Siao Chang out on the Great Plain. As James preached in the church and Eric's mother, Mary, helped teach school, Eric would sometimes dress in a blue padded jacket and pants like the rest of his Asian friends. He spoke perfect Chinese, but when he took off his cap, anyone could tell he wasn't Asian—he had straight blond hair and big blue eyes.

Eric's parents had come to China before he was born. They were married in Shanghai and then sent by the London Missionary Society to work in Mongolia, remaining in the northern region because "Boxers," a group of Chinese people who hated and killed foreigners, had targeted Mongolia for persecution. In Siao Chang, the Chinese Christians welcomed and protected the Liddell family.

After nine years in China, the London Missionary Society decided the family should return to Scotland on furlough. Eric's older brother was excited about going home. But Eric was confused—he thought China *was* home. It was the only home Eric knew, and it was a home he had grown to love and enjoy. He did not share his family's excitement as they packed up and took a long boat journey back to Scotland.

The days of the blameless are known to the LORD, and their inheritance will endure forever.

PSALM 37:18

Though Scotland proved to be full of new surprises and adventures for Eric and Robert, they were saddened to learn that their parents were going to leave them there to attend boarding school while they returned to China with their younger sister, Jenny. (It was seven years before Eric and Robert saw their parents and sister again.) Extremely shy, Eric would always let his brother, Robert, do the talking. Lonely for their parents and their China home, they often wrote letters to their parents and told them of their life at school.

One relief and joy the brothers found at school was the opportunity for vigorous exercise and sports. The boys played rugby in winter and cricket and track events in the summer. Eric wrote his father, "I don't think much of lessons, but I can run." As the years went on, Eric and his brother excelled more and more at sports. By 1918, when Eric was sixteen and Robert was eighteen, the boys were the athletic stars of the school. In fact, Eric was voted outstanding sportsman and given the Blackheath Cup, later becoming captain of both the cricket and rugby teams. Eric became renowned all across the country, collecting trophies, ribbons, and awards. Yet his headmaster noted that he was "entirely without vanity."

In 1921, Eric's father returned again to the United Kingdom. Together again, James asked his son what he wanted to do once he finished studying for his degree in math and science. Eric admitted that he wasn't sure. He was sure of only a few things. He loved Jesus, he loved to run, and he loved China.

Though Eric was a strong Christian, he was still terribly shy and afraid to share his faith—unlike his gregarious, talkative brother, Robert. One day a friend, David Thomson (or DP as he was known to most people), approached Eric and asked him if he would speak about Christ to a group of rugby players. Eric chaffed at the idea, but after consideration, agreed. He spoke about how God was in control of his life and how he accepted whatever happened to him as God's best for that time. He also spoke about God's love for him and everyone who was there. He thanked the players for listening and then sat down. To Eric's surprise, every newspaper in Scotland carried a photo and story of the speech. The man who disliked drawing attention to himself was now a nationally known spokesperson for Christ.

In early 1923, Eric tried out for the Olympic team and easily qualified. He was elated until he received a list of the events he was entered in. Beside each event were the times and dates for the heats and the finals. Beside the heat for the 100-meter sprint—his best event—was one fateful word: *Sunday*. He had never run on a Sunday and was not about to start. His religious convictions wouldn't let him. His parents had always taught him that Sunday was a day of rest and reverence for God. All his life, Eric had honored that teaching. Sadly, Eric informed the British Olympic Committee that he couldn't run in the 100-meter sprint. As a compromise, they suggested he run the 200-meter and 400-meter events, even though he was not favored to win. Eric accepted.

At about the same time as the Olympic Games, Eric decided to follow in his father's footsteps and become a missionary to China. He wasn't sure where he would go, but he planned to first go to Tientsin, where he had been born and his parents were now stationed. There, he would live with his family while he got established. He wrote to the Anglo-Chinese College in Tientsin to ask if they needed the services of a science teacher or a sports coach. He knew they wouldn't reply for months and figured he'd run his races in the meantime—for now the Olympics and his country needed him.

At the start of the 400-meter race final at Colombes Stadium, Eric Liddell lunged forward in the worst possible position—the outside lane. A 100-meter sprinter, Eric was up against American favorite and world record holder Horatio Fitch. Next to Fitch was Joseph Imbach, a Swiss runner, who had also broken the world record in his qualifying heat. The battle belonged to these two men—not Eric.

As the runners raced down the back straightaway, Eric had the lead. Everyone assumed he would fade as the race progressed. A sprinter, Eric didn't know how to pace himself for an event four times the length of his normal race. Amazingly, Liddell ran the first half in a speedy 22.2 seconds.

As Fitch and Imbach closed in on him, Eric knew he had to give it everything he had. Coming down the front stretch, Fitch closed to within two meters, but Eric burst to life again and ran the second half of the race faster than the first! Crossing the finish line, Eric threw his head back and his arms into the air, a full five meters ahead of Horatio Fitch! Eric not only won the race but he also broke the old record by two-tenths of a second!

At a victory celebration back in Scotland, Eric revealed his future before a shocked audience. According to *Eric Liddell: Something Greater Than Gold* by Janet and Geoff Benge, he said, "Since I have been a young lad, I have had my eyes on a different prize. You see, each one of us is in a greater race than any I have run in Paris, and this race ends when God gives out the medals. It has always been my intention to be a missionary, and I have just received word that I have been accepted as a chemistry teacher at the Anglo-Chinese College in Tientsin, China. From now on, I will be putting my energy into preparing to take up that position."

A year later, after studying theology at Congregational College, Eric took a train to London. On the way, he read letters from his father about the deplorable conditions now present in his beloved China. Undeterred, Eric took the newly completed Trans-Siberian railroad from Holland to China, where he met his father and began his new life serving the Lord. Eric served faithfully until he died of a brain tumor at age forty-three.

James Liddell gave his son a love of China and the Chinese people; and through his example of quality, Christian leadership, and parenting, taught Eric that fame and glory are fleeting, but a life of obedience to Christ lasts forever.

A Father of Influence teaches his children that giving their lives to God's work is the greatest glory of all.

J. R. R. Tolkien

1892–1973

John, Michael, Christopher, and Priscilla Tolkien.
Author and English literature professor J. R. R. Tolkien
relied on his children for help and inspiration, allowing him
to create one of the greatest works of the twentieth
century, the Lord of the Rings trilogy.

J. R. R. Tolkien longed for the days when his children could be
active readers and participants in his stories. He wanted a ready
audience for his invented worlds. Once, when Tolkien's five-
year-old son Michael lost a favorite toy dog, the as-yet-unpublished
author invented a tale to cheer up his sad boy. Tolkien wrote down a
story about a dog named Rover who was transformed into a toy dog
named Roverandom by a magical wizard. Roverandom had many
adventures, including meeting a sand sorcerer and riding to the
moon up a moon path. Another time, Roverandom hitched a ride on
a seagull. As Tolkien told this story to his son, Michael's sadness
turned to joy. And this became the very first recorded story by the
writer of *The Hobbit* and *The Lord of the Rings*.

To spend more time with his family, Tolkien, a professor of
English Literature at Oxford, often met with students at his home.
Always coming home for lunch and tea, he took his job as head of the
family very seriously. He let his children come and go from his study
at any time, except when he was meeting with students there. Tolkien
often hurried between home and campus several times each day, riding his bicycle, wearing long, black, flowing robes.

It was neither his love of languages nor his fascination with the past that pushed Tolkien to write fiction. It was rather his children who inspired him to invent tales. Each night they asked him for another story. Each night his children asked to learn about particular characters. They wanted to hear about elves, dwarfs, and magical treelike creatures called the Ents.

Parents rejoice when their children turn out well; wise children become proud parents. So make your father happy! Make your mother proud!

PROVERBS 23:23 MSG

His son Michael said about Tolkien's bedtime stories in an interview in *The Sunday Telegraph* in 1973: "They were infinitely more exciting and much funnier" than any published children's books. Michael believed his father's stories were of such quality because of "that reality of being inside a story and so being part of it." Unfortunately, these first "bedtime stories" were never written down—until the story of Roverandom.

Tolkien's children first heard "hobbit" stories in the late 1920s, and yet it wasn't until 1930 that Tolkien wrote down the first words of *The Hobbit* on the blank page of a student's examination paper. The author insisted he never really wrote his stories but simply typed them on the page. He believed he merely described a world that already existed. At first, Tolkien did most of his own typing, but his sons Michael and Christopher helped him as they grew older.

After eight years of toil, the author finished *The Hobbit* and dedicated the work to his four children for their help and inspiration. Tolkien wanted a perfect manuscript and paid his son Christopher two pennies for each mistake that he found. Writing the book in the early hours of the morning, Tolkien shared sections of it with his children as bedtime stories. As the children grew older, the author worked on the manuscript less and less. It took his friend C. S. Lewis, author of *The Chronicles of Narnia*, to motivate him to finish it. When he did, word spread around Oxford. Publisher Sir Stanley Unwin showed the manuscript to his son Rayner, who read it and gave it a glowing report. *The Hobbit* was published in September of 1937, and by Christmas of that year the first printing had sold out.

Sir Stanley Unwin asked Tolkien to write a sequel or follow-up book and the author agreed. At first, Tolkien offered his unfinished work, *Book of Lost Tales*, renamed *The Silmarillion*. He had begun *The Silmarillion* while lying in a hospital bed during World War I recovering from trench fever. Sir Stanley's son, Rayner Unwin, however, compared it to a necklace of jewels lacking a string, and the work was shelved. (In fact, *The Silmarillion* took more than fifty years to complete.)

Before his demise, the author asked his son Christopher to finish *The Silmarillion*. Tolkien knew he could do it because Christopher had also studied languages at Oxford. Christopher knew and understood the world of Middle-earth better than anyone. (And later, Christopher became an Oxford don, just like his father.)

Little did Sir Stanley Unwin know he would not see the requested sequel, *The Lord of the Rings*, for seventeen years. When World War II broke out in 1939, all the Tolkien children were grown except for Priscilla. John, the eldest, had become a Catholic priest. Michael and Christopher were fighting in the war. Tolkien often wrote to his son Christopher, who was stationed in the Royal Air Force (RAF) in South Africa, and described new characters who had entered the world of Middle-earth.

By the time *The Lord of the Rings* was finished, Rayner Unwin had grown up, graduated from Oxford, and was now working for the publishing company. He read the manuscript and loved it, but felt that it would lose money for the publishing house. Rayner decided it must be separated out and printed as a trilogy. The three volumes were released in 1954 and 1955, becoming an instant classic and inspiring the imaginations of generations of students, young people, and all who read them.

A former student of Tolkien, S.R.T.O. d'Ardenne said what she remembered most about the man was his great love of family. He often wrote her about his concern for the children. Their health, comfort, future, success, and perfecting were important to him.

After Tolkien died, his son Michael wrote in the Sunday *Telegraph*, "I, together with my two brothers and my sister, have not only lost a father who retained a close interest in every detail of our lives ... but a friend of half a century's standing, for he possessed the rare talent of combining fatherhood and friendship." Perhaps the best description of the author comes from his son Michael, who summarized his father with one word. When he joined the army, Michael had to fill out an entry form. Asked his father's occupation, the younger Tolkien wrote: "Wizard."

A Father of Influence shares his vision with his children.

Dr. James Dobson

1936–

James Ryan Dobson. Through his popular ministry Focus on the Family, Dr. James Dobson teaches America's parents how to raise godly children. Dr. Dobson found his own parenting skills put to the test when son Ryan's undiagnosed learning disability took its toll on their relationship. Now Ryan stands as a committed Christian with his own speaking and writing ministry.

Since the inception of Focus on the Family in 1977, Christians the world over have come to rely on the firm but loving parental advice of its founder and primary spokesperson, Dr. James Dobson. Heard on more than three thousand radio facilities in North America and in twenty-seven languages around the world, Dr. Dobson dispenses practical advice on how to raise boys and girls, dare to discipline, and offer tough love. One could easily assume he runs his own family with ease and that Dobson is no stranger to the "in-the-trenches" efforts it takes to be a parent in today's world. The conviction and stability Ryan exhibits today are a testament to Dr. Dobson's ability to apply his own words to the making of a man.

After the birth of their daughter, Danae, doctors told Dr. James and his wife, Shirley, that she would be unable to bear any more children. Yet, wanting to round out their family with another member, the couple adopted James Ryan on the same day James Dobson released his first (and perhaps most controversial) book, *Dare to Discipline*. Both events changed his life completely.

It quickly became evident that Ryan suffered from Attention Deficit-Hyperactivity Disorder (or ADHD). He was so restless that he would wake up ravenous with hunger after a night's sleep. Dobson realized his young son had a problem, but in the seventies the only available medications were sedatives. And, as was customary among medical professionals at the time, Dobson believed his son's restlessness would disappear when he reached puberty.

Dobson allowed his son to expend his rambunctious energy on sports. When Ryan was fourteen years old, the two rappelled down high cliffs in the Sierra Nevada. While Ryan descended the mountain quite easily, Dobson prayed and struggled all the way down.

Though Ryan wasn't a particularly good student and didn't express much interest in going to college, Dobson insisted that his son enroll in Olivet Nazarene University in Bourbonnais, Illinois. To help him make the adjustment, he also provided the means for his son's best friend to attend the college. He even managed to secure the release of Ryan's buddy from a four-year obligation made to the U.S. Navy just a week earlier.

Coming from metropolitan Southern California, Ryan felt out of sorts in rural Illinois, and he struggled at Olivet. Dobson pulled his son out of school, helped him move to Colorado, set him up in an apartment with a month's rent, and then told him he needed to fend for himself. Once Ryan was able to excel at a handful of nonacademic jobs, he gained the courage and confidence to ask his parents to give him another opportunity at higher education. They agreed and Ryan enrolled at Biola University in suburban Los Angeles. He knew this would be his last opportunity.

Initially, Biola wasn't working out either, and Ryan began to despair. That Thanksgiving, Ryan remembers, "I had more stress and angst in my life than ever before." Ryan asked his father if he could see a counselor, and Dr. Dobson sent him to the dean of Rosemead School of Psychology, the Biola-affiliated graduate school that had been founded by one of Dobson's mentors. After countless tests revealed a genius-level IQ along with strong disabilities in math and languages, the psychologists told Ryan he had ADHD. Finally, Ryan had an understanding of his difficulties.

Ryan says this about his father's reaction to the news: "Discovering that changed lots of things in our relationship. It took the pressure off and said that 'whatever happens, happens'—which was a big deal." Ryan began taking Ritalin, his grades improved, and he graduated from Biola in 1995. According to *Family Man: The Biography of James Dobson* by Dale Buss, Ryan said, "I couldn't believe how understanding my parents were during what had to be a very difficult time. I wasn't a very good student, and my parents accepted me no matter what my grades looked like."

Post-college, Ryan tried to get his footing in the real world. He wasn't able to settle on a career even though his gift for public speaking emerged. "I went through a major life crisis when I moved back to California. I had quit my job and at the time, I just didn't care if I got another one."

In 2002, Dobson asked his son to help with a Focus on the Family event, the National Bike Ride for the Family. The gig not only engaged Ryan in a fulfilling activity, but also gave him a new appreciation for his father's ministry. Ryan got rid of all his anger during those bike rides as he met people who told him how important his father was to them. What really restored him was his parents' love and support. At his lowest moments, they were there. They were determined to let their son know that they wanted his best. Ryan knows his father holds his son's success in top priority, not necessarily business or wealth prosperity, but spiritual well-being. As James and Shirley made it very clear to Ryan that they would do everything they could to see him through, everything changed.

This constant support helped shape Ryan into an accomplished author and speaker. His parents never prodded or pushed him to enter Christian work. They merely encouraged him to do whatever he believed God was calling him to do.

In 2003, Ryan joined the Ambassador Agency in Nashville, and speaking engagements lined up. Before an event at a crisis pregnancy center in Tampa that year, Ryan felt others were expecting him to be as good as his dad on stage. Realizing their age difference, he satisfied himself with doing his best for God, and then recognized that in the past three years, he had turned into a pretty good speaker. By the end of 2003, Ryan Dobson had become one of the nation's premiere speakers to Christian youth.

> *Love never gives up.*
>
> 1 CORINTHIANS 13:4 MSG

Ryan dedicates his 2003 book *Be Intolerant: Because Some Things Are Just Stupid* to his father. In its pages, he talks about how his father always stands up for what is right. As for himself, Ryan says he is completely intolerant to sin. Though he knows some people may call him narrow-minded or Bible thumping, he doesn't care. Like his father, he makes a practice of standing up and saying things are right, like loving Jesus Christ with all you have.

Within *Be Intolerant*, he expounds, "I see intolerance in my dad who takes a stand on a daily basis no matter what anybody says. He does what God wants him to do, even though people don't like it—a *lot* of people. They put him down and take him off the air because he makes a stand for Christ. And he does it anyway. He could take the easy way out. When he was on the gambling and pornography commission, we got threats from the Mafia. He could have said, 'You know what? Enough of this.' But he did what God wanted him to do." Two years later, Ryan came out with his second book, *2Die4,* and continues to influence youth culture with his straight-up, no-nonsense message.

Despite the uncertainty and difficulty of raising a son with a learning disability, Dr. James Dobson not only maintained a thriving ministry during that time but also was able to provide a firm and solid foundation for his struggling son. Through effective parenting backed up by wise biblical counsel, Dr. James Dobson pulled his son through a dark and uncertain youth to a brighter, more confident adulthood, one that is touching youth in ways the elder Dobson could never do.

A Father of Influence stands by his children during their struggles.

James R. Jordan

1936–1993

Michael Jeffrey Jordan. James R. Jordan foresaw greatness within his son, NBA great Michael Jordan, widely considered the greatest basketball player of all time.

Michael Jordan made the game-winning shot in the 1982 NCAA basketball championships. He knew how meaningful the game was, but he didn't understand its full implications. Michael was a freshman at North Carolina, and they were playing Georgetown starring basketball legend Patrick Ewing. As Michael and his team rode to the arena, Michael remembers falling asleep on the bus, daydreaming about scoring the winning shot. Feeling calm and relaxed, he was neither awake nor asleep. He was somewhere comfortably in between. He saw himself as the hero of the game. He imagined hitting the game-winning shot. He could see his teammates James Worthy, Sam Perkins, and Coach Dean Smith. But Michael didn't know if this event would be against the upcoming Georgetown team or against another team in another year. The dream wasn't that specific. But after they beat Georgetown, Michael told his father about the dream. Pausing to reflect, James then told his son that life was never going to be the same—life was going to change.

Initially, Michael thought his father was just being encouraging—after all, who could know what would happen. But he remembered his father's words when success began to stalk him.

Michael Jordan's life did change, in a colossal way that would forever alter the face of basketball and redefine him as the greatest athlete the sport has ever seen. In his book *For the Love of the Game: My Story*, Michael writes, "When I think of my career, where I have come from, where it all began, and all that I have accomplished along the way, I realize everything did change after that game. Not just basketball, but my life. I think my father saw some things in me that I couldn't see in myself. At first, I just thought it was a father's pride, the voice of hopes and dreams for a son to be successful. I saw his comments more in the context of a motivational speech a father might give a son. I do believe my father knew. I believe he saw things unfolding in a way that no one, not me, not the Chicago Bulls, or anyone else saw. I believe that's a father's gift."

Michael is the fourth of five children, born in Brooklyn, New York. He has two older brothers, a younger and older sister.

While Mrs. Jordan was pregnant with Michael, her mother died unexpectedly, and she came close to having a miscarriage. The doctors kept the expectant mother bedridden as a precaution. Everyone worried that Michael might not make it to full term. He made it safely into the world but almost suffocated when he fell behind his parents' bed. Later as a toddler, he picked up two wires in the rain next to the car that his father was working on. The shock threw young Michael about three feet back. Many events in Michael's young life could have altered his future, preventing him from becoming a basketball great.

After Michael was born, his parents decided to move to Wilmington, North Carolina. They felt the small, laid-back town would be a better place to raise their family. Once settled in Wilmington, Mr. and Mrs. Jordan began to show their children the benefits of hard work.

Michael wanted to attend USC but wasn't offered a basketball scholarship, so he attended the University of North Carolina instead. After the 1982 NCAA championships, Jordan was nominated player of the year—from that point on his professional basketball career was on track. After winning the Naismith College Player of the Year award in 1984, he left school early to enter the NBA Draft and was selected by the Chicago Bulls in the first round as the third pick overall. That same year, he won Olympic gold for the USA basketball team. During the 1984–85 season, he won Rookie of the Year. Throughout the mid to late '80s and early '90s, Jordan wowed NBA fans, earning titles and awards while meeting and breaking individual records. During this time, he and the Bulls achieved the first of two three-time, consecutive NBA championship titles.

Then, in October 1993, Jordan announced his retirement, citing a lost desire to play the game. By the beginning of 1992, Michael was starting to feel like he was under a microscope. He was a father and husband at home, but everywhere else he was Michael Jordan. It seemed like everyone had an idea of what was expected of him, and he didn't like it. By all accounts, his life and the way he perceived it were changing rapidly.

On July 23, 1993, Michael's father, James Jordan, was brutally murdered while returning from the funeral of a friend. He had pulled into a rest area off of Interstate 95 near Lumberton, North Carolina, for a nap. Two local criminals—Daniel Green and Larry Martin Demery—shot the elder Jordan in the chest and stole his Lexus, a gift from Michael. The perpetrators made several calls from Jordan's cell phone and were quickly captured.

The death of James Jordan ended one of the most successful yet challenging periods of Michael's life. Michael and his father were best friends, and James knew everything about his son. Michael recognizes that the happy, joyous side of his personality came from his father. James was a real people person and he had a great sense of humor. He taught his son many life lessons, and one of those was that everything happens for a reason.

After retiring from basketball, Jordan spent the next year pursuing a childhood dream—professional baseball. He signed a minor league contract with the Chicago White Sox of the American League, but only achieved lackluster results. When the professional baseball strike occurred in 1994, Michael returned to basketball and rejoined his old team, the Chicago Bulls. At his press conference he said only two words, "I'm back." He continued to amaze everyone with his on the court prowess, racking up another three consecutive NBA titles with the Bulls, while continuing to set individual records.

With Bulls Coach Phil Jackson's contract expiring, and in the latter stages of an owner-induced lockout of NBA players, Jordan retired for a second time on January 13, 1999. After a year as the GM of the NBA team, the Washington Wizards, Michael again stepped onto the court as a player. He finally announced his permanent retirement at the end of the 2003 season, though his numbers and performance only decreased slightly. He continued to perform as a dominant player until the ripe old age of forty.

> *"I know the plans I have for you,"* declares the LORD, *"plans to prosper you and not to harm you, plans to give you hope and a future."*
> **JEREMIAH 29:11**

Michael's accomplishments would impress even the most critical sports analyst. "M. J." ended a career of fifteen seasons with a regular-season scoring average of 30.12 points per game, the highest in NBA history (higher than Wilt Chamberlain's 30.06). With the Chicago Bulls, he won six NBA championships (during which he won all six NBA Finals MVP awards), ten scoring titles, and was named league MVP five times—as well as the All-NBA First Team ten times and All-Defensive First Team nine times. He led the league in steals three times. Jordan has appeared on the front cover of *Sports Illustrated* forty-nine times (a record), and was named the magazine's "Sportsman of the Year" in 1991. In 1999, he was named "the greatest athlete of the twentieth century" by ESPN, and placed second on the Associated Press list of top athletes of the century. His leaping ability, vividly illustrated by dunking from the foul line and other feats, earned him the nicknames "Air Jordan" and "His Airness." In living-room and barroom debates, he is often placed next to Muhammed Ali as the greatest athlete of all time.

James R. Jordan almost intuitively knew his son Michael had the seeds of greatness within him. He nurtured this greatness with friendship, humor, and a strong sense of destiny.

A Father of Influence envisions a great future for his children.

George Washington

1732–1799

Father of our country. Though he never had children of his own, George Washington rose from no formal education to defeat the British army and guide America through its perilous first years of existence.

The tale of George Washington is a tale of many fathers. His own father, Augustine, died when George was only eleven years old. After his father's death, George was raised by his older half-brother, Lawrence, who became a hero and father figure to him. As a commander in chief of the newly formed Continental Army, George fathered the soldiers under his charge. Then as the first president of the United States of America, sworn in on April 30, 1789, Washington stood over a fledgling nation defining office responsibilities and ushering in a new age of democracy for the fragile, emerging republic.

George Washington came from a long line of American-born landowners. His great-grandfather, John, his grandfather Lawrence, and his father, Augustine, all added land to the family holdings. All three men had been a justice of the peace, a member of the Virginia House of the Burgesses, and an officer in the Virginia militia. And all enjoyed at least a few years of schooling "back home" in England.

George's father, Augustine Washington, was a prosperous tobacco farmer. Known to friends as "Gus," the elder Washington also bought and sold land for profit and was part-owner of an ironworks operation. Prior to George's birth on the shores of the Potomac River in Virginia, Augustine was married and had three children, among them a son named Lawrence. When Augustine's wife died, he married a young woman a year later named Mary Ball. George was the first of their four children.

At six years of age, George and his family settled at Ferry Farm, along the Rappahannock River, near Fredericksburg, Virginia. There, George grew up in a crowded household—thirteen beds and a couch were packed into six rooms.

The familiar story about George Washington chopping down the cherry tree as a six-year-old and then telling his father "I can't tell a lie, Pa; I did it with my hatchet" is likely fiction. It comes from an early biography of Washington by Mason Locke Weems, who, ironically, was trying to teach young readers that "honesty is the best policy."

As a successful tobacco farmer, Augustine was able to send his two older sons to England to study. George hoped to study there too, but when his father died, everything changed. George's two older half-brothers inherited most of his father's property, more than ten thousand acres. As a younger son, George received five hundred acres and ten slaves. At Ferry Farm, George was the oldest son but as head of the household, he would not be traveling to study in England.

Without his own father to guide him, George's older half-brother, Lawrence, became an increasingly important father figure. An officer in an American regiment of the British army, Lawrence thrilled his younger brother with military stories and exploits. Under Lawrence's tutelage, George began to study military subjects and hoped to become a British military officer one day himself. At fifteen years of age, George moved permanently into Lawrence's home, Mount Vernon. There, George continued his military education as well as dreamed of travel and adventure as a surveyor.

In Belvoir, a grand estate home near Mount Vernon, George also found another father figure, Lord Fairfax, a neighborhood patrician and English nobleman. Lawrence had married one of the Fairfax daughters, and George was soon a regular guest at Belvoir. There, George learned card games, dancing, and lessons in civility.

One day, Lord Fairfax offered George an extraordinary opportunity. Only sixteen years old, he joined a surveying party orchestrated by Fairfax to explore and map unsettled western parts of the Virginia colony. Fairfax paid him well, and George was able to buy land of his own.

When George was nineteen, his brother Lawrence grew ill with tuberculosis. George and Lawrence traveled to Barbados, where this time, George took care of his brother, but Lawrence did not recover. After brief deployments in the French and Indian War, George returned to Mount Vernon and rented the residence from Lawrence's widow until she too died. He then inherited Mount Vernon and became its permanent, full-time caretaker.

As a home and land owner, Washington was ready to start a family. He married Martha Dandridge Custine, a widow with two small children and a large estate inherited from her deceased husband. Washington enlarged Mount Vernon, bought furniture, purchased more slaves (it wasn't until later that his opinion on slavery changed), and personally oversaw the hundreds of details needed at the plantation. One of his first changes of order was to stop growing tobacco and instead plant corn and cereal grains. This fed the workers at Mount Vernon and allowed Washington to direct some of the workers to make other necessary goods, such as cloth.

Soon Washington was following in his forefather's footsteps by serving as a justice of the peace and representative in the Virginia House of Burgesses. But the political climate was changing and American colonialists were becoming increasingly frustrated with England and its new tax laws. After the Boston Tea Party, Washington openly declared he would rally a thousand troops and lead them north to Boston himself.

Colony leaders, known as the Continental Congress, gathered to discuss the troubles with Britain. The delegate from Virginia, Washington wore his military uniform. As war between Great Britain and the colonies seemed imminent, the Continental Congress understood they would need an experienced soldier to lead them—so they chose Washington as commander in chief. Washington accepted but felt that he did not equal the position to which he had been charged.

Within days, Washington was traveling to Boston where the Battle of Bunker Hill had just taken place. What he found left him disheartened. Soldiers were untrained and ill-equipped. They had little sense of order or discipline. Washington quickly began to get them into shape, and though the soldiers resented taking orders from a Virginian, their strength increased as well as their respect for the man. In time, the militia drove the British troops out of Boston.

> *Let all who take refuge in you rejoice; let them sing joyful praises forever. Spread your protection over them, that all who love your name may be filled with joy.*
>
> **PSALM 5:11 NLT**

Washington's next task was to defend New York City. This was a very tricky assignment because congressional delegates had signed the Declaration of Independence. No longer was the war about taxes, but for sovereignty itself. If Washington was captured, he would be considered a traitor and executed. For the next six months, Washington lost troops and faced defeat, routed on Long Island, driven out of New York, and chased across New Jersey. He needed a victory soon or his discouraged men would not reenlist and the revolution would be doomed.

On Christmas Day, 1776, Washington led twenty-four hundred American soldiers across the Delaware River near Trenton, New Jersey. They attacked and defeated the Hessians (British hired German soldiers). More than a thousand Hessians were taken prisoner. Washington was delighted—as were his men.

Washington continued to lead his men into battle, including Valley Forge and Yorktown. At Yorktown, Washington cornered Cornwallis, who eventually sent word that he wanted to surrender. Eventually, the Treaty of Paris was signed and the Revolutionary War was over. Washington gathered with his fellow officers in New York City, embracing them and saying good-bye with tears in his eyes. According to *George Washington* by Brendan January, he said as he resigned his commission, "Having now finished the work assigned to me, I now retire from the great theater of action."

If he never performed a single public service again, Washington would have secured his place in American history. But America wasn't finished with him yet. The thirteen states agreed to the Articles of Confederation, but each state wanted to act like its own separate country. This worried Washington. He thought these United States could not last long as a nation without some kind of unifying force that could apply to the entire union. Reforms to the Articles were necessary to provide for a stronger national government.

Washington attended the Constitutional Convention, which rallied others to attend. Elected president of the Convention, Washington guided the debates, and together, the delegates wrote an entirely new document. Slowly, they created the Constitution of the United States. Among the articles was a provision to create a new executive office called the "presidency." There was little disagreement about who the first president should be—Washington was the natural choice.

On April 30, 1789, Washington gave his inaugural address in New York City at Federal Hall. Washington worried that his countrymen would demand too much of him. As Washington went to work, everything had to be decided upon for the very first time. For example, Washington created the cabinet, a group of advisors. Everything he did was debated and criticized, but he still enjoyed overwhelming support.

That support by his fellow Americans came to a head when in 1790, he lay gravely ill with a raging fever. At one point, his breathing grew shallow and many thought he was near death. Washington rallied, however, and returned to good health to serve two terms as president and establish many of the practices still held by presidents today.

George Washington not only served his country as its first president, he fought for its very right to exist and helped shape its laws and governance. He is truly a founding father and a great architect of freedom and democracy. On his death in 1799, his friend Henry Lee described him as "first in war, first in peace, first in the hearts of his countrymen." It truly can be said, without Washington there would be no United States of America. As a founding father of America, George Washington ranks on top of the list.

**A Father of Influence watches over and
protects his own.**

Hermann Einstein

1847–1902

Albert Einstein. Electrical engineer Hermann Einstein encouraged exploration and discovery for his son Albert, one of the greatest minds of the twentieth century.

One thing that always fascinated Albert Einstein was science. When he was about five years old, his father, Hermann, gave him a compass. This simple instrument completely fascinated the youth, who couldn't understand why the needle always pointed north. Albert reasoned there must be a mysterious invisible force that acted on the compass needle causing it to hold its position.

This curiosity reflected the same aptitude held by his father, who also loved science and mathematics. As a Jew in the German state of Wurttemberg, Hermann could only receive an education in the city of Stuttgart. However, after finishing his education, he moved to the old cathedral city of Ulm and sold feathers for mattress stuffing, all the while building an electrochemical enterprise.

In 1876, twenty-nine-year-old Hermann married eighteen-year-old Pauline Koch, the daughter of wealthy grain traders. In March of 1879, the couple gave birth to their first child, a son named Albert. Family legend holds that when Albert was born, his head was so large and angular that his mother thought he was deformed.

In fact, Albert hardly spoke until he was three—causing his parents to question his mental abilities. Albert, himself, claims his earliest memories were rehearsing entire sentences in his head before speaking them out loud just to get them right. His first such sentence was when he was two years old. He was promised a toy by his parents on the birth of his sister, and when he saw her for the first time, he declared, "But, where are its wheels?"

As Albert grew older, he continued to be quiet and uncommunicative, but his father noticed he had unusual concentration for a child. One of his favorite activities was building a house of cards, at times up to fourteen stories high.

Even before that event, however, Hermann believed in his son's potential and allowed him an extraordinary degree of independence. When Albert was no more than four years old, Hermann allowed, even encouraged him to make his way through the streets of Munich.

When Albert began his formal education, he immediately bristled at the idea of rote memorization. Nevertheless, at his school, the Luitpold *Gymnasium*, he excelled in mathematics. Hermann, sensing that the financial future would be brighter in Italy, sold the family home and moved south. But he decided Albert should stay behind to continue his education at the *Gymnasium*. Albert didn't like this idea at all, but his father insisted, feeling that his son's potential was crying out for education.

Not long after his parents moved, Albert was able to convince his teachers and the headmaster to let him go (for health reasons) and join his family in Italy. (Albert was also eager to leave Germany to escape the mandatory military service for all eighteen-year-olds.) Though disappointed at his son's supposed "illness," Hermann allowed Albert to educate himself by touring the art centers of Italy.

After the art tour, Hermann wanted his son to help in the family business as an electrical engineer. Albert thought otherwise and considered a career as a teacher of philosophy. Either way, he would need a college diploma. Hermann encouraged him to apply at the Federal Institute of Technology in Zurich. Albert was only seventeen, a year younger than the required age, but he was allowed to take the entrance exam—and failed!

So, Albert enrolled at a small Swiss country school for one more year to obtain his high school diploma and study to retake the entrance exam. This time, Albert sailed through with perfect marks for history, geometry, and physics. He was ready to start school in Zurich.

In the spring of 1896, Mileva Marić arrived at the University of Zurich. She began as a medical student, but after a term switched to mathematics and physics, the same section as Einstein and the only woman that year to study for the same diploma. Albert spent countless hours studying with the Serbian beauty and their relationship developed into romance.

> *Live creatively.*
> GALATIANS 6:1 MSG

Throughout college, Albert developed a reputation as a brash young man, which irritated most of his professors and made it very difficult for Albert to find a teaching post after graduation. Yet, the father of a classmate helped him obtain employment as a technical assistant at the Swiss Patent office in 1902. There, Einstein not only determined the worth of inventors' patents, particularly ones with electromagnetic devices, but he also had lots of free time to think and develop his own theories. He stayed there until 1909, long after he had established himself as a renowned scientist and began to receive offers for academic posts.

In early 1903, Albert and Mileva married. It was both a personal and intellectual partnership. He has called her "a creature who is my equal and who is as strong and independent as I am." She also gave him the solitude necessary to accomplish his work. She, in fact, has often been hinted at as a silent partner in his award-winning PhD papers of 1905, which detail molecular movement and composition.

That same year, when he wasn't working on taking care of his new family, Albert wrote four articles that helped to create the foundation of modern physics. Amazingly, he completed them with very limited scientific literature to reference and few scientific colleagues with whom he could discuss the theories. And yet many physicists agree that three of those papers (on Brownian motion, the photoelectric effect, and special relativity) deserved Nobel prizes. His fourth paper titled "Does the Inertia of a Body Depend upon Its Energy Content?" showed the famous equation demonstrating the equivalence between matter and energy. The energy equivalence (E) of some amount of mass (m) is that mass multiplied by the speed of light (c)

squared: $E=mc^2$. It was this equation that rocked the scientific world and established Einstein's reputation as a genius.

Though Albert Einstein went on to become an unsalaried teacher at a university in Bern, Switzerland, a member of the Prussian Academy of Sciences, a published author of many other significant works, and holder of esteemed posts at various universities, it wasn't until 1921 that he was awarded the Nobel Prize for physics. Ironically, though his most famous work was on his theory of relativity, it was his earlier work on the photoelectric effect that earned him the prize. His work on relativity was still being argued by physicists, and the Nobel committee decided that his less-controversial theory would gain more acceptance from the scientific community.

Hermann Einstein loved mathematics and electromagnetism. Though he was never able to nurture a successful business in this field, he was able to encourage his son, Albert, to become a Nobel Prize–winning physicist and the greatest thinker of his time.

A Father of Influence encourages his children to develop their minds and realize their potential.

James Earl Carter Sr.

1894–1953

Jimmy Carter. Young James Carter always sought his father's approval, and Earl gave it to him. After a career as a young naval officer, Jimmy entered politics first as the governor of his native Georgia and then as the thirty-ninth president of the United States.

O f his two parents, young Jimmy Carter was especially fond of his father, and he hungered for his father's approval. One day when Jimmy was only four years old, his father took him, his mother, and younger sister, Gloria, to see their newly purchased farmhouse. The door was locked because Earl Carter had forgotten the key. Earl pried open a window and asked Jimmy to slide through the narrow opening. Jimmy did and opened the door from the inside. It was a small thing, but he was proud to be able to save the day for his dad.

On another occasion, Jimmy let his father down, and the sting stuck with him for years. Every Sunday, Earl gave his son a penny to put into the collection plate at church. That afternoon, Earl found two pennies on Jimmy's dresser. That meant that instead of putting a penny into the plate, Jimmy had taken one out. Jimmy got a swatting, but the pain of disappointing his father was even more painful. From that day on, Jimmy never stole anything again.

Earl Carter taught Jimmy to fish, hunt, and play baseball. But most of all, Earl esteemed his son and taught him the value of hard work. Earl didn't heap praises on his son, but when Jimmy heard his father call him Hot Shot, he knew he had done well.

At twelve years of age, Jimmy got a long splinter stuck in his wrist trying to catch a chicken for the family dinner. For days, he could not bend his wrist or move his fingers without intense pain. It was mid-summer and every hand was needed to pick cotton, but Jimmy's injury kept him from working. Earl didn't appreciate the rest of the family working while Jimmy lay there in the house reading a book. Jimmy knew his father was unhappy, so after his father left, Jimmy gritted his teeth, fought through the pain, and forced the splinter out. Then he bicycled down to the fields to join the others. Thrilled, his father welcomed him back with a greeting and a joke. Jimmy smiled in return.

Jimmy's parents, Earl and Lillian Gordy Carter, owned 350 acres of cotton, pecan, and peanut farmland near the village of Archery, about three miles from the town of Plains in southwest Georgia. Jimmy was expected to work hard on the farm, but he didn't consider it a hardship. To him, childhood was happy, filled with hard work, rough play, and a nurturing family. After the midday dinner, Jimmy often relished lying down next to his father on the floor for a quick rest.

Jimmy and his siblings, sisters Gloria and Ruth and brother Billy, initially grew up in a house without indoor plumbing or electric light-ing. They had to go outside to use the outhouse and employed kerosene lamps for lighting. They even had to use a battery-powered radio to hear their favorite radio programs. When Jimmy was eleven, his father installed a windmill to provide running water for the kitchen and bath-room, and then he installed electricity for lighting and heating.

Jimmy graduated from Plains High School in 1941 and would have been the valedictorian of his class had he not skipped school on senior day. As a result, his grades were lowered. Years later, his father wrote a congressman from Georgia, hoping that he would appoint Jimmy to the Naval Academy. Unfortunately, the congressman had already chosen his candidate for admission. Undeterred, he enrolled at the two-year Georgia Southwestern College in Americus.

When the empire of Japan attacked Pearl Harbor that December, Jimmy was even more determined to join the navy—specifically, he wanted a post as a submarine commander. The next summer the con-gressman recommended Jimmy for appointment to the Naval Academy for the following year.

When Jimmy came home on leave during the summer of 1945, his sister Ruth invited Rosalynn Smith to help them clean up the Pond House, a family cottage that Earl had previously built on a nearby lake. Jimmy teased Rosalynn a lot that day and as they worked on the grounds, he got up the courage to ask her out. After only one date, he returned to tell his

Let us consider how we may spur one another on toward love and good deeds.

HEBREWS 10:24

parents, "She's the girl I want to marry." The two wrote each other while Jimmy was at Annapolis, and when he came back home again, he asked her to marry him. To his surprise, Rosalynn said no. She loved Jimmy, but she had promised her dying father that she would finish college. The two continued to write and date, and when the time was right, he asked her again. This time she said yes. Just one month after his graduation, Jimmy and Rosalynn were married in Plains.

The newlyweds made their home in Norfolk, Virginia, where Jimmy had aspired to become chief of Naval Operations. In order to achieve that goal, he attended submarine school and soon had duty aboard a submarine. Navy life looked promising for the young couple, and they had even started a family.

But then in early 1953, Jimmy received some terrible news—Earl was dying of pancreatic cancer. Jimmy was devastated. His father's morality, industriousness, and recent foray into politics impressed him deeply. He dropped all his big plans and drove to Georgia to spend time with his father. They talked endlessly about family history, business, and life. Jimmy always told others about the astonishing accomplishments and varied interests of his father.

After his father's funeral, Jimmy told Rosalynn he wanted to leave the navy and go back to Plains to run the family farm. He wanted to have influence in a community and possibly enter politics—just like his father. Return they did and Jimmy found he was working sixteen-to-eighteen-hour days, throwing himself into the farm with the same determination he had shown during his time in the navy.

Jimmy also joined the Lions Club and headed the Community

Development Committee. He helped start a new medical clinic in Plains too, and got a public swimming pool built.

In 1962, Jimmy was elected to his first public office as a member of the Georgia State Senate and served from 1963–67. He was elected governor of Georgia and served in that position from 1971–75. After President Nixon resigned from office in 1974, Vice President Gerald Ford became president. Ford was never able to shake the shame of the Watergate scandal and in 1976, Jimmy Carter ran against him and was elected president of the United States.

Some of Jimmy's major actions as president included declaring amnesty for Vietnam War draft evaders, establishing a new Department of Energy, and announcing the Camp David Accords between Israel and Egypt. He also completed successful negotiations to free U.S. hostages in Iran.

Many historians believe that Carter's post-presidency work has been greater than his presidential actions. He has been a tireless crusader for Habitat for Humanity and overseen several democratic elections in foreign nations. In 1998, he received one of the first United Nations Human Rights prizes. That same year, he won the Presidential Medal of Freedom, the highest civilian award granted by the U.S. government. And, in 2002, he was awarded the Nobel Peace Prize for his tireless efforts through the decades to find peaceful answers to international difficulties.

Earl Carter loved his children and affirmed them throughout his life. His influence on his son Jimmy contributed greatly to Jimmy's unwavering belief that everything should be done with excellence and diligence. This belief led Jimmy to a successful career in the navy, an outstanding career in politics, and then as a Nobel Peace Prize winner.

**A Father of Influence motivates his children to greatness
by expecting the best from them.**

George Walton Lucas Sr.

Unknown–1991

George Walton Lucas Jr. A hardworking businessman, George Walton Lucas Sr. gave his son the tools and resources needed to help him create the most financially successful movie franchise in the history of motion pictures, the six-movie Star Wars story.

I n the 1950s, Modesto, California, was a sleepy town of hardworking people who merely wanted the American dream for their families. George Walton Lucas Jr. had an idyllic youth with lots of friends who lived on his block. They created a lot of carnivals and circuses, and built lots of forts, funhouses, and soapbox race cars. It was simple, old-fashioned fun.

When George Jr. was ten years old, his father bought the family a television set. George was riveted by shows like *Adventure Theater*, *Tailspin Tommy*, *Flash Gordon*, and *Buck Rogers*. This sense of adventure and fun was punctuated by George's reading list. He devoured adventure novels like *Treasure Island, Robinson Crusoe*, and *The Adventures of Tom Sawyer* and *Huckleberry Finn*. He also amassed a comic-book collection and read biographies of General Custer and Thomas Edison.

At the time of his birth to Dorothy and George Walton Lucas Sr. in May 14, 1944, Modesto had a population of less than twenty thousand people. The family owned L. M. Morris, a local office supply store. George Jr. made deliveries for his father after school, and George Sr. couldn't help but dream that one day his son would take over the family business.

When Disneyland opened in Anaheim in 1955, the Lucas family headed for Orange County and stayed there for a full week. They enjoyed themselves so much that it became their favorite vacation destination.

In the late 1950s, George Sr. moved his family to an outlying ranch-style house set on thirteen acres of walnut trees. George Jr. had difficulty adjusting to the new surroundings. For a while his grades suffered until he took an interest in motorcycles and automobiles. At fifteen, he started driving, initially just around the ranch. But once he turned sixteen, he obtained his license and drove around on the streets. Cruising consumed his life from that point on.

George wasn't a particularly good student while attending Thomas Downey High School. After all, he loved to cruise and dreamed of becoming a professional race-car driver. On June 12, 1962, he crashed his car, a Bianchina. He was thrown from the car as it rolled over. Had the harness not snapped, he would most likely have been crushed to death by the steering column when the car smashed into a walnut tree—a circumstance that left him thinking about his life. Soon after, he decided to apply himself academically, and enrolled in Modesto Junior College with the hope of studying psychology, anthropology, and philosophy. He didn't lose his passion for automobiles, but instead of racing them, he started photographing them.

George Sr. bought his son a 35 mm camera and allowed him to set up a darkroom at home, encouraging what he thought was just a hobby. When his son turned eighteen, George and his father had a talk about the family business. When George explained that he wasn't the kind of person who could do the same thing every day, his father was worried and angry. He feared his son would become some sort of pitiful, starving artist, especially since he still didn't know exactly what he wanted to do with his life.

George enrolled at San Francisco State University to major in anthropology, but a friend persuaded him to go to the University of Southern California instead and join the school of cinematography. George Sr., impressed that USC was a fine school, dropped his objections.

Early into the program, George Jr. realized the movie-making process was exactly what he had been searching for. He was in love with it all.

At USC he made a number of short films, including an early version of *THX 1138* (which with the help of his friend Francis Ford Coppola, was made into a feature film in 1971).

> *Righteousness guards the man of integrity.*
>
> **PROVERBS 13:6**

After graduating with a BFA in film in 1966, he attempted to enter the Air Force as an officer, but was turned down because of his numerous speeding tickets. He was later drafted by the army—but diabetes put a stop to that as well. Unable to serve, Lucas enrolled as a graduate student in film production at USC. While there, he and Coppola cofounded the studio American Zoetrope in the hope of creating a liberating environment for filmmakers to direct outside the perceived oppressive control of the Hollywood studios.

Lucas's second feature film, the low-budget *American Graffiti* (1973), became the most successful film of its time and won numerous awards. Yet Universal Studios thought *Graffiti* was so bad they weren't going to release the film at all until Coppola intervened and the studio relented. Produced for $775,000, the movie went on to earn nearly $125 million.

Despite the success of *Graffiti*, George Jr. was unable to find financing for his next project, a movie called *Star Wars*. This space fantasy was based in part on the childhood TV serials he so loved. Unable to find the technicians or technology he needed to create the special effects he wanted, Lucas assembled a team and set up his own studio, Lucasfilm, housed on a compound called Skywalker Ranch. The rest is history—the movie spawned five sequels and created one of the most successful film franchises of all time. Other ventures, including Skywalker Sound and Industrial Light and Magic pioneered and invented numerous technological advances in the cinematic arts now used by filmmakers worldwide.

Lucas Jr. conceived of the Skywalker Ranch as an anti-Hollywood establishment. In his mind, Hollywood was evil, greedy, and encouraged mediocrity. Skywalker Ranch, on the other hand, would be an ideal studio, respecting human values, innovation, and creativity. Much of Lucas's disdain for Hollywood was a result of his father's influence. He viewed lawyers and film executives as "sharpies" and referred to Hollywood as Sin City.

George Jr. looks back on his beginnings with humility and paternal respect. He says he inherited his father's fiscal moderation, the common-sense wisdom he uses to succeed in the business world. As the son of a small-town businessman, George Jr. says he's fiscally conservative, just like his father.

In his biography *Skywalking*, George Jr. says, "My father provided me with a lot of business principles—a small-town, retail-business ethic—and I guess I learned it. It's sort of ironic because I swore when I was a kid, I'd never do what he did. At eighteen, we had this big break, when he wanted me to go into the business and I refused, and I told him, 'There are two things I know for sure. One is that I will end up doing something with cars, whether I'm a racer, a mechanic, or whatever; and two, I'll never be president of a company.' I guess I got outwitted." After the success of the first Star Wars movie, George Jr. was able to finance the second and third films himself, and then he built the ranch.

Today George Jr. claims modest goals. All he really wants to do is make movies and raise a family. When he makes money on a film or product sales, he puts it right back into the company. He claims he doesn't feel a need for material things, doesn't care about living extravagantly or partying, and has no desire to hold power over others.

George Lucas Jr. never wanted to join his father in the family business, but on reflection of his life and career, one can clearly see the stamp his father has impressed upon his son. By exemplifying quiet, solid, small-town business ethics, he showed his son how to amass a loyal following both among employees and customers. Thanks in large part to his father's influence, George Lucas Jr. has become one of the most successful and innovative filmmakers of all time.

A Father of Influence shows his children how to succeed in business without compromising their core values.

Herbert Aaron

Unknown

Henry Aaron. Herbert Aaron taught his son Henry "Hank" Aaron the importance of excellence, education, and patience. Henry would go on to hit 755 home runs over a 23-year career to become the major league's all-time home-run king.

It seemed from the start that Henry Louis Aaron was destined for baseball greatness. He was born in Mobile, Alabama, the hometown of baseball great Satchel Paige, on February 5, 1934, exactly one day before Babe Ruth's thirty-ninth birthday.

Henry's father, Herbert Aaron, loved sports but knew that opportunities for black and white athletes varied greatly in the segregated South. Herbert told his son that there weren't any "colored" players in professional baseball, and at the time, he was correct. A shipbuilder by trade, Herbert encouraged all his children to play ball by starting with the Toulminville Whippet sandlot team.

In the book *Chasing the Dream*, Henry commented that years of watching his father labor long and hard for his family taught him the value of patience and respect. These were traits that young Henry would emulate, especially later in his career as he faced persecution and racial hatred while nearing Babe Ruth's home-run record.

In the early 1940s, the Aaron family moved from the congested slums of the Down the Bay district of Mobile to the more habitable neighboring community of Toulminville. Herbert purchased two empty lots and hired a team of carpenters to build a six-room house— the cost was just two hundred dollars.

When the walls and roof went up, they moved in, rent and mort-gage free. A proud family, they figured the only people who owned their own homes were rich folks. And they owned theirs outright.

Unlike Babe Ruth, who had a turbulent childhood, Henry grew up in a close, nurturing family, where he was expected to behave, respect elders, cut firewood, and go to church on Sundays. Herbert and his wife raised their children in a loving home with their greatest good in mind.

When Henry was eleven years old, Jackie Robinson signed with the Brooklyn Dodgers to break the color barrier in the major leagues. This sparked great dreams in Henry's heart—a dream that he, too, could one day make it into the big leagues.

Herbert Aaron claimed his son was always crazy about playing baseball. He never thought about him becoming a player until the Brooklyn Dodgers came to Mobile for an exhibition game. He took Henry out to see the game, and his son told him that night that he would become a big-league player before Jackie Robinson retired.

Henry was well into his teens before he got involved with organ-ized baseball. The schools he attended and towns where he lived simply didn't have a Little League team for him to join. His initial encounter came when he joined an all-black, fast-pitch softball league sponsored by the town's recreation department.

Henry would often cut classes and go down to the local pool hall to listen to the Brooklyn Dodgers on the radio. When Herbert learned of Henry's truancy, he became furious. But rather than angrily con-fronting his son, he reminded him of the sacrifices he was making every day for his family. He explained that he provided lunch money for each of his children each day—fifty cents apiece—while he kept only twenty-five cents for himself. He felt that if he could sacrifice for his children, they could thank him by graduating from high school. Henry agreed.

That same day, Bobby Thomson hit a three-run homer that lifted the New York Giants over the Brooklyn Dodgers for the National League pennant. The one-two punch of that dramatic day reinforced Henry's desire to play in the majors. Because scouts weren't exactly scouring the South for black players at that time, Henry reasoned the quickest way to the major leagues was through the Negro League.

One day when Henry was only sixteen years old, a man approached him and asked if he would like to join a local semi-pro team, the Mobile Black Bears. Initially, Henry turned down the offer because the team played ball on Sundays. But he eventually agreed and his professional career began.

> *Those who hope in the LORD will renew their strength. They will soar on wings like eagles; they will run and not grow weary, they will walk and not be faint.*
>
> **ISAIAH 40:31**

Henry was then recruited to play for the Negro League's Indianapolis Clowns. Henry's parents were excited but insisted that he wait a year to finish school. Henry thought he would never hear from the recruiter again, but a year later, Henry signed on with the Clowns.

The following year, Henry was acquired by the Boston Braves and played for their farm team, the Eau Claire Bears. In 1954, Henry Aaron broke in with the Milwaukee Braves after outfielder Bobby Thomson broke his ankle sliding into second base. He hit a home run on the first game in spring training. In 1957, at age twenty-three, Aaron won the MVP award by hammering a home run that captured the pennant and led Milwaukee to its first world championship.

While with the Braves, Henry started meeting and surpassing home-run hitting milestones. In 1960, he hit his 200th home run, in 1963, his 300th. In 1966, the Milwaukee Braves moved south to become the Atlanta Braves, and it was there that he hit his 400th home run. His 500th in 1968 also came in Atlanta. On July 30, 1969, Aaron hit his 537th home run to move into third place as the best career home-run hitter, surpassing Mickey Mantle. Only Willie Mays and Babe Ruth remained in his path. Aaron was now on the radar, fans and media touting him as the guy with the goods, the home-run king.

In 1971, Henry Aaron hit his 600th home run, and a year later, he surpassed Willie Mays to become the second-place career home-run hitter.

But not everybody appreciated his achievements. Racist hate mail flooded in. From the stands, protestors shouted vile words in his direction. Some sports writers even wrote obituaries just in case. Babe Ruth's widow, Claire, condemned the hatred and said her husband would be proud to know that Aaron would attempt to surpass him. Aaron endured the scorn quietly and valiantly. Despite daily hounding by the media and fans, Aaron said he felt no pressure while pursuing the record.

Then, with the largest crowd in Braves history watching (53,775 in attendance), Hank Aaron broke the record on April 8, 1974, with a home run in the fourth inning off Los Angeles pitcher Al Downing. The ball actually landed in the Braves bull pen where reliever Tom House caught it. After hitting the record-breaking home run, Herbert Aaron yelled from the stands, "He's mine! He's mine!" and nearly lost his hat in the excitement. Hank's mother rushed the field to attend to her son, thinking he had been shot after hearing celebration cannon fire.

Babe Ruth had reigned as the all-time home-run king for more than fifty years before Hank Aaron surpassed him that night. Hank told the press and his fans afterward that he thanked God it was over. That night at home, he privately got down on his knees and again thanked God for His watchful care through the whole ordeal.

Herbert Aaron gave his son a love for the game and taught him to valiantly prioritize his life. He modeled for his son a quiet resolve that endured racism and hardship. Henry Aaron took his father's steady demeanor with him wherever he went, and drawing from it, he kept his focus on becoming one of the greatest ball players of all time and the greatest home-run hitter the major leagues have ever known.

A Father of Influence teaches his children to patiently endure distractions while wholeheartedly pursuing their goals.

Moses Carver

1812–1910

George Washington Carver. At the end of the Civil War, white Moses Carver exercised a redeeming love and adopted black George Washington Carver as his own son. He gave him an appreciation for botany, influencing George to benefit the lives of thousands by finding hundreds of uses for the simple peanut.

Born into slavery at the end of the Civil War, in Diamond, Missouri, George Washington Carver and his mother, Mary, belonged to Moses Carver, a German immigrant, frontiersman, and homesteader. Moses Carver himself was opposed to slavery, but hiring labor for his Newton County farm proved difficult. So in 1855, he bought Mary from one of his neighbors to help around the farm. At that time, she was thirteen years old and over the next decade bore at least four children.

The actual identity of George's biological father is not known, but he was probably a slave on a nearby farm—a man who died around the time George was born. The man was killed while hauling wood with an ox team. Somehow, he fell under the wagon and was crushed from the load as the wheels passed over him.

Unfortunately, George never really got to know his mother either. They were separated shortly after his birth. Moses Carver and his wife, Susan, were Union sympathizers. As such, their farm was frequently raided by Confederate "bushwhackers."

On one occasion, the raiders tied Moses to a tree by his thumbs, burned his feet with hot coals, and demanded to know where he had hidden his money. Despite the torture, Moses didn't tell them the location of his stash, and they left. When the "bushwhackers" struck again, they kidnapped Mary and young George and took them to Arkansas, a Confederate state twenty miles to the south. A kindly Union scout agreed to find and retrieve the kidnapped slaves. The scout found George but was never able to find Mary. What became of her was never known. Happy to have the boy back home, Moses rewarded the scout with a racehorse.

Near the war's end, President Lincoln issued the Emancipation Proclamation, freeing all the slaves. Having no children, Moses and Susan raised George as their own. Under the protection and care of this white couple, the boy was given a good home and opportunities that most black children were not afforded.

Young George continually contracted respiratory ailments and the malady excused him from doing some of the hardest chores around the farm. When he didn't have to stay indoors to do light housework, he was exploring outside, studying the adjacent woods and wildlife. George wrote later, "I wanted to know every strange stone, flower, insect, bird, or beast." Eventually, Susan and Moses Carver recognized that George's curiosity made him special. Here was a child eager to learn.

George particularly liked plants and spent long hours in his adoptive parents' garden. With their help, he started a garden of his own. He made careful note of the conditions that enabled his plants to grow and thrive and became known around the neighborhood as the "plant doctor." People frequently called him to nurse sickly flowers and plants back to health.

George also came to love and worship the God of creation. Every plant and animal was evidence that God was a magnificent craftsman. George saw God's handiwork everywhere. As an adult, George credited "the Creator" for any successes he had in the laboratory. By the time George was ten years old, he had become a Christian.

George craved a more formal education and begged Moses and Susan to find a school he could attend. Though blacks were now allowed an education, the Carvers found it difficult to find one that would accept him. Finally they hired a private tutor for George, and soon he was asking more questions than the tutor could answer. The following year, he was admitted to a school for blacks in Neosho, the county seat.

Each man has his own gift from God; one has this gift, another has that.

1 CORINTHIANS 7:7

A year later, George traveled to Fort Scott, Kansas, hoping to find a school that met his expectations—one that could challenge him and meet his thirst for knowledge. This also lasted only a year. The boy was horrified when he witnessed a white mob lynching a black man and refused to stay in Fort Scott. Eventually, he found a good school and welcoming folks in another Kansas town. There he added to his botanical knowledge and also learned music and painting.

George tried to attend college but was refused admission when they saw he was black. Instead, George tried his hand at his father's profession: homesteading. George claimed a parcel of land in Beeler, Kansas, and was accepted into the community. He would later thank the people of Ness County for their contributions to his accomplishments. He felt they gave him every opportunity to fully develop his skills and interests.

He remained a homesteader for two years before the education bug hit him again. He enrolled in Simpson College in Indianapolis—an institution that didn't care what race its students were. George became its sole male fine arts scholar. But there, George worried what kind of future he could have as an artist. Another student noticed he often painted flowers and spoke of plants, so she encouraged him to attend Iowa State University, where her father taught agriculture. After praying about the matter, George realized that God had a special work for him to do and left Simpson for Iowa.

Despite racial bigotry at Iowa State, his career as a botanist and plant biologist took off. George was highly regarded by his teachers for his ability to graft plants and cross-pollinate. One professor described him as the ablest student in the school. George received a bachelor's, then a master's degree in agriculture before becoming the director of agriculture at Tuskegee Institute in Alabama. There he picked up the moniker "Wizard of Tuskegee."

Among his many accomplishments, George Washington Carver managed the institute's two farms, ran its agricultural experiment station, and expanded Tuskegee's research program to include poor black farmers in the South. In fact, he became a living legend as he sought to improve the fortunes of other blacks. A creative chemist, he found hundreds of new uses for the peanut and demonstrated many of these uses to the U.S. House Ways and Means Committee. A movie was made in his honor titled *The Story of Dr. Carver*, and a museum at Tuskegee documents his accomplishments.

Carver was more than a hero and role model for children of his race. He was an inspiration to people of all ages and races, especially to orphans and those from humble, disadvantaged beginnings. George Washington Carver once said his desire was "to help the 'man farthest down.'" His father, Moses, redeemed him twice and gave him the best upbringing he could. Furthermore, Moses recognized his God-given talent and genius and helped him learn more about his primary interest: the world of plants.

A Father of Influence teaches his children to recognize their God-given talents and use them for the good of all people.

Bob Hewson

1925–2001

Paul David Hewson, aka Bono of U2. Bob Hewson

financed his son's musical ambitions and gave him

the gift of song.

Before they were signed, in the very early years of the Irish rock band U2, front man Bono welcomed a representative from a recording company to a practice. In the book *Bono: In Conversation with Michka Assayas*, Bono writes, "This big shot came over to see the band and offered us a publishing deal. It was a big moment for us, because we were really flat broke. And with the money that he was offering, we booked a tour of the U.K. But on the eve of that tour, the publisher rang up and halved the money, knowing we had to take it. We went to our families and asked them for five hundred pounds each. My father gave it, Edge's father gave it, and I think Larry's father gave it."

Bono's father, Bob Hewson, came from a working-class Irish family, which included an older brother, two younger brothers, and a sister. When not working, family members enjoyed playing cricket and listening to the opera. For a time, Bob entertained the idea of being an opera singer, but instead, worked his entire career as a postal carrier.

Bob Hewson was taken out of school when he was fourteen. His teachers begged Bob's mother not to remove him, because as a good student, they loved watching him learn. Yet Bob was put into civil service at fifteen, which offered the family a secure, steady income. And he stayed in that job until he retired.

Bono's father, Bob, was a Catholic, and his mother, Iris Hewson, was a Protestant. They grew up on the same street, a working-class area in a district called Cowtown on Cowper Street. Son Norman was born first, and then Bono in 1960. Bono was given the birth name Paul David.

When Paul was three years old, his parents saw him playing in their backyard garden. The couple watched with both horror and fascination as their toddler lifted honeybees off the flowers with his finger, talked to them, and then put them back on the petals without ever getting stung.

Young Paul formed his embracing, ecumenical, but unorthodox views of faith and religion by observing his parents. He saw how his parents could get along and still hold different views on religion and God, and therefore concluded that religious doctrine and dogma could get in the way of a real relationship with God.

Today, Bono makes no apologies for his faith in Christ. His spiritual lyrics and humanitarian work stem directly from his understanding of Scripture. In his book, he says, "I'm holding out that Jesus took my sins onto the cross, because I know who I am, and I hope I don't have to depend on my own religiosity. The point of the death of Christ is that Christ took on the sins of the world, so that what we put out did not come back to us, and that our sinful nature does not reap the obvious death. That's the point. It should keep us humble. It's not our own good works that get us through the gates of heaven."

When Paul was fifteen, his mother died unexpectedly, just four days after attending her father's funeral. The three Hewson men lived together, trying to process their grief and showing proper emotion. The result, however, was often frustration and anger. Life wasn't easy in the motherless Hewson household. Her death affected Bono's confidence, and he felt abandoned. After the school day, he would return to his house but never felt it was a home without her.

Paul received his nickname "Bono Vox" from a high school chum named Guggi, who stole the moniker from a hearing-aid store on O'Connell Street in Dublin. Fittingly enough, Bono Vox means "good voice" in cockeyed Latin. Paul later shortened it to Bono, which remains his name to this day.

In high school, Paul's natural talkative nature and dramatic personality allowed him to move within nearly every school circle and experiment with a variety of artistic mediums. Bob paid for his son's guitar lessons, but Bono struggled with the instrument. Later, Bono learned that his father regretted that he himself hadn't become a musician and a singer.

> *[God] hath put a new song in my mouth, even praise unto our God: many shall see it, and fear, and shall trust in the LORD.*
>
> **PSALM 40:3 KJV**

In 1983, Bono married his no-nonsense, dark-headed sweetheart, Alison Stewart. The couple have two girls, Jordan and Memphis Eve, and two boys, Elijah and John Abraham.

The band U2 formed in 1976, when Bono answered an ad posted on a bulletin board at the Mount Temple Comprehensive School in Dublin. The poster asked would-be musicians to meet at the house of Larry Mullen Jr. to audition for a band.

Larry served as the talented drummer and catalyst for the group's formation. The other members were a guitarist/guitar builder named Dave Evans, nicknamed "The Edge"; an amateur bassist named Adam Clayton; and finally, Bono, who couldn't play guitar or really carry a tune (at that time), but whose earnest charm, intense poetic songwriting, and theatrical persona ultimately won him the position as the band's front man and songwriter.

As the band was struggling to be a success, Bob Hewson gave his son one year of free room and board. Then, at the end of this year, Bob insisted if things weren't happening with the band, his son had to find a job. Bono agreed to his father's terms, considering them more than generous. But success came quickly for U2. Their first album, *Boy,* came out in 1981.

One time in the 1980s, Bono flew his father to New York to see a U2 show. As Bob Hewson watched, Bono wondered what his father thought. Following the show Bono turned around, and saw his father standing backstage. After the performance, he offered his son a congratulatory handshake. Bono was pleased.

International success created by intense touring, radio play, and their skillful, impassioned performances catapulted U2 to stardom. Albums *War, The Unforgettable Fire, The Joshua Tree,* and *Rattle and*

Hum, displayed their penchant for spirituality, intensity, and the ability to forcefully move an audience. The '90s marked their foray into electronica and new musical incarnations, exemplified by such records as *Auchtung Baby* and *Pop*. Today, Bono is known as much for his humanitarian activism as he is for his music.

In 2001, Bob Hewson contracted cancer, and did not recover. According to his book, Bono spoke of his father at the funeral, "Thank you for giving me my voice." He also said, "Our house was filled with music. It was the kids who had to ask the father to turn it down."

Bono wrote about him in the song "Sometimes You Can't Make It on Your Own" from their album *How to Dismantle an Atomic Bomb*. The lyrics credit his father for giving him the reason to sing.

Bono had a difficult time dealing with the loss of his father. One Easter morning, he attended a small church, fell to his knees, and let go of all the anger he still harbored against his father from the years after his mother died. Today, he thanks God for his father and the gifts he gave him.

On faith and what mattered in life, Bono writes in his book, "Occasionally, my father would ask a real question, meaning I had to give him a real answer. It was always about my belief in God. 'There's one thing I envy about you,' he said to me one time. But think about it: I was singing, doing all the things he would have loved to have done, had a creative life. He said, 'You really do seem to have a relationship with God.'"

Bob Hewson worked hard all his life as a postal worker, raising two sons as a widower. Though he had a difficult time finding hope and faith in his own life, he provided his son with the resources necessary to help make him a success in the music business. Bob Hewson's legacy lives on in Bono Vox, a man who has stirred the world with impassioned lyrics rooted in faith in Christ and offered tireless compassion to the world's poor.

A Father of Influence gives his children the gift of music.

Johnny Cash

1932–2003

John Carter Cash. Country music icon Johnny Cash
learned from his mistakes to offer exceptional, gentle, faith-
filled parenting to his youngest child and only son, John
Carter, who would later become a close spiritual companion
and record producer.

When Johnny Cash's youngest child and only son, John
Carter, was eleven years old, armed robbers broke into
Cinnamon Hill, the family's Jamaican vacation home.
Inside, the Cash family was celebrating Christmas. The family's joy
turned to horror as three men with stockings over their heads burst
through the open doors and demanded all their money and valuables.
For four terrifying hours, the thieves held them hostage, forcing them
to lie on the floor. The robbers selected John Carter as their intended
murder victim if Johnny didn't meet all their demands. Though
frightened during the ordeal, Johnny didn't panic, remaining extraor-
dinarily calm. The robbers made off with many of their valuables
(they were later apprehended) and John Carter was not harmed. It
was agreed that Johnny's steady presence in the midst of a horrifying
ordeal probably saved his young son's life.

Of all Johnny's children, John Carter benefited the most from
Johnny's new and improved parental skills. By the time John Carter
was born, Johnny had married June Carter Cash, kicked his addiction
to drugs, and begun to take his Christian faith much more seriously.
Johnny often took his son on the road with him. When they weren't
on the road, Johnny took his son on hiking or fishing trips. Johnny

was determined not to make the same mistakes his own father, Ray Cash, had made with him, or the mistakes he himself had made with his four daughters earlier in his life.

Faith, farm, and family were always big in Johnny Cash's family tree. His grandfather, William Henry Cash, was a farmer and minister, a circuit rider traveling preacher serving four widely scattered congregations. He never took any money as a preacher, but his barn was filled with livestock and produce his parishioners had given him. His twelve children never lacked for food.

At five years of age, Johnny worked in the cotton fields, singing along with his family as they worked. They often sang hymns to take their minds off their aching backs and bleeding hands.

When he was twelve, Johnny gave his life to Christ. That same year, his brother Jack was killed while working at a local sawmill. All day long, Johnny had a sense of foreboding. On his deathbed, Jack said he had visions of heaven and angels. That life-altering experience may be why many of Johnny's songs resonate with universal themes like sorrow, pain, redemption, and moral struggles.

Johnny joined the U.S. Air Force after graduating from high school, serving for several years in Germany before receiving an honorable discharge. Soon after, he met Marshall Grant and Luther Perkins, who with Johnny became the Tennessee Three; married Vivian Liberto; and auditioned for Sam Phillips at Sun Records all in the same year. A year later, Johnny's recording and performing career really took off with his first hit, "Hey! Porter." It was the beginning of a meteoric rise in popularity for Johnny. However, his relationship with Vivian suffered as a result of his constant touring and they divorced. While touring he met June Carter, whom he would later marry in 1968.

In 1979, when John Carter turned nine, Johnny presided over his son's baptism, performed in the Jordan River by Hendersonville Church of God pastor John Cobaugh. That day Johnny was also baptized for the third time in his life.

When John Carter became a young adult, he and his father wrote songs together and the younger Cash frequently made suggestions to the elder. Conversely, Johnny would sometimes write songs for and about his children. During the *American Recording* sessions, John Carter performed as associate producer.

Fathers, do not provoke your children to anger, but bring them up in the discipline and instruction of the Lord.

EPHESIANS 6:4 NASB

On June's death in 2003, John Carter and his wife, Laura, returned the gentleness his father had shown them. In *The Man Called Cash*, Laura says, "Many times John and I would sit with him for long periods with no words spoken. I believe it was a comfort to him to have someone there who didn't feel it necessary to talk."

Following the mourning period, Johnny knew he had to get back to work. He told his son that he had to get back into the studio. At first, Johnny recorded a collection of Carter Family songs. Then he did an album referred to as *American V*, with John acting as associate producer. Producer and friend Jack Clement attended these recordings and was proud of the way John Carter rallied and supported his father. Eventually, Johnny couldn't see well enough to read the lyrics. So John would sing them to his father so Johnny could sing them back.

On August 21, 2003, Johnny recorded his last song, "Engine 143." It was produced by John Carter at Cash Cabin Studio.

At 2:00 a.m., September 12, 2003 (four months after June's death), Johnny died from intense respiratory problems. The only people with him were John and Johnny's daughters Rosanne and Kathy. Afterward, as documented in the book *The Man Called Cash*, John Carter commented to the press on the moment: "He had purpose. He had belief, and he had a peace in spite of himself that God granted him. I think this is what the grace was in his life and that is where the redemption lay."

John Carter shares his father's Christian beliefs. The two were close spiritual companions, spending many hours together praying and discussing the Bible. On his father's legacy and faith, John has said his father was like Peter, a great tortured soul who was in misery and pain but had something in him that brought him close to Christ.

Johnny Cash was a father many times over. He had four daughters with his first wife, Vivian Liberto, and one son with his second wife, June Carter Cash. June brought two daughters from her previous marriage into the relationship. With them, he avoided punishments, praised them endlessly, and often professed his love. He preferred to correct their misbehavior by talking with them or writing them letters.

From his autobiography, *Cash*, Johnny writes, "I'm thankful for my family—thankful for my daughters and grandchildren and a son who loves me, and thankful that their love is unconditional. Finally, I'm thankful that God has inspired me to want to write, and that He might possibly use me to influence somebody for the good."

Asked how he'd like to be remembered in a hundred years, Johnny said, "I'd like to be remembered as a good daddy."

A Father of Influence is a gentle, godly presence in his children's lives.

Reverend Denzel Washington Sr.

1911–1992

Denzel Washington Jr. The Reverend Denzel Washington limited the movies he allowed his children to watch, and yet he gave his children the gift of story, inspiring his son Denzel Jr. in his award-winning acting career.

In the 1950s and '60s, the Reverend Denzel Washington made sure that his three children were not exposed to the vulgarities of many Hollywood films. That meant his middle son, Denzel Jr., saw only a few movies—mainly Disney films or biblical epics.

Instead, young Denzel learned from an early age to love God and value hard work. At twelve years of age, he worked part-time at a local barber shop and enjoyed earning his own money. He also spent countless hours in his father's church.

It wasn't all work and no play. Growing up in Mount Vernon, New York, Denzel Washington was surrounded by children from various ethnic and racial backgrounds. He had friends who were West Indians, blacks, Irish, and Italians. He learned about many cultures.

As the head of his household and the leader of a Pentecostal church, the Reverend Denzel brought a levelheaded, reverential spirit into his home. A hard worker, he also held down other jobs including work at the water department and a local department store, so that his family could be financially secure.

At the age of fourteen, tragedy rocked young Denzel's world. His parents separated and eventually divorced. (Six years would pass before Denzel would see his father again, in an emotional but healing reconciliation.) Despite the blow, Denzel's upbringing and sense of self-worth prevented him from getting into any serious trouble.

Still his mother decided to enroll him in Oakland Academy, a prestigious prep school for boys in upstate New York. He was an average student, but excelled in extracurricular activities such as band and sports—especially football.

After high school graduation, Denzel knew that he wanted to attend college. He finally settled on Fordham University in the Bronx. He majored in journalism, sensing that he had a gift for storytelling after years of listening to his father's sermons.

During the summer, Denzel took a job coaching sports at a YMCA camp in Lakeville, Connecticut. He was also in charge of putting on the camp talent shows. It was probably then that he realized he had a serious interest in acting.

When he came back to Fordham, he joined a theater workshop run by Robinson Stone, a professional actor who was in the 1953 movie *Stalag 17*. One time during class, Denzel told Stone that he wanted to be the greatest actor in the world.

Denzel performed in several stage plays at Fordham, and Stone convinced several film agents to see Denzel's performances. Remarkably, Denzel was offered a professional TV role before even graduating from college, a part in *Wilma*, as Olympic track star Wilma Rudolph's boyfriend.

His big break came when he starred in the popular television hospital drama *St. Elsewhere*. What he thought would be a thirteen-week run turned into a six-year job. Though a lead on the show, he still had opportunity to act in minor theatrical films and stage roles. His big film role came when he starred as South African anti-apartheid campaigner Steve Biko in Richard Attenborough's *Cry Freedom*. In this role, he gained his first Oscar nomination for Best Supporting Actor.

With that breakthrough performance, Denzel went on to a successful film career as a forceful leading man in many film roles such as *A Soldier's Story, Philadelphia, Courage Under Fire, The Preacher's Wife, He Got Game, The Hurricane, Antwone Fisher,* and *Man on Fire*.

One of the most notable was the title role in *Malcolm X*. He credits his father's preaching as a major influence for the speaking cadence he found to make the role authentic. According to the biography, *Denzel Washington*, Denzel's sister Lorice said after seeing the film: "[Denzel's] hand gestures and the rhythms of his voice were Daddy's." Unfortunately, the Reverend Denzel never got to see his son perform in this role because during filming, he died at the age of eighty-one years.

> *Using the boat as a pulpit, he addressed his congregation, telling stories.*
>
> Matthew 13:2–3 msg

Although Denzel Sr. had been absent from his son's life for a long time after the divorce, their relationship had been improving for some time. The actor was devastated by the loss and poured that emotional energy into the role. His performance captured the attention of the Academy and they nominated him for Best Actor.

Though he is a dashing leading man, Denzel does not like to shoot love scenes. One day while shooting *Mo' Better Blues*, he felt tense and irritable. He went up to director Spike Lee and refused to take off his shirt. Denzel told Spike, "I'm a family man. I don't want to do that." Since then, Denzel has said that love scenes make him uneasy and he prefers not to do them.

Denzel is also bothered by the violence and mayhem in many action films. He even regrets doing the violent movie *Ricochet*. He doesn't like to perform or appear in movies with mindless or gratuitous violence. On another occasion, the actor has simply said that he doesn't like action movies because there's too much running and jumping and not enough talking. He doesn't think it is acting. Denzel has, however, gone on to star in action movies like *Crimson Tide* and *Inside Man*, but claims those movies are more substantial than most action fare.

Denzel went on to win Academy Awards for Best Supporting Actor as Private Tripp in 1989's *Glory* and the Best Actor honor as Detective Alonzo Harris in 2001 for *Training Day*. He is the only African American actor who has won Oscars in both categories.

According to his biography, Denzel has said, "I'm very proud to be black, but black is not all I am. That's my cultural historical background, my genetic makeup, but it's not all of who I am nor is it the basis from which I answer every question."

Nevertheless, Denzel will fight for dignity when it comes to racial issues. According to a 1995 article in *Premiere Magazine*, Denzel had a heated debate with writer/director Quentin Tarantino when he visited the set of *Crimson Tide*. Quentin had performed an uncredited rewrite of the script, and Denzel lambasted Tarantino about his use of racial slurs in his films. Tarantino was embarrassed and wanted to move the conversation to a more private area, but Denzel refused. Though he admired Tarantino, he could not ignore what had been done.

Denzel is a rare Hollywood actor who has said that God is his hero. When asked to prioritize his life, he stated simply, "God, family, work, football." Denzel and his wife, Pauletta, are also frequent attendees and regular givers at their church, the West Los Angeles Church of God in Christ.

On his career, he has said publicly: "Acting is just a way of making a living, the family is life." Finally, on his talent, he reflects, "I remain thankful for the gifts that I've been given and I try to use them in a good way, in a positive way."

As the national spokesperson for the Boys and Girls Club, Denzel promotes the idea of being a father to the fatherless, nurturing children to achieve their full potential. He is featured in print advertisements for the club and a firm believer in the organization's goal: helping the future of America by helping its children.

Though Denzel's father didn't let him watch many movies, he taught him the power of story and gave him the grounding to be a major star without losing touch with the priorities of life. Denzel has proven to the world that you can find success in Hollywood without losing your faith or your footing.

**A Father of Influence teaches his children
the power of story.**

William Carey

1761–1834

Father of modern missionaries. One of the founders of the Baptist Missionary Society, William Carey wrote that the Great Commission was still in effect today, detailed the role of the missionary, and led by example by establishing a mission in India, still inspiring missionaries today.

William Carey was born to Edmund and Elizabeth Carey, weavers by trade in the village of Paulerspury in Northamptonshire, England. Raised in the Church of England, he was naturally inquisitive and keenly interested in natural sciences, particularly botany. Fortunately, these interests were nurtured and approved of by his father, who was appointed parish clerk and village schoolmaster when William was six. The young Carey possessed a natural gift for languages and taught himself Latin.

Edmund apprenticed William to a shoemaker when he was fourteen years old at the nearby village of Hackleton. There, a fellow apprentice would influence William to leave the Church of England and join other Dissenters to form a small Congregational church in Hackleton. As a shoemaker, William also taught himself Greek with the help of a local villager who had a college education. At a young age, William took an interest in God, academics, and languages—the seeds of the missionary mind-set.

When his master shoemaker died, William went to work for another local shoemaker, Thomas Olds. Olds himself died soon afterward and William took over his business. While working on the shoes, William studied Hebrew, Italian, Dutch, and French, somehow managing to focus on two tasks at once.

Carey joined a local association called Particular Baptists and became acquainted with such Christian luminaries as John Ryland, John Sutcliff, and Andrew Fuller, men who would become close friends in later years. They invited him to preach at their church in nearby Barton every other Sunday. William accepted and there developed his speaking style. In 1783, he was baptized by Ryland and from then on committed himself to the Baptist denomination.

His academic credentials increased when he was appointed as schoolmaster for the village of Moulton two years later. The local Baptist church also invited him to pastor. In these years, he shaped his thoughts on spreading the gospel by reading the works of Jonathan Edwards, David Brainerd, and his friend Andrew Fuller. Carey was outspoken in his belief that it was the duty of all Christians to preach the gospel of Christ throughout the world. Remarkably, some renowned Christian scholars opposed him on this now commonly accepted biblical principle.

When Carey served as the full-time pastor of a small Baptist church in Leicester, he published his seminal missionary manifesto, *An Enquiry into the Obligations of Christians to Use Means for the Conversion of the Heathens*. Consisting of five parts, the first part is a theological justification for missionary activity. He argued that the command of Jesus to make disciples of all people still remains in effect for all Christians. In the second part, Carey outlined the history of missionary activity, starting with the early church and ending with John Wesley. The third part had tables listing areas, populations, and religion statistics for every country in the world—the first compilation of its kind. The fourth section answered objections that others had about sending missionaries, like the difficulty of learning languages and the dangers presented by foreign lands. Finally, the fifth part asked for the formation of a Baptist missionary society and described how it could be partially supported. The work became the basis for missionary activity and is still used today.

Later, William preached his pro-missionary sermon, the so-called

"Deathless Sermon." Within it, he repeatedly said, "Expect great things from God; attempt great things for God." This would become his most famous and repeated quote. This sermon became the catalyst for the Particular Baptist Society for Propagating the Gospel among the Heathen (now the Baptist Missionary Society), founded in 1792. There they discussed practical matters such as raising funds, as well as deciding where they would direct their efforts.

> *[Jesus] said to them, "Go into all the world and preach the good news to all creation."*
>
> **MARK 16:15**

One of the first missionaries to come under their umbrella was a medical doctor named John Thomas. He had spent some time in Calcutta and was raising funds in England so that he could return. After Thomas received society approval, Carey decided to accompany him.

Once in Calcutta, Carey briefly studied the Bengali language and then took a job managing an indigo plant in order to provide financial support for the mission and establish a base of operations. During his employment, he completed the first revision of a Bengali New Testament and established principles for his missionary community, including communal living, financial self-reliance, and the training of indigenous ministers. Many of these practices are upheld by missionaries yet today.

In time, many more missionaries from the society came to India. A house in Serampore was purchased to accommodate the men and their families. A print shop was set up there as well so the group could print the Bible in Bengali. When their first convert came to Christ, a Hindu named Krishna Pal, the group decided that they should no longer observe the caste system. While the caste system said some classes of people were better than others, Carey and his team knew that all people were equal, created in God's image. Subsequently, Pal's daughter, a Sudra, married a Brahmin man, a taboo for that society.

William also wrote grammars of Bengali and Sanskrit and began to translate the Bible in Sanskrit too. He also translated native works into English to make them accessible to his own countrymen. One of his greatest contributions may have been influencing the locals to discontinue certain pagan practices such as infant sacrifice.

During his life, William's mission printed and distributed the Bible in whole or part in forty-four languages and dialects. His other accomplishments on the subcontinent are many. He introduced the steam engine to India. He brought the idea of a savings bank there, and discouraged usury or lending with interest. He promoted the humane treatment of India's leprosy patients. Furthermore, he founded India's Agri-Horticultural Society, and introduced the study of astronomy.

William Carey had a fierce desire to reach the Indian people not only with the good news of Jesus Christ, but the good news of Christian culture. He preached Christ, but also the difference Christ makes on society as a whole. With his written works and his principles and bylines for the missionary lifestyle, he inspired, motivated, and provided a priceless model for countless others who chose to preach and live the Great Commission.

A Father of Influence teaches his children to lead others to faith in Christ.

Henry Ford

1863–1947

Edsel Ford and Henry Ford II. Raised a farm boy outside Detroit, Henry became one of the great captains of industry, and created a family dynasty still ruled by Ford family members today.

As a young boy, Edsel Bryan Ford exhibited artistic flair, a trait his father, auto industrialist Henry Ford, noticed and looked upon with pride. Henry Ford told painter Irvin Bacon in 1910 to shake hands with his son because he was the artist in the family.

Also a skilled engineer, Edsel played with cylinders and spark plugs in his earliest years. His father, Henry, stocked workshops for his son at multiple locations, and it was Edsel who rolled up his sleeves and went to work on his father's Model T car when it broke down during their 1915 drive across America.

Henry's only son, Edsel married Eleanor Lowthian Clay in 1916 and moved to Indian Village, a fashionable new neighborhood where many wealthy young Detroiters were settling. Then in September 1917, Henry Ford II was born, followed by one more son, Benson, a daughter, Josephine, and a baby brother, William Clay.

By 1918, the Model T Ford had been in production for ten years, and half of all the cars in America were that model. On December 31, 1918, Henry turned over the presidency of the Ford Motor Company to twenty-eight-year-old Edsel, who had been working full time for his father's company since he left school six years earlier.

Edsel's first assignment was extreme, but he handled it with ease. He was to buy out the Dodge brothers and other minority shareholders to regain full ownership of the company. In the 1919 reorganization, Edsel Ford personally held just more than 40 percent of Ford Motor Company shares.

As Edsel assumed the presidency of the Ford Motor Company, Henry proudly posed for pictures alongside his son—visiting the Rouge River plant, inspecting cars, and visiting Greenfield Village together. Henry particularly liked one photo: father and son in the Village's Plympton House sitting together side by side in an old, high-backed wood bench, their faces warmly lit by a flickering log fire. In fact, Henry liked it so much that he used it as a Christmas card. It captured the best that both hoped for in their relationship—intimacy, warmth, and partnership.

Father and son spent several hours each day in each other's company, talking and working together. When they couldn't meet, they talked on the telephone. A direct private line connected the study of Henry Ford at his home on Fair Lane with Edsel's study on the other side of Detroit, and the line was often busy at night.

Edsel's other responsibilities involved taking care of sales, marketing, and keeping the books. He also personally contributed to the Ford car design, concentrating on the more peripheral aspects of the Model T like its shape, the position of the instrumentation on the dashboard panel, and the configuration of accessories. It was Henry's habit to have Edsel take responsibility for all the artistic and aesthetic details.

If executives ever came to Henry Ford questioning decisions that Edsel made, Henry insisted they follow his son's wishes because Edsel ran the company.

By 1927, sales of the Model T had plummeted. A new model was needed, so Henry and Edsel went to work. Henry designed the engine, chassis, and other mechanisms, while Edsel developed the body design and a sliding-shift transmission. The result was the highly successful Model A, produced through 1931.

In 1936, Henry and Edsel created the Ford Foundation with a broad mission to promote human welfare. Henry split his stock into a small number of voting shares, which he gave to his family, and a large number of nonvoting shares, which he gave to the foundation. It grew immensely and by 1950 reached out to benefit the needy beyond America's borders.

In his youth, Edsel's son, Henry II, had little financial worry or care for his family's business. Besides schooling, Henry II enjoyed family vacations and visits from international luminaries such as the Prince of Wales in 1924. All the students and teachers at Detroit University School were in awe of the young Henry, as if he were of royal blood. Some called him "spoiled," but Henry II didn't know what that meant.

Don't just do the minimum that will get you by. Do your best. Work from the heart for your real Master, for God, confident that you'll get paid in full when you come into your inheritance. Keep in mind always that the ultimate Master you're serving is Christ.

Colossians 3:23–24 msg

Detroit University School was followed by Hotchkiss, an East Coast boarding academy, which prepared the young rich for the Ivy League. The life of privilege continued there. Edsel would often send telegrams to his son telling him that the chauffeur would arrive at a given time by the front porch main school building to drive him to the Ritz Carlton.

After Hotchkiss, Henry II attended Yale and began to do quite well at his studies—a fact his father recognized and applauded. Additionally, Henry II began to take responsibility for his actions, exemplified by a car accident where he assumed responsibility.

In July, 1940, Henry II married Anne McDonnell, and Edsel approved of the union, knowing that the marriage would further stabilize and mature his son. War further disciplined Henry II when he joined the navy.

In May of 1943, tragedy struck the Ford family. Edsel died of heart complications. The elder Henry, at age seventy-nine, momentarily took over the presidency, and Henry II was released from the navy to become an executive vice president. The company saw hard times during the next two years, due primarily to war demands and transitional growing pains. In 1945, Henry Ford II took over the presidency—two short years before his grandfather died.

Not wanting to see the Ford Motor Company flounder or fail, a newly determined and ready Henry II hired a brilliant group of young executives known as the "Whiz Kids," and transformed Ford Motor Company into the fourth-largest industrial corporation in the world.

Back in 1873, at ten years of age, Henry Ford saw his first self-propelled machine, a stationary steam engine with a drive chain connected to its wheels. Fascinated, Henry took his passion, left the family farm, and by 1891, became an engineer with the Edison Illuminating Company. Through promotions, he found he had enough time and money to devote attention to his personal experiments on gasoline engines. These experiments culminated in the quadricycle, a self-propelled vehicle he created in 1896. With even more experiments, trial, error, grit, and determination, Henry Ford improved the quadricycle, ultimately leading to the creation of the Ford Motor Company and its famous Model T.

Creator of the Model T, the moving assembly line, the five dollar workday, and the peace ship, Henry Ford demonstrated the near limitless capabilities of human achievement. Rewarding and taking care of family, Henry promoted his only son, Edsel, to the presidency of the company he founded, and later saw his grandson assume the same position. Henry Ford exemplified and led a family work ethic transforming and transporting generations of Americans.

A Father of Influence teaches his children to be creative and industrious.

Jim Henson

1936–1990

Jim Henson's five children and children everywhere.

With boundless enthusiasm and creativity, Jim Henson inspired three of his five children to take over Jim Henson Productions, i.e. The Muppets, while delighting children of all ages the world over.

Four years prior to his death at age fifty-three, Jim Henson wrote a letter to each of his children to be read upon the event of his death. He told them about the type of funeral service he would like. He said, "I suggest you first have a friendly little service of some kind. It would be lovely if there was a song or two ... and someone said some nice, happy words about me." He asked that no one wear black and requested that a Dixieland band play the song, "When the Saints Go Marching In." He finally wrote that he hoped the world would be a better place because he had been in it. He wrote to his son Brian, "Please watch out for each other and love and forgive everybody. It's a good life, enjoy it," all this according to the book *Jim Henson: Puppeteer and Filmmaker.*

More than five thousand mourners dressed in bright colors crowded into the Cathedral of St. John the Divine in New York to attend Jim Henson's memorial service. As they entered, mourners passed an old green coat missing a frog-shaped piece of cloth, in honor of Henson's most famous character, Kermit. Also in attendance were two thousand foam butterflies placed on rods, which attendees fluttered in the air. The Dixieland band played Jim's request, and the organist played the *Sesame Street* theme "Sunny Day." In death as in life, warmth and joy radiated from Jim Henson. They were his memory and legacy.

The creator and lead puppeteer of The Muppets, Jim Henson was born in a small Mississippi town. (Kermit the Frog always said he came from a small swamp in Mississippi.) As a child, he loved to play in the cotton fields and fish along Deer Creek. In the fifth grade, he and his family moved to Hyattsville, Maryland, a suburb of Washington DC, where Jim's father worked for the Department of Agriculture.

In the 1950s, Jim discovered television and was entranced by it. He thought it was incredible to see a live picture transmitted from somewhere else. He fell in love with the medium, and one of the first shows he ever watched was a puppet show called *Kukla, Fran and Ollie*.

At University Park High School, Jim's main interest was art. He made posters for school dances, drew cartoons for the school newspaper, and acted in several school plays. He also joined a puppet club. Jim wrote about the merge of his love of television and puppetry. As soon as he was old enough to get work, he set out and approached all the local studios in Washington to see who would accept him. When he heard a small station was looking for a puppeteer, he built some puppets with an associate and was hired.

As a result of Jim's unique design and natural puppeteering ability, the show received good reviews from critics. Even so, the show was cancelled after three weeks. Before disappointment could set in, however, a nearby NBC affiliate hired him and his puppets for their local program. At this time, he still planned to pursue a career in commercial art.

Now enrolled at the University of Maryland, he took classes in acting, stagecraft, scene design, and puppetry. He also continued to draw and paint. After his freshman year, he was offered his own show called *Sam and Friends*. It was a late-night five-minute spot before *The Tonight Show*.

The Muppets, a take-off on both the words "marionette" and "puppet," began when he combined features of hand puppets, rod puppets, and marionettes. He used foam rubber because it was pliable,

more expressive than harder materials. Steve
Allen caught *Sam and Friends* one evening and
invited Jim to perform on *The Tonight Show.*
Jim showed up with Kermit (then more like a
lizard) and a creature that would evolve into
the Cookie Monster.

A cheerful heart fills the day with song.
PROVERBS 15:15 MSG

From there, Jim went on to commercials, a European tour, and
even collected an Emmy Award for Best Local Entertainment
Program for *Sam and Friends*. Additionally, the Muppets were gaining
widespread recognition and were in demand. Jim made a short film
called *Time Piece*, which would garner an Oscar nomination for Best
Short Film. Then, in 1969, the Children's Television Workshop came
calling and the famed and celebrated *Sesame Street* began.

After Jim died, his twenty-six-year-old son Brian inherited the
business. Brian wrote in the book about his father, "My father had
wonderful goals and wonderful dreams. And when he died, I realized
they had become mine." Brian took over as president of Jim Henson
Productions.

Emotions were raw at the company after Jim's death. There was a
substantial period of mourning. But in the end, Jim's absence hard-
ened their drive. They felt strongly that they should keep his dreams
alive. With that resolve, they found a passion to keep working with
Brian as their leader.

Brian believes it was easier to continue the dream after his father's
death because of the way he ran the company when he was alive. Jim
wanted the company to run with minimal supervision so that he
could continue to perform and direct. Therefore, he chose talented
people who loved the work. It was also important to him to be a
father figure to his employees rather than a boss.

Show business and the creative bug also bit two of Jim's other
children. Brian's sister Cheryl, second of Jim's children, is president
of the Jim Henson Foundation and a director of the Jim Henson
Company. She is also a puppeteer and author. Lisa Henson, Jim's
oldest daughter, helped develop the Storyteller series and is now co-
CEO and cochairman of the Jim Henson Company.

Jim believed in taking a positive attitude toward people and his work. He always thought he was in the world for a purpose. He wasn't sure if everyone had a purpose, but he was convinced he did. He always tried to find in himself whatever it was that he was supposed to be. Though he found it difficult to keep his focus on those thoughts throughout the day, he always began each day with positive ambitions in mind.

Jim believed that life is basically a growth process. He thought everything worked out for some benefit. He drove some people mad with his ridiculous optimism, but it always helped him live his life. To Jim, life was a constant learning process, full of opportunities to express gratitude.

This positive mental attitude carried Jim beyond *Sesame Street* to other TV programs such as *The Muppet Show* and *Fraggle Rock*. Additionally, he made several movies with the Muppets including *The Muppet Movie* and *The Muppets Take Manhattan*, and the fantasy films *The Dark Crystal* and *Labyrinth*. A true pioneer and inspiration to children everywhere, Jim lived a life of creative, positive imagination.

A Father of Influence brings joy and an enthusiasm for life to his children.

John Wooden

1910–

His players and children everywhere. John Wooden, voted "Coach of the Century" by ESPN, followed his father's seven-point creed, winning admiration, respect, and more national college basketball championships than any other coach in history.

Exemplifying his care for his basketball players as if they were his own kids, legendary UCLA coach John Wooden writes, in his autobiography *They Call Me Coach* of one star player he had to remove for bad performance in a championship game. "Pushing open the dressing room, I ran right into Fred Slaughter. He had evidently been waiting for me. 'Coach,' he said, 'before someone gets the wrong impression, I want you to understand. You had to leave Doug in there because he played so well, and I didn't. I wanted to play in the worst way, but I do understand, if anyone says I was upset, it's not true. Disappointed, yes, but upset, no. And I was very happy for Doug.'"

Wooden realizes there are a lot of peaks and valleys in every coach's life. But to him, that moment was the ultimate. He and that team had won their first NCAA title by beating Duke 98 to 83 and they finished the 1964 season with a perfect 30 and 0 record. Any concern he had for Fred was dissolved at that moment.

Fred Slaughter lacked height as a center, but he had other attributes that made him a leader. A quick man, he often set others up with great shots and great rebounding skills. As a former high school track athlete, he had quick anticipation. But mainly, he had intelligence on the court.

John Wooden's own father hailed from Hall, Indiana, where he worked a variety of jobs including tenant farmer and rural mail carrier. His father worked hard and made sure his children also kept busy. This work ethic had a profound influence on John, who says his father greatly influenced his life and coaching philosophy. John respected his father, even as a small boy, because his father was always fair with him and wanted his best.

This fairness was demonstrated when Wooden's father whipped both he and his brother Cat over an altercation out in the barn. There was no favoritism in the Wooden home. A true gentleman, Wooden's father read the Bible daily, and expected his children to read it too. They did, and at least in John's case, believed it. Even today, Coach Wooden keeps a well-marked, well-read copy of the Bible in his desk.

After little John graduated from the country grade school, his father gave him a piece of paper on which he had written a creed that he suggested John live by. According to his autobiography, it read:

1) Be true to yourself.
2) Make each day your masterpiece.
3) Help others.
4) Drink deeply from good books, especially the Bible.
5) Make friendship a fine art.
6) Build a shelter against a rainy day.
7) Pray for guidance, count and give thanks for your blessings every day.

Coach Wooden carried that original handwritten note in his wallet for many years. When it wore out, he had copies made. He still keeps a copy in his wallet.

Coach also learned basketball from his father, who always made sure they had some play mixed in with their work. On the farm, when he was a kid, John developed his love of sports. He first learned about basketball when he was only eight years old. His father made a basket out of an old fruit basket. He knocked the bottom out of it and nailed it up on a wall near the hayloft in the barn. By the time

John was in third or fourth grade, his father forged a ring out of iron for the basket.

Prior to high school, Coach Wooden actually favored baseball over basketball. But in high school, he led Martinsville High School to the state championship final for three consecutive years, winning the tournament in 1927. At Purdue University, he was a three-time All-American guard and a member of their 1932 national championship team. Humorously, Wooden was named "The Indiana Rubber Man" because he fearlessly dove after balls on the hardcourt. He first earned an English degree at Purdue, and then earned his master's degree at Indiana State Teacher's College. After a brief professional career with the Indianapolis Kautsky's, he enlisted in the navy, where he gained the rank of lieutenant during World War II.

After the war, Wooden coached at Indiana State University in Terre Haute, Indiana, from 1946 to 1948. In 1947, Wooden's basketball team won the conference title and received an invitation to the NAIB National Tournament in Kansas City. Coach Wooden refused the invitation citing the NAIB's policy banning African American players. A year later, the NAIB changed this policy and Wooden guided his team to the NAIB final, but lost to Louisville. John Wooden was inducted into the Indiana State University Athletic Hall of Fame on February 3, 1984.

In 1948, Wooden began his legendary coaching career at UCLA, where he gained lasting fame, winning 665 games and 10 NCAA titles in 12 seasons, including 7 in a row from 1967 to 1973. His UCLA teams won 88 games in a row, 4 perfect 30-0 seasons, and they also won 38 straight games in the NCAA Tournament. Nicknamed "The Wizard of Westwood," Wooden retired immediately after his 10th title in 1975.

UCLA was actually Wooden's second choice for a coaching position in 1948. He wanted a coaching position at the University of Minnesota, and it was his and his wife, Nellie's, desire to remain in the Midwest. But inclement weather prevented Wooden from

I meditate on your precepts and consider your ways.

Psalm 119:15

receiving the scheduled phone offer from the U of M, and thinking they had lost interest in him, he accepted the UCLA position. He was married to Nellie for fifty-three years before her death in 1985.

One of Coach's best players, 1974 UCLA graduate and 1993 Hall of Fame inductee Bill Walton, writes in the forward of *They Call Me Coach*, "At 92, John Wooden is happier, more positive, more upbeat than ever. There is not a bit of cynicism, not an ounce of bitterness, absolutely no jealousy or envy. He is still the same teacher, the same positive force, the person we would all like to become, only better."

Voted "Coach of the Century" by ESPN, Coach Wooden is listed as both a player and a coach in the Basketball Hall of Fame. He is also an author, writing his own biography, several life advice books including *A Lifetime of Observations and Reflections On and Off the Court*, and the children's book *Inch and Miles: The Journey to Success*. A father figure to many, he was voted "California Father of the Year" and "California Grandfather of the Year" by the National Father's Day Committee. The very next year, he was voted the "California Sports Father of the Year." A true national hero, John Wooden exemplifies success and achievement.

**A Father of Influence gives his children
precepts to live by.**

Martin Luther

1483–1546

Father of all Protestants. Though originally a law student, Martin Luther became a monk, studied the Scriptures, and began to preach salvation through faith in Christ, inspiring the Protestant Reformation.

Growing up as a small boy in Germany, the religious establishment taught Martin Luther that he was watched by a great and just God, powerful enough to make lightning strike a boy for any small sin. Martin believed that no matter how well he lived, in the eyes of God he was always sinful. Martin learned that only the Virgin Mary and the saints could pardon his sins.

Years later, this burden still waged against his soul. The Black Plague ravaged Europe. Millions died and the living wondered what God must be doing and thinking. While attending the University of Erfurt, Martin walked near the village of Stotternheim during a thunderstorm. He collapsed to the ground at the clap of thunder and a strike of lightning. Fearing for his life, Martin cried out, "Ah, do but help me, Saint Anne, and I will straightaway become a monk!" As the rain poured, Martin rose and discovered he was not harmed. When he reached the home of his friends, he told them of his promise to Saint Anne. They thought he was jesting. But he didn't waver. "I have made my choice. I am going into a monastery."

Martin's father, Hans, recognized his son had talent, so he wanted him to receive an education. Hans himself struggled, first as a farmer and then as a coal miner. Martin began studying at the cathedral school when he was seven. It was an unhappy place where boys sat in dark, cold, dirty rooms doing the bidding of a teacher who did not care if the boys learned or not. Oftentimes, the teachers would whip the children for minor infractions. As Martin strove to learn Latin, mathematics, and Greek, his father's work began to prosper in the mines. Hans began to plan. He wanted to buy a smelting furnace of his own and planned a brighter future for his son Martin.

Martin became familiar with the monastic life when he joined a reasonably priced school run by Franciscan monks. A happy time, Martin's good friend John Reinicke also joined him there. When Martin was eighteen, he enrolled at the University of Erfurt. His father was proud of his son and glad to support him. The furnaces were making money, and it looked more promising than ever that Martin would be able to pursue a career in law. During his first year, Martin excelled at playing the lute, and studied Roman literature and philosophy. He earned the nickname, "the philosopher."

Martin's first inclination that he would lead a life of ministry came during these college years. He fell and injured his foot. Though a physician bound the wound, he became gravely ill and was expected to die. Tossing about with a high fever, a priest came and sat quietly beside him. Martin opened his eyes and the priest told him to be of good cheer because he would not die. The priest also told him that God was going to make him into a great man, who would be of comfort to many people. Martin did recover, studied hard, and at the end of his first year, obtained a bachelor of arts degree.

As Martin began more advanced studies, he discovered the Bible. Chained to its stand, the book was almost unused. Even the religion studies students weren't encouraged to read it. But Martin opened it up and was riveted by what he read—even though it was written in Latin.

Martin obtained his master of arts degree, but his father still wanted him to study law. In fact, on graduation, his father bestowed him a gift of expensive law books including *Corpus Juris* or "Body of the Law." But it was not to be. He discontinued his law studies and entered an Augustinian monastery in Erfurt.

For a full year, Martin studied and prayed until he was ready to say his first mass. He invited his father to come and was delighted when

Hans said he would attend. By that time Hans had become a more important man in the village, one of the *Vierherren*, the Four Citizens, who represented his fellow townsmen on the town council. The furnaces were doing well, Hans now owning at least six mines and two foundries. He rode to the monastery like a well-to-do man with a company of twenty horsemen. He even made a monetary gift to the monastery.

Martin tried desperately to gain God's favor at the monastery by fasting, good works, flagellations, prayer, and pilgrimages. He became gaunt and depressed. The more he tried to please God, the more he became aware of his own sinfulness.

God has us where he wants us, with all the time in this world and the next to shower grace and kindness upon us in Christ Jesus. Saving is all his idea, and all his work. All we do is trust him enough to let him do it. It's God's gift from start to finish!

EPHESIANS 2:8–9 MSG

The other monks hated to see him so anguished, so they ordered him to pursue an academic career to distract him from excessive rumination. Martin was ordained into the priesthood and then began teaching theology at the University of Wittenberg, eventually receiving his doctorate of theology.

There at the monastery, Martin finally received his own Bible, bound in red leather. Nothing he had ever received in his life meant so much to him. He especially found the life of the apostle Paul meaningful. He marveled at how such a proud, learned man could come to a relationship with Christ by faith alone. With the knowledge of law in the back of his mind, Martin came to realize that no one could earn his or her way into heaven. Instead, forgiveness and acceptance by Christ could only come through faith.

As Luther studied and researched the Bible, he began to question the contemporary usage of terms like *penance, righteousness,* and *indulgences* used by the Roman Catholic Church. He became convinced the church had lost the central truth of justification by faith alone. Drawing from his knowledge of law, Luther began to distinguish between the law and the gospel, a distinction he believed the church of his day didn't recognize, and the root of its many theological errors.

Luther's writings and teachings became so controversial that the pope gave him a papal bull, or official church document, stating he risked excommunication unless he recanted his words. On January 3, 1521, Pope Leo X excommunicated Luther. However, Luther's friends prevented the execution of the ban. Luther was summoned to renounce or reaffirm his views and given a guarantee of safe passage by Emperor Charles V at the imperial Diet of Worms (an assembly or "diet" of people of nobility, clergy, and commoners in the small town of Worms). The book *Martin Luther* says that he was plainly asked the question, "Will you reject your books and the errors they contain?" He replied as quoted, "Unless I am convicted by Scripture and plain reason—I do not accept the authority of popes and councils, for they have contradicted each other—my conscience is captive to the Word of God. I cannot and will not recant anything, for to go against conscience is neither right nor safe." He would stand on that position, convinced he had no other recourse and nothing else to say. On this pronouncement, Luther left himself to God's mercy. Remarkably, Luther escaped Worms but was declared an outlaw and all his literature was banned.

Through his life and work, Luther emphasized that a person is saved by God's merciful kindness through the work of Christ, not by any human effort. Luther also penned the beloved hymn, "A Mighty Fortress Is Our God," inspiring congregational singing practiced by churches everywhere today. Furthermore, his marriage and child rearing reintroduced the practice of clerical marriage. (Marriage is still banned among Catholic clergy.) A Bible translator, he encouraged the common man to read the Scriptures and discover for himself the message of life-affirming faith within its pages. Today, nearly seventy million Christians claim to belong to Lutheran churches worldwide, and another 320 million Protestants trace their history back to Luther's reforming work.

A Father of Influence teaches his children that salvation is by faith in Christ alone.

Thomas Lincoln

1778–1851

Abraham Lincoln. Thomas Lincoln moved his entire family to a different state because he opposed slavery, teaching his son, Abraham, sixteenth president of the United States, to value freedom and liberty for all.

O ut in the fields of Hardin County, Kentucky, Thomas Lincoln tended to his farm. Born in Virginia, Thomas moved with his family as a child to Kentucky (then a part of Virginia). There in a small cabin on the farm near Hodgenville, Thomas and his wife, Nancy, gave birth to a son named Abraham, named after his grandfather.

Before Abraham was two years old, the family moved to another Kentucky farm. But the moves weren't over. Seven-year-old Abraham was quickly proving himself to be a knowledgeable and inquisitive child when the family moved across the Ohio River into Indiana. Thomas openly opposed slavery and felt he had a better chance of succeeding in a state that prohibited the practice.

Young Abraham learned about slavery and its implications from his father, and he watched his father carefully as he put feet to his belief that all men are created equal. The sentiments of freedom for all were set before Abraham at a young age, and he retained them throughout his life.

Only a year after the move, Abraham's mother died of accidental poisoning, and the loss was harshly felt by the Lincoln family. Thomas returned to Kentucky to find a wife, and there met Sarah Bush Johnston, a widow he had known before marrying his first wife.

Thomas and Sarah married and young Abraham now had a new mother. Abraham worked on his father's farm, which left him little time for schooling. Still, Lincoln loved to read and walked miles to borrow books at his stepmother's prompting.

In 1828, nineteen-year-old Lincoln left the family farm and sold farm goods in New Orleans. He returned for a short while before heading out again to explore the world.

After failing to gain his first pursuit at elected office as a member of the General Assembly in New Salem, Illinois, and failing as a general store owner, he fell on further bad times when he fell in love with Ann Rutledge, who died before a serious romance could develop. Lincoln was eventually elected to the General Assembly, and after much study received his license to practice law. He would practice law off and on in Illinois until he was elected president in 1861.

Public office came calling again, and in 1846 Lincoln was elected on the Whig ticket to the U.S. House of Representatives. He first hinted at his attitudes toward freedom and pursuit of happiness for all people when he opposed President Polk's attack on Mexico during the U.S.-Mexican War.

In 1854, Lincoln debated Stephen Douglas, and began a six-year political sparring match with him. In his speech, Lincoln shaped and articulated his opinions on slavery and freedom by talking about whether a Negro is or is not a man. If African Americans were men, then the words of the Declaration of Independence, which stated that all men are created equal and have the rights of life, liberty, and the pursuit of happiness, applied to them. This speech attracted the attention of the Republican Party, who realized that Lincoln could be one of their most powerful champions.

In 1858, Steven Douglas faced reelection in the U.S. Senate, and the Republican Party nominated Abraham Lincoln to run against him. He made his position on slavery even clearer by quoting Scripture. Lincoln said, "A house divided against itself cannot stand. I believe this government cannot endure; permanently half *slave* and half *free*. I do not expect the Union to be *dissolved*—I do not expect the house to *fall*—but I *do* expect it will cease to be divided. It will become *all* one thing, or *all* the other." Thousands came to hear the debates, which lasted three or more hours. The debates focused on one subject: slavery. Lincoln lost the election but sealed his position as the spokesperson for the Republican Party and gained a taste for high public office.

> *Wherever the Spirit of the Lord is, there is freedom.*
>
> **2 CORINTHIANS 3:17** NLT

In 1860, Lincoln won the presidential election, striking fear in the Southern states. They worried Lincoln would attempt to end slavery. In anticipation of this, the Southern states began to secede from the Union to form the Confederate States of America. Before he even assumed office, Lincoln faced a national crisis—dissolution of the country he had been elected to govern. In his inaugural address, quoted in the biography *Abraham Lincoln: America's 16th President*, the president said of the Southern states, "We are not enemies, but friends. We must not be enemies. Though passion may have strained, it must not break our bonds of affection."

When Confederate forces attacked the Union-controlled Fort Sumter in Charleston, South Carolina, the Civil War began. The North thought the South should be taught a lesson, and with its superior manpower and industry, also thought the war could be over in a few weeks. Of course, the war would continue on four more years with unspeakable casualties. Major battles occurred at Vicksburg, Mississippi; Atlanta, Georgia; Petersburg and Richmond, Virginia; and Gettysburg, Pennsylvania.

Lincoln made his most concrete action for freedom and against slavery by issuing the Emancipation Proclamation on January 1, 1863. The document declared the slaves in the Confederacy were "forever free." Scoffing at the move, Southern states did little to effect the law.

In Gettysburg, Pennsylvania, Lincoln accepted an invitation to attend a dedication of the cemetery there. In two minutes, he succinctly and brilliantly articulated the struggle the United States faced and the struggle he championed. He said in what is known today as the Gettysburg Address: "We here highly resolve that these dead shall not have died in vain—that this nation, under God, shall have a new birth of freedom—and that government of the people, by the people, for the people, shall not perish from the earth."

By the next election, the nation was weary under the weight of the war. Republicans did not believe Lincoln could win reelection. Though his opponent won 45 percent of the popular vote, Lincoln was given a second term.

In January of 1865, Lincoln introduced the Thirteenth Amendment to the Constitution, which officially abolished slavery in the United States. It passed in both the House and the Senate. Yet it did not go into effect until after it was ratified in December 1865, more than seven months after Lincoln's assassination.

During his second inaugural address in March of that year, Lincoln again issued a verbal salve in an effort to heal the wounds of the nation. He said, "With malice toward none; with charity for all; with firmness in the right, as God give us to see the right, let us strive on to finish the work we are in; to bind up the nation's wounds; to care for him who shall have borne the battle, and for his widow, and his orphan—to do all which may achieve and cherish a just, and a lasting peace, among ourselves, and with all nations."

War's end came when General U. S. Grant overran Petersburg and federal troops occupied the Confederate capital of Richmond. While Lincoln toured Richmond, Grant pursued General Robert E. Lee, who finally surrendered to Grant at the Appomattox Court House. Lincoln urged Grant to set kind and generous conditions for the surrender.

On April 14, 1865, Abraham Lincoln performed his final deed for freedom by becoming a martyr for its cause. As the Civil War gasped in its final days, the battle-weary president and his wife sought to relax and attend a play at the Ford Theater. There, as the audience laughed at a particularly funny line, Confederate sympathizer John Wilkes Booth fired a single pistol shot into the back of the president's head, knocking him unconscious and mortally wounding him. Lincoln died nine hours later in a house across from the theater. The Union mourned and millions lined up along the railroad tracks as his body was carried from Washington to its final resting place in Springfield, Illinois.

The Civil War was as much about preserving the United States of America as it was about freeing the slaves. But for those who love freedom everywhere, especially the disenchanted, enchained African Americans who knew the bondage of forced servitude, Abraham Lincoln became a savior and champion of liberty and freedom. And it all stemmed from a family move across state lines—a move his father, Thomas, insisted on as a matter of protest and principle.

A Father of Influence teaches his children to value freedom for all.

Bishop Milton Wright

1828–1917

Orville and Wilbur Wright. Bishop Milton Wright gave

his sons the intelligence, creativity, and spirit of exploration

needed to resolve the problem of human flight as they

successfully launched the first self-propelled airplane at

Kitty Hawk, North Carolina.

The earliest letter written by either Wilbur or Orville Wright, the inventors and pilots of the first airplane, came from Orville, age nine, to his father in Omaha when the Wright family was living in Cedar Rapids, Iowa. He wrote, "Dear Father—I got your letter today. The other day, I took a machine can and filled it with water then I put it on the stove. I waited a little while and the water came squirting out of the top about a foot." The freedom with which Orville wrote of his experimentation exemplifies the spirit of freedom and invention that existed in the Wright home.

The third and fourth of five children, Orville and Wilbur Wright caught the aviation bug early when their father, a bishop with the United Brethren Church, gave them a toy helicopter. Coming home from an itinerant preaching excursion, Bishop Milton first concealed the toy then tossed it into the air for their delight. The helicopter was made of cork, bamboo, and paper, activated by a twisted rubber band. This event became a sort of baptism into flight for young Orville and Wilbur. The boys played with the toy until it wore out, but it inspired them in subsequent months and years to build other toy helicopters of various sizes and designs. They were astonished to discover that the larger they made them, the more poorly they flew.

They were determined to make a flying machine large enough to carry a man.

Their father was a kind but strict patrician, who always encouraged the keeping of the Sabbath in his home. Play and work were discouraged, but Sunday reading and letter writing were not. (In later years, Orville and Wilbur refused to permit Sunday flights out of consideration for their father.) Everyday card-playing was forbidden, not because it was a sin, but because it was considered to be a waste of time. Santa Claus was outlawed, but not fairy tales, and simple gifts made an appearance every Christmas morning. Orville and Wilbur regularly attended Sunday school at the United Brethren Church, but they also read the writings of agnostics and other literature found in their father's library.

Not ones to settle in any one place for too long, the Wright family moved to Richmond, Indiana, close to the home of Grandpa Koerner. It was quite possible that the two boys developed their mechanical aptitudes there, as they prowled about the outbuildings and investigated the foot-powered lathe in his carriage and wagon shop. After the family moved to Dayton, Ohio, they received their high school educations, but never obtained diplomas. They dabbled in printing and the newspaper business before opening the Wright Cycle Company in 1892. There they manufactured and repaired bicycles. Throughout the years, the brothers thought often of aeronautical pursuits, many times at the expense and neglect of the business.

The boys were also avid travelers. Years earlier, in his late twenties, Bishop Milton Wright began his travels as a church missionary, visiting Philadelphia, New York, Panama, San Francisco, and Portland, Oregon. This yearning to travel took Orville and Wilbur not only to Kitty Hawk and the Outer Banks of North Carolina to do their flight experiments, but also on subsequent trips throughout America and Europe as they promoted flight and perfected their planes.

Wilbur wrote of his desire to travel in 1900 in one of many letters to his father: "I am intending to start in a few days for a trip to the coast of North Carolina in the vicinity of Roanoke Island, for the purpose of making some experiments with a flying machine.... At any rate, I shall have an outing of several weeks and see a part of the world I have never before visited."

As the Wrights were traveling back and forth to Kitty Hawk between 1900 and 1903, a matter back home almost prevented Wilbur from making another trip to the Atlantic shore. He felt duty bound to help his father in a potentially scandalous church problem. A layman connected with the church publishing business had mishandled funds. Bishop Wright would not tolerate the dishonesty and wanted to see the man removed, if not prosecuted. Yet one faction of the church sought instead to oust the bishop. Wilbur set to work on the books to seek proof of the dishonesty. Then he wrote a blistering memo, setting forth the facts, clearing his father's name, and implicating the guilty man. The whole Wright family became as interested in this matter as they were in aviation. Bishop Wright was never deposed, but the fight went on for a long time. The brothers finally decided to continue their work and built a new glider at Kitty Hawk.

For four long years, the brothers toiled and then on December 17, 1903, Orville mounted the motorized glider, Wilbur started it up and watched as his brother gathered enough speed to lift off the ground and travel aloft for 59 seconds. The two would take three more flights that day before a wind gust smashed a wing.

On successfully completing their flight, they sent a telegram to their father to tell him the news. The housekeeper, Carrie Grumbach, received the messenger, signed for the telegram, and took it upstairs to the bishop. In a little while, he came downstairs and calmly said, "Well, they've made a flight." He showed no excitement but looked pleased. Later that night, Milton and their sister, Miss Katherine, were in high spirits, not because of the successful flight, but because the boys would be home for Christmas. Stuffing the turkey had always been Wilbur's privilege, and the way he did it was something special.

That afternoon, Bishop Wright gave the telegram to his son Lorin, who took it to the Dayton representative of the Associated Press. The press man said, "59 seconds?! If it were 59 minutes, it might be worth mentioning." So, he didn't mention it. It didn't run in the paper the next day. Yet, after reading about it in the

Cincinnati Enquirer, the editor woke up and finally ran the story.

Following the success of that flight, Bishop Wright warned his famous children that some would try to take advantage of them or steal their glory. When Wilbur was in France in 1907, Bishop Milton wrote, "It behooves you to be watchful of your interests, and to be certain of any move you may make. And you may be sure that all dealing with you will try to reach into you as far as possible. Men of wealth generally have exercised their shrewdness pretty well."

The brothers wrote back assurances to their father, especially with regard to revelry and alcohol consumption. According to *The Wright Brothers: How They Invented the Airplane*, Orville wrote his father that year from Paris, "We have been real good over here. We have been in a lot of churches, and haven't got drunk yet!"

> *Write these commandments that I've given you today on your hearts. Get them inside of you and then get them inside your children. Talk about them wherever you are, sitting at home or walking in the street; talk about them from the time you get up in the morning to when you fall into bed at night.*
>
> DEUTERONOMY 6:6–7 MSG

Wilbur wrote similarly of that same trip, "As to drinking and dissipation of various kinds, you may be entirely easy. All the wine I have tasted since leaving home would not fill a single wine glass. I am sure that Orville and myself will be careful to do nothing which would disgrace the training we received from you and from Mother."

Temperance and restraint also extended to other areas as well. Bishop Wright wrote his sons telling them how glad he was they observed Sunday and abstained from tobacco. He said this moral behavior would do them more good than what they would get from their invention. Bishop Milton encouraged his children to be wary of fame. He wrote a witty letter warning Wilbur to be wary of the French who treated him as if he were Christopher Columbus resurrected.

On May 25, 1910, Orville took his father, then eighty-two years old, for his first trip in a flying machine. The bishop enjoyed it immensely, begging his son to take him higher and higher.

In 1912, Wilbur succumbed to typhoid fever and died. He wrote of his father in his will, "My earnest thanks for his example of a courageous, upright life, and for his earnest sympathy with everything tending to my true welfare." Bishop Wright wrote of his third son in his journal: "In memory and intellect, there was none like him. He systemized everything. His wit was quick and keen. He could say or write anything he wanted to. He was not very talkative. His temper could hardly be stirred. He wrote much. He could deliver a fine speech, but he was modest."

Between Wilbur's death and his own death in 1917, Bishop Wright would visit Wilbur's grave, read the *Encyclopedia Britannica*, and work on family genealogy. On April 3, 1917, Bishop Milton Wright died in his sleep at age eighty-eight.

Two simple, modest mechanics with no more formal education than a high school diploma received support, strength, inspiration, encouragement, faith, and self-restraint from their father, Bishop Milton Wright. Through his fine parenting skills, their ideal youth allowed them to strip away any pretenses that might otherwise entangle them in their pursuit of manned flight. Bishop Milton Wright trained his children properly, wrote and communicated often with them, and encouraged them to soar.

A Father of Influence writes and communicates often with his children.

John Osteen

1921–1999

Joel Scott Osteen. John Osteen rose from poverty to pastor of Lakewood Church in Houston, Texas. After John's death, under his son Joel's leadership, Lakewood has become America's largest and fastest growing church congregation, averaging approximately forty-six thousand adult attendees each weekend.

Pastor of Lakewood Church in Houston, Texas, Joel Osteen may have his best life now, but back in his youth times were tough. His own father, John, also a pastor, had barely enough food to get along, yet during special services they would host guest ministers at their home for up to an entire week. One Sunday, during such a week, a businessman in the church approached the elder pastor Osteen and gave him some money to use personally, just to help out. He handed over a check for a thousand dollars, nearly equal to ten thousand dollars in today's money.

John was overwhelmed by the man's generosity but was so limited in his thinking at the time that he held the check by the edge at the corner, as if he might become contaminated if he clutched it any tighter. He told the businessman that he could never receive the money and insisted it go into the church offering.

God was trying to teach the elder Osteen that he wanted something better for him. While it is not God's intention that His servants should be controlled by money, He does want to bless and prosper those who live in faithful obedience to Him.

It was a lesson John would eventually learn and teach his son Joel. This is the kind of positive, prosperous thinking that has led Joel to lead the largest and fastest growing church in America.

In his book *Your Best Life Now*, Joel Osteen writes about his father's humble beginnings. John Osteen was raised in a poor cotton-picking family in the Deep South during the Great Depression. At the age of seventeen, John gave his heart to God.

After initially becoming ordained as a Southern Baptist minister, John Osteen received what he describes as the baptism in the Holy Spirit in 1958. This experience energized his ministry and transformed it into a worldwide outreach for Jesus Christ. He subsequently traveled extensively throughout the world, taking the positive message of God's love, healing, and power to people of all nations. On Mother's Day, 1959, John Osteen founded Lakewood Church in Houston, Texas, widely known as "The Oasis of Love in a Troubled World."

When John Osteen first started ministering, he was not an experienced student of the Bible. In fact, no one in his family had ever been a church leader or Bible teacher. This deficit took on a humorous tone when he preached an entire message on Samson one Sunday, realizing after the fact that he had been calling the hero of the story "Tarzan"!

Through the years, John Osteen improved his delivery and was able to develop Lakewood into a body of about six thousand members. The church administered an active television ministry, crusades, conferences, missionary support, and food distribution. He coined the motto for his congregation: "No Limits."

John's success often translated to special favor for his son Joel. In his book, Joel writes, "John Osteen, my dad, was well respected and highly influential in our community. Many times people did good things for me simply because they loved my dad. One time as a teenager, I got pulled over by a policeman for speeding. I had just recently received my driver's license, and I was extremely nervous when I saw those flashing lights pull up behind me, and then the ominous looking officer looming outside my window. But when that officer saw my license, he recognized that I was John Osteen's son. He smiled at me as though we were long-lost buddies, and he let me go with just a warning. The point is, of course, that I received preferential treatment, not because of me, but because of my father."

In 1999, Joel suddenly found himself face-to-face with both favor and responsibility. His father developed kidney stones and then underwent dialysis. Then, a pacemaker was implanted in his chest. Not long after, Joel and Christians around the world grieved as John experienced further complications and died of a heart attack. It was a difficult time, but Joel, despite having only preached one sermon in his life—the week before his father's death, succeeded him as pastor of Lakewood Church on October 3, 1999.

I can do everything through Christ who gives me strength.

PHILIPPIANS 4:13 NLT

Joel writes in *Your Best Life Now*, "When Daddy passed away in 1999, and I took over as pastor of Lakewood Church in Houston, people often approached me and asked, 'Joel, do you really think you can keep it going? Do you think you can hold down the fort? You've got some real big shoes to fill.' I knew God doesn't want one generation to shine and then the next generation to fade into obscurity. I knew I didn't have to fill my dad's shoes. I had only to fill my own shoes. I just had to be the person God made me to be. I believe I'm going to do more than my dad."

Joel is off to a rousing start, quickly surpassing his father's reach. Joel's low-key, positive style has resonated with crowds, and Lakewood began to hold six weekly services in its seventy-eight-hundred-seat sanctuary. This facility became too small, however, so Lakewood took over the former Compaq Center in July of 2005. That facility can seat more than sixteen thousand people at one time. There, Joel Osteen gives positive messages emphasizing the goodness of God. The congregation itself is ethnically and racially diverse, where all people, regardless of background or economic status, are encouraged to achieve their fullest potential. Joel has even adopted a slogan, like his father, "Discovering the Champion in You."

In addition to being seen at Lakewood's services, Joel Osteen can be seen via his weekly television broadcast on numerous national cable networks. His programs are carried internationally in more than one hundred nations including CNBC Europe, Vision Canada, CNBC Australia, and Middle East Television. Recently Nielsen Media Research rated Joel Osteen's broadcast as the number-one inspirational program nationally, based on average television viewers per market.

Reaching beyond the audio/visual format, Joel's book *Your Best Life Now* quickly became a national best seller. On the opening page, Joel writes, "This book is dedicated to my father, John Osteen (1921–99). My dad's integrity, humility, love and compassion for all people left an indelible impression on my life. I will be eternally grateful for his example."

John Osteen gave his son a legacy of faith in God's goodness and generosity. He encouraged him to dream big and reach out to others with the love and saving power of Christ.

A Father of Influence gives his children a vision for a limitless future.

William Franklin "Billy" Graham

1918–

William Franklin Graham III. Franklin Graham, the son

of the world's most famous evangelist, Billy Graham,

grew out of a rebellious period to become a respected

evangelist and world-relief practitioner as

the head of Samaritan's Purse.

William Franklin Graham III couldn't wait on his busy father and came into the world according to his own schedule in 1952. His father, Billy Graham, was talking with Jon Cordle and F. Roy Cattell, leaders of the Evangelical Alliance of Britain, in Ruth Graham's hospital room when she went into labor. Billy writes of the event in his autobiography *Just as I Am*, "I loved my three daughters—Anne, Gigi, and Bunny—with all my heart, but we were hoping and praying for a boy this time. When Ruth's labor pains began in earnest, the nurse took her out. A couple of hours later, another nurse came to tell me that we had a son. I was thrilled and emotional, but I also felt terribly guilty that I had not been with her, but with those two men. We named our son William Franklin Graham III, but we would call him Franklin. Eventually, I accepted the invitation for a London Crusade to begin on March 1, 1954."

After their son Ned was born in 1958, the Graham family was complete. Each child was unique and special, with joyous and challenging personality traits. Life for little Franklin and his siblings must have been a challenge, as their father was in great demand the world over. They had difficulty maintaining their privacy as Billy's ministry grew in size and popularity. People approached them all the time, disrupting normal family life.

To gain more privacy, the family moved to Montreat, North Carolina, a mountain resort village only accessible by four-wheel drive vehicles. There they created a comfortable Appalachian log-frame residence in the woods. Ruth Graham was able to make the place a happy home for the children and a real sanctuary for Billy.

Another challenge Billy faced as a young father was his constant travel. He worried what impact long absences would have on his children. He knew he was missing out on watching them grow up. Ruth and the children alone truly understand what those extended periods away from Billy meant to them.

In 1957, Franklin was five. During the lengthy Madison Square Garden Crusade, Ruth would tuck Franklin into bed every night. One night, after he thanked God for his father and for the team in New York, he also thanked God for letting his mother stay home.

Life as the son of Billy Graham began to take its toll on young Franklin in his teen years. Billy initially objected to his son's long hair, but Ruth reminded her husband that long hair wasn't a moral issue. So Billy never talked about it again. Grinning, Ruth also commented that Franklin looked like one of the prophets or the apostles.

Franklin continued to struggle and this led his parents to send him to Stony Brook School, a Christian boarding school in Long Island, New York. But that experience didn't last long. He dropped out his junior year and came back to finish high school in North Carolina. Franklin then attended LeTourneau College (now University), but was expelled for keeping a female classmate out past curfew. He continued his higher education at Montreat College and finally graduated at Appalachian State University near his childhood home.

Throughout this time, Franklin lived his "rebel years" drinking, doing drugs, smoking, and chasing girls. He said his parents didn't really know about these escapades in his life, but Billy knew what was going on. In 1974, Billy assured his son that he loved him no matter what he did, where he traveled, or how his life turned out. He told him he could always make a collect phone call home from anywhere in the world. He also told him he could come home whenever he wanted because the door would always be open. Ruth and Billy let Franklin know they always prayed for him. Finally, during a trip to Jerusalem, Franklin made a firm decision to follow Christ.

> *[Jesus said,] When he was still a long way off, his father saw him. His heart pounding, he ran out, embraced him, and kissed him.*
>
> LUKE 15:20 MSG

Later that same year, Franklin married Jane Austin Cunningham. And shortly after that, he joined Dr. Bob Pierce, founder of Samaritan's Purse, on a six-week mission trip to Asia. During this trip, Franklin was deeply moved by the people he met and the sights he saw. He decided to focus his ministry efforts on world relief. In 1979, after the death of Dr. Pierce, Franklin became the president of Samaritan's Purse.

Thrilled, Ruth and Billy were grateful their son became involved in Africa through Samaritan's Purse, an emergency aid organization that gives to the needy in the name of Christ. After disasters, the group works alongside local church or mission organizations. They have provided famine relief in Ethiopia and Mozambique and medical care in war-torn Rwanda. Franklin also began to join his father on evangelistic trips to Leningrad (now St. Petersburg), Tallinn (in Estonia), Moscow, and Novosibirsk (in Siberia).

Billy's good friend and fellow evangelist Roy Gustafson played an integral role in Franklin's spiritual journey. Billy helped Franklin grow spiritually and encouraged him in his evangelism skills. Roy invited Franklin to participate in several trips and taught him many religious and political things about the Middle East. Since then, Franklin has visited the prime minister of Israel, the king of Jordan, and other leaders in the area.

Other mentors have come into Franklin's life as well, such as Canadian evangelist Dr. John Wesley. Billy asked him to mentor Franklin with his spiritual growth and encourage him in his evangelistic skills. Because of that relationship, Franklin has stepped in as an associate evangelist with his father's team. Subsequently, Billy thinks his son is a better preacher than he was at that age.

Franklin joined the board of the Billy Graham Evangelistic Association (BGEA) in 1979. In 1995, the board took great pride in unanimously electing Franklin as first vice chair. The goal was that he would one day assume leadership of the BGEA on Billy's incapacity or death. Though no one could fill Billy's shoes, Franklin has matured into his own with his responsibilities and preaching. An evangelist in great demand the world over, Billy never dreamed his own son would rise to such levels. The BGEA will continue because of Franklin's commitment to the ministry.

Growing up the son of the world's most famous evangelist must not have been easy for Franklin Graham, but God's hand and his father's influence and example played a major role in pulling Franklin out of rebellion into obedience and leadership. Today, Franklin carries on the family ministry and, in the true sense of being the hands, feet, and mouthpiece of Christ, is carrying God's Word to millions around the world.

A Father of Influence never gives up on his children.

Frederick Douglass

1818–1895

Lewis Douglass. American abolitionist, editor, orator, author, statesman, and former slave provided a new model for African Americans and taught his son Lewis how to live as a free man.

The Civil War was over. The Thirteenth Amendment, officially abolishing slavery, had been ratified. The South, facing reconstruction, groaned and reeled against new realities. Northern armies occupied the once slave-filled lands to enforce the decrees of congress. Frederick Douglass, ardent abolitionist and former slave, was overjoyed to see the end of slavery in his lifetime, but he quickly discovered he couldn't ease back into a quiet life of obscurity. More work was left to do.

A new president, Andrew Johnson, had assumed power after the brutal assassination of Abraham Lincoln. Unlike his predecessor, this new president clearly had no interest in ensuring the freedom of Southern blacks. The Union army could only offer limited protection to ex-slaves. New southern state legislators passed laws that continued to keep blacks in poverty and positions of servitude. Ex-slaves who had no steady employment could be arrested and ordered to pay stiff fines. Prisoners unable to pay the sums were kept in slavelike servitude. Blacks couldn't purchase land or receive fair wages either. Furthermore, hate groups like the Ku Klux Klan emerged and rose to power using terrorist, fear tactics to keep blacks under control.

In February 1866, Douglass and his son Lewis addressed President Johnson and told him their concerns. Specifically, they wanted to tell him about the need for change in the Southern state governments. Unfortunately, the president did most of the talking and told the Douglasses that he intended to support the interests of Southern whites and continue to block the right for blacks to vote. Gravely disappointed, the Douglasses left with greater resolve to take their case to the American people, to ensure freedom for their race and liberty to express themselves as full American citizens.

Frederick Douglass continued to write and speak out for the rights of black Americans and achieved some success. The public mood turned away from Johnson and his attempts to instill antiblack governments in the South. Finally in June 1866, congress passed the Fourteenth Amendment, granting a guarantee to blacks under the earlier Civil Rights Bill ensuring constitutional protection. Sensing the change in public attitude, President Johnson asked Frederick Douglass to be in his administration, but Douglass refused, detesting the true heart and policies of the president.

Lewis Douglass always admired the goals and position of his father. Born in 1840, he enlisted in the Union army after his father recruited young black men for the cause, having written an editorial, "Men of Color, to Arms," urging blacks to earn their equality and show their patriotism.

Lewis himself was a young man of strong, clear sense, who inherited his father's focus and drive. An astute observer, he was invited by his father to speak with the president because Lewis witnessed firsthand the difficulty that blacks had in the months directly following the close of the war. As a Union soldier, Lewis returned to the North, finishing his tour of duty, and wrote these words to his father as recorded in the biography *Frederick Douglass* by William S. McFeely. "The white people will do anything they can to keep the blacks from advancing. There seems to be a combination among the white people to keep the blacks from buying land. Large tracks of woods that the whites will neither use nor sell to the blacks is idle, and wasting. There are a great many colored people who would buy land if the whites would sell."

Frederick defended his son's decision to take a low-paying job outside of the jurisdiction of black unions. At war's end, Lewis looked for work for months on end and found none. Lewis eventually had to take low-paying work just for survival. Frederick, in turn, denounced well-paying business jobs that denied jobs to young men of good character simply because they were black. He told his son's accusers that it is no crime to stay alive. Both the younger and elder Douglass knew that social change would come slowly. They also knew the advocated isolationism from American social institutions by the black unions wouldn't be productive in the cause of equality for the black man.

Stand fast therefore in the liberty wherewith Christ hath made us free, and be not entangled again with the yoke of bondage.

GALATIANS 5:1 KJV

In all, Frederick Douglass and his wife, freewoman Anna Murray, had five children—Rosetta, Lewis, Frederick, Charles, and Annie. The entire Douglass family knew what was at stake in such a precarious time in America's history. By his death at age seventy-seven, Frederick Douglass had witnessed enormous change for black men during his lifetime. And, by taking his son Lewis with him to important meetings and standing up for him during struggles, he reinforced his strongest beliefs and set a shining example for all to live, not under bondage, but as free people.

A Father of Influence teaches his children to live as free men and women.

Harry S. Truman

1884–1972

Margaret Truman. The thirty-third president of the United States maintained a cool, calm protective presence, assuring the nation at the end of World War II and the onset of the Cold War. This same demeanor provided a stable environment for his only child, Margaret.

In September 1948, Harry S. Truman, his wife, Bess, and daughter, Margaret, sped across the Kansas plain aboard the caboose on the presidential train, the *Ferdinand Magellan*. The next day, Harry would be making an important speech in Denver, fighting to keep his position as the Democratic presidential candidate in the next national election. Though politically Truman's role was tense and precarious, domestically all was well—even serene.

Along the way, the engineer let out the throttle all the way. Perhaps someone had told the engineer to take no chances on arriving late, but by all observations, the Trumans were traveling at an unusual rate of speed. Harry looked at a speedometer on the wall and said to Margaret, "Look at that." The dial read 105 miles an hour. Though Margaret rushed to the window to look at the blurred countryside, Harry frowned. He asked his daughter matter-of-factly, "Do you know what would happen if that engineer had to make a sudden stop?" Truman continued, "We would mash those sixteen cars between us and the engine into junk." He added, "Don't say a word to your mother. I don't want her to get upset."

Truman hailed his press secretary and asked him to tell the conductor to slow down. He said they didn't need to get to Denver that fast, because 80 miles an hour was fast enough.

This calm, quiet, unflappable leadership exemplified Harry S. Truman inside and outside of the White House. Aides, the American people, and especially his family benefited from his assured style and manner.

Margaret expounds on her father's temperament in her biography of her father, *Harry S. Truman*. "In our home, he rarely raised his voice, never used profane or even harsh language, and made a point of avoiding arguments. I am not claiming that Dad never lost his temper, or never used salty language when talking man to man. But it was very, very seldom that he thought circumstances warranted it. Ninety-nine times out of a hundred he preferred to play the calm peacemaker's role. Constant consideration for others, the total lack of egotism with which Dad conducted the day-to-day affairs of the White House was the real source of the enormous loyalty to those around him. To him humility meant never blowing your own horn, never claiming credit in public for what you did or said, above all never claiming you were better, smarter, tougher than other people."

On that same whistle-stop tour, Margaret took it upon herself to throw the emergency brake on the rear platform to prevent a rollback of the cars after they had come to a halt at the station. Truman quietly reprimanded Margaret and told her that she was liable to start a panic in the crowd.

Truman showed his concern for the people when the *Ferdinand Magellan* scared a horse whose rider was moving with him through a crowd. The rider was having trouble controlling the animal, creating a real danger for those on foot. While the White House aides and Secret Service agents wondered what to do, Truman stepped down from the rear of the platform, walked over to the jittery animal, and seized the bridle. Truman told the rider he had a fine horse. Then he calmly led the animal over to one of the Secret Service agents, who led it away from the bystanders.

> *Let all who take refuge in you rejoice;*
> *let them ever sing for joy,*
> *and spread your protection over them,*
> *that those who love your name may exult in you.*
>
> PSALM 5:11 ESV

Truman also showed great concern for the people who worked under him. He told his staff he planned to travel all over the country to campaign at every whistle-stop along the way. He expected it to be tough duty on everybody, but he couldn't see any other way around it. He knew he could take it, but he worried that it might take a cruel toll on his workers.

After speaking at each whistle-stop, Truman would introduce his wife and daughter. Bess was introduced as "the boss," and Margaret as "the one who bosses the boss." This cute, demurring way of honoring the women in his life was not appreciated by Bess or Margaret, and they tried to stop him to no avail.

A father's greatest worry is that something might happen to his children, and the worry that haunted Truman the most was the fear that his daughter might be kidnapped. In the 1930s, when Truman was a judge, he stood up to the Ku Klux Klan on more than one occasion and Klan animosity toward Judge Truman was high in Missouri. One day, when Margaret was in the first grade, an odd-looking character appeared at her school and told the teacher he had been sent to take Mary Truman home. Mary is Margaret's legal first name, but everybody who knew the Trumans knew that nobody called her Mary. So, the teacher called the Truman home, and Harry sent police hustling to the scene. Margaret didn't learn about the incident until she was older, but from that day on, Mr. or Mrs. Truman or an available uncle or aunt drove her to and from school.

This calm reserve to preserve and protect his own was also evidenced in one of the most important decisions President Truman ever had to make—the heartrending decision to drop the atomic bomb on Japan in order to end World War II. During a lecture in 1965, Truman explained his rationale. "It was a question of saving hundreds of thousands of American lives. I don't mind telling you that you don't feel normal when you have American boys who are alive and joking and having fun while you are doing your war planning. You break your heart and your head trying to figure out a way to save one life. I could not worry about what history would say about my personal morality. I made the only decision I ever knew how to make. I did what I thought was right."

Harry S. Truman went on to win the 1948 presidential election by the narrowest of margins. He had already served three years of President Roosevelt's term after his death in 1945.

His many accomplishments include serving as a captain during World War I, keeping a lean, efficient military budget during World War II, signing America as a charter member of NATO (North Atlantic Treaty Organization), and defending South Korea during the Korean War. He was one of America's greatest defenders and protectors. With folksy charm and steely resolve, Truman constantly assured his staff, the American people, and especially his daughter of his confident leadership, giving her safety in uncertain times.

A Father of Influence calmly protects his own.

James Alfred Wight
(James Herriot)

1916–1995

Jim Wight. Scottish country veterinarian and best-selling author James Herriot, aka Alf Wight, took his son, Jim, with him on house calls, instilling in him a love of animals and urging him toward his own career as a vet.

Long before the publication of *All Creatures Great and Small* and its sequel, *All Things Bright and Beautiful*, James Alfred "Alf" Wight was a simple, poor, country veterinarian. He would often take his two children, Rosemary, James, and their dog, Danny, on house calls with him, when he needed to visit a farm with a sick animal. Not only was this quality family time with father and children, but the kids played a valuable role in helping their father with his work. Their jobs were many. They opened gates for their father, carried equipment, and if it was dark outside, carried the flashlight as they slogged their way through mud, grime, and up slopes to reach the animals needing care. Alf's great love of animals and his enthusiasm for his job rubbed off on his children, especially young Jim.

Jim was able to study his father as he went about his work and to appraise the ins and outs of veterinary medicine. Jim saw how conscientious and caring his father was with each patient. Jim especially enjoyed watching his father manage the calving and lambing, procedures the elder Wight performed with extreme gentleness. Alf Wight told his son many times that lambing ewes was easily his favorite part of the job. One afternoon, Alf lambed sixteen ewes in three hours.

In the biography of his father, *The Real James Herriot*, Jim Wight writes, "My father was pleased that I showed an interest in his work at such an early age, but he needed to be very patient with me. Much of my assistance in the car was of dubious value. I kept up a fairly non-stop conversation, asking such meaningful questions as 'Dad, what's the fastest? A magic train, or a phantom motorcar Dad? ... *Dad?* ... DAD?!'"

If the children couldn't join their father, Alf would try to get home to them before they went to bed. He would read them bedtime stories by the fire, even if he had had a long, exhausting day. The children loved to play practical jokes on him, and if he became agitated, they would cluck at him like old hens. They went fishing, on long walks with the dogs, or hiking somewhere to gaze at a beautiful view. In summers, they visited the beach. When the younger Jim became a teenager, father and son would hike and go "hostelling," staying at inexpensive youth hostels. The Wight children always felt that their father made time for them.

James Alfred "Alf" Wight became James Herriot when he started his writing career late in his life. He never felt comfortable "advertising" himself through his stories, and though they are based on his experiences, they are largely fictional. A lover of European football, or soccer to the Americans, Alf Wight chose the pen name James Herriot named after a star player he enjoyed watching on the "telly."

Jim nearly lost his desire for animal medicine when he was fifteen years old. His father asked his teenage son to inject a sow pig. Terrified, Jim pushed the needle into her leg, and the animal erupted from its straw bed with a roar. Jim jumped back out of the pen, as the needle still hung from the pig's thigh. The elder Wight scolded his son for being afraid. Jim soon learned to stand up to the surly beasts.

Rosie went on to practice human medicine, but Jim Wight, born

> *God spoke: "Let us make human beings in our image, make them reflecting our nature So they can be responsible for the fish in the sea, the birds in the air, the cattle, and, yes, Earth itself, and every animal that moves on the face of Earth."*
>
> **GENESIS 1:26** MSG

in 1943, followed in his father's footsteps at the Glasgow Veterinary College. After graduating in 1966, he joined the practice of Sinclair and Wight in Thirsk, working alongside his father and Donald Sinclair for the next twenty years. Throughout that time, Jim's help at the practice allowed Alf time to write his novels.

Though technically still a member of the practice at Sinclair and Wight, Jim Wight has since taken up writing, just like his father. But he's never lost or wavered in his love for animals, a love nurtured and sustained by observing and joining his father many years ago.

A Father of Influence teaches his children
to care for animals.

Forrest Dale Bright

Unknown

Dr. William "Bill" Bright. The founder of Campus

Crusade for Christ and the producer of the *Jesus* film, Bill

Bright was able to organize one of the world's largest

evangelistic efforts by using the hard work and leadership

skills learned from his father, Dale.

O ne of seven children, Bill Bright experienced a busy childhood. He worked and played hard on his family's
five-thousand-acre ranch outside the town of Coweta in
northeast Oklahoma. Two generations earlier, Bill's grandfather,
Samuel Bright, had settled the land during the Oklahoma Indian
Territory land grab. Forrest, known as Dale, maintained the farm with
conscientious diligence.

While Dale was a fair, just, and faithful father, Bill's mother, Mary
Lee, actually offered Bill his first religious education. She led by example and often was up reading her Bible and praying long after all the
children had gone to bed. On Sundays, Mary Lee took her children to
church, while Dale typically discussed business and politics with several townsmen.

Yet Bill loved his father and admired his father's abilities. Dale
could ride the wildest broncos and steers, and had a gift managing
livestock. Dale could also enter a corral and tame a herd of wild
horses.

Bill also looked up to his grandfather Samuel, the ranch founder
and elected mayor of Beggs, Oklahoma. Samuel was bold and popular,
and owned a new, immaculate house, which impressed young Bill

(although the abode was not a mansion by today's standards). Samuel was warm, fun, and kind. He would buy Bill store-bought ice cream, a real treat in those days.

Together, Dale and Samuel conducted business deals with nothing more concrete than a word and a handshake. Dale and Samuel were very fair. Once, Samuel refunded money out of his own pocket to several partners after an oil property failed to produce. Another time, Samuel refused to accept a large settlement and opted to accept an amount only one-third the size of the original offer. With such integrity and honesty, Bill knew he had strong standards in his blood.

Bill also learned generosity and sharing from his father, Dale. During the Depression, when life was difficult for many farmers, Dale let other farmers and ranchers use his new threshing machine whenever they needed it.

In school, Bill wasn't necessarily a good student, but he loved all things sports. It wasn't long until he'd sustained an injury. While just a freshman on the football team, Bill injured his left eardrum while attempting to tackle a giant fullback. Concerned for his son, Dale forbade Bill to continue in sports. This disappointed the boy, but it gave him an opportunity to explore other interests. He helped organize a 4-H Club in Coweta and was elected its president. This gave him the confidence to take on other leadership roles. Bill then turned to dramatics and speech work, winning first prize in oration at the Interscholastic Meet in Tahlequah, Oklahoma. Leadership in other scholastic organizations soon followed. By the time Bill graduated from high school, he was named the best all-around student in his thirty-three-member senior class.

Meanwhile, Dale Bright served as the chairman of the Republican Party of Waggoner County and arranged for candidates to speak as they visited the area. Bill often served as the master of ceremonies for these events, getting opportunities to meet many influential people.

Bill began his collegiate studies four miles away at Northeastern State University. He had several goals: Be elected president of his class, become editor of the school yearbook, and be selected as the college's most outstanding student. He eventually met all three goals. Originally premed, Bill decided to be a rancher, obtain a law degree, own a newspaper, and then run for congress. He had a deep desire to serve his fellow man. All this time he

We have gifts that differ according to the grace given to us: ... the leader, in diligence.

ROMANS 12:6, 8 NRSV

remained like his father: a humanistic, materialistic, and self-sufficient person.

Halfway through his junior year of college, the Japanese attacked Pearl Harbor. Bill wanted to join the war effort, but every time he tried to enlist, he was refused because of his perforated eardrum. With his father's assistance, he tried to appeal to Washington, but they wouldn't listen. Discouraged, Bill went home to help his father by assuming many of the farm and ranch duties. Finally, Bill figured that if he tried to join the war at a busier recruiting office, perhaps they wouldn't notice his injury. So, Bill packed up and headed west to Los Angeles.

On his very first night in Los Angeles, Bill gave a young man a ride. The man asked Bill where he was staying and Bill said he didn't know. The young man invited him to spend the night where he lived, at the home of the Navigators, an evangelistic ministry. That night, Bill ate at the home of Dawson Trotman and was exposed to several bright, well-spoken Christians. Bill attended a birthday party for Dan Fuller whose father, Charles E. Fuller, founded Fuller Theological Seminary. After the party, Bill spent the night with the Trotmans and then left in the morning for the LA draft board.

Again, Bill flunked the physical exam. Dejected, he bounced around at a few odd jobs and then started a specialty foods business. Though he sometimes worked eighteen- to twenty-hour days, Bill also found time to study drama, do amateur radio on Sunday mornings, and ride horseback in the Hollywood hills on Sunday afternoons. Still, he hadn't realized his need for Christ.

That finally changed when Bill's landlords invited him to Hollywood First Presbyterian Church. There, Bill met Dr. Henrietta

Mears and they developed a friendship. She introduced him to many successful, articulate people who loved Christ. Her dynamic personality and love of God were infectious, and one day, Bill returned to his apartment ready to give his life to God. Bill was soon elected president of Hollywood Presbyterian's Sunday school for college students and young professionals.

Bill had been praying for his father's salvation since the day of his own conversion. He urged his parents to attend a revival meeting at a local Oklahoma Methodist church and went home to attend the meetings with them. On the third night, Dale finally told his son he was ready to accept Christ. Bill led his father through the sinner's prayer and from that day forward, Dale was a totally different man.

The Oklahoman rancher strongly influenced his son's work ethic, encouraged him to sharpen his leadership skills, and urged him on toward greatness. His diligence resulted in Bill's success in organizing and leading the largest evangelistic ministry in America, Campus Crusade for Christ.

A Father of Influence teaches his children to be capable leaders.

Yitzhak Rabin

1922–1995

Noa Ben-Artzi Pelosoff. A former military man,

Yitzhak Rabin became prime minister of Israel twice,

won the Nobel Peace Prize in 1994, and on his

assassination, inspired his granddaughter Noa to continue

pursuing peace activism.

Tragically, on November 4, 1995, Yitzhak Rabin was assassi-
nated by a right-wing Israeli radical who vigorously opposed
Rabin's signing of the Oslo Accords during the previous year.
The Oslo Process was the result of peace negotiations aimed at resolv-
ing the Israeli-Palestinian conflicts, involving compromises by both
Rabin and Arafat, the Palestinian leader. Rabin's murder shocked
many of the Israeli public, who loved and esteemed their Nobel
Prize–winning leader. They held memorials and eulogies near the
assassination site, Rabin's home, and at the official state funeral. In
attendance at the funeral were U.S. President Bill Clinton, Egyptian
President Hosni Mubarak, and King Hussein of Jordan. Also attending
were Rabin's extended family, including his eighteen-year-old granddaughter, Noa Ben-Artzi Pelosoff.

With wisdom and eloquence beyond her years, she tearfully said, as
quoted in her book, *In the Name of Sorrow and Hope*, "I know we are talking in terms of a national tragedy, but how can you try to comfort an
entire people or include it in your personal pain, when Grandma doesn't
stop crying and we are mute, feeling only the enormous void that is left
by your absence? Grandfather, you were, and still are our national hero.
I want you to know that in all I have ever done, I have always seen you

before my eyes. Your esteem and love accompanied us in every step and on every path, and we lived in the light of your values. You never neglected anyone. And now you have been neglected—you, my eternal hero—cold and lonely. And I can do nothing to save you, you who are so wonderful. People greater than I have already eulogized you. But none of them had my good fortune to feel the caress of your warm, soft hands and the warm embrace that was just for us."

This beloved national hero and grandfather never meant to be a political man, much less a martyr for the cause of peace. Born in Jerusalem (then a part of Palestine) in 1922, he studied at the Kadoorie Agricultural College, where he graduated with distinction. He aspired to be an irrigation engineer.

As the world entered war in 1941, Rabin joined a fighting force, the Palmach, a section of the Haganah. (The group was formed with the help of the British to protect Palestine from the growing Nazi threat.) Over the next six years, Rabin rose to the position of chief operations officer. The following year marked Israel's independence, and Rabin's marriage to his wife, Leah.

Peaceful thoughts between Israel and Palestine materialized in Rabin's heart in 1948, when against his wishes, he was ordered to participate in the forced evacuation of fifty thousand Palestinians by the Israel Defense Force (IDF). Nevertheless, for the next twenty years, he served in the IDF and by 1964, became its chief of staff, even commanding the IDF during the 1967 Six-Day War.

The next year, Rabin decided diplomacy was the preferred route and retired from the IDF to become the Israel ambassador to the United States. Afterward, he returned to Israel and joined the Labor Party. In 1974, he succeeded Golda Meir as the prime minister of Israel. His primary objective during that tenure was to improve Israel's economy and tackle its social problems.

Rabin met a tremendous challenge in 1976, when Israelis were hijacked aboard an Air France flight. The prime minister orchestrated "Operation Entebbe," resulting in only three deaths of the 103 hostages.

In 1992, Rabin once again was elected prime minister. During this tenure, PLO Chairman Yassar Arafat sent Rabin a letter renouncing violence and officially recognized Israel as a Jewish state. Rabin returned the gesture and sent Arafat a letter recognizing the PLO. This mutual recognition laid the foundation for the Israel-Jordan Treaty of Peace in 1994, a motion that polarized Rabin's image in Israel—some seeing him as a hero for advancing the cause of peace and some seeing him as a traitor for giving away land they saw as rightfully belonging to Israel. The action ultimately led to Rabin's assassination.

> *Blessed are the peacemakers, for they shall be called sons of God.*
>
> **MATTHEW 5:9 NKJV**

According to Noa's brother, the prime minister never missed a school ceremony in which she played a role. Noa's mother, Dalia, agrees and says he was also always there during illnesses and special needs. He was a concerned father.

Noa would recall that whenever her grandfather had to make an important decision, he would drum his fingers on the table or the arm of a chair. Though he had so much on his mind, he still would take the time to talk with her even about trivial matters like movie stars or soccer players.

After Rabin's death, CNN asked Noa, "How do you promote peace in a region that has experienced fighting for centuries?" Noa replied, "First of all, never stop hoping and dreaming for peace. Second, if it was the way you describe it, as a country which will probably never know peace, then there's nothing to live for or expect, there's no tomorrow. I think that the Oslo Process was about taking the peace process step by step, in order to build mutual trust—first between the leaders, and then among the people, and only after that, to reach reconciliation. And I think this is the right way to do so. You cannot expect reconciliation overnight." Noa continues to speak for her generation on campuses, promoting peace, inspired by her grandfather, peacemaker Yitzhak Rabin.

A Father of Influence teaches his children to make peace.

Gadla Henry Mphakanyiswa

Unknown–1930

Nelson Mandela. The son of a tribal chief, Nelson Mandela was born of "royal blood," groomed to counsel rulers, and establish kings. After years of suffering imprisonment under Apartheid's unjust laws, Mandela would be released to become president of all South Africa.

His great-great-grandfather was King Ngubengcuka, ruler of all Thembus when the land belonged to them and they were free from the oppression called Apartheid. His father, Gadla Henry Mphakanyiswa, was a chief by both blood and custom, confirmed as a chief of Mvezo by the king of the Thembu tribe, a member of the Madiba clan. As chief, Henry had the authority to counsel and recommend kings, and on the untimely death of Jongilizwe in the 1920s, Henry was consulted and suggested that Jongintaba be elected king on the grounds he was best educated. Nelson Mandela had leadership in his blood.

In 1918, when Henry's son Nelson was born, he was given the name Rolihlahla, which in Xhosa literally means "pulling the branch of a tree," but its colloquial meaning is "troublemaker." Henry sired thirteen children in all—four boys and nine girls—of which Nelson was the youngest son. He was not in line to assume his father's role as chief. That assignment fell to Nelson's brother, Daligqili, who died in the 1930s.

The name "troublemaker" apparently applied to Henry as well because a dispute eventually deprived him of his chieftainship. As chief, he had to give an account not only to King Jongintaba but also to the local magistrate. One day, Henry challenged the magistrate over some relatively trivial tribal matter, behavior considered the height of indolence. The magistrate deposed Henry, ending the Mandela family chieftainship. Nelson writes in his autobiography *A Long Walk to Freedom*, "My father possessed a proud rebelliousness, a stubborn sense of fairness that I recognize in myself."

> *[Learn] what's right and just and fair.*
>
> PROVERBS 1:3 MSG

Henry often told his sons stories of historic battles and heroic warriors, legendary tales that came down through the generations. These stories stimulated Nelson's childish imagination and usually contained some moral lesson.

Henry befriended two brothers from the amaMfengu clan, educated Christians. Their influence over the family led to Nelson being baptized in the Methodist church and sent to school. One of the brothers approached Henry and told him his youngest son was bright and should go to school. Henry, despite his own lack of education, immediately agreed. Henry gave his son his first pair of trousers for school. At this place of learning, run by British teachers, young Rolihlahla received the Christian name Nelson.

Then, when Nelson was nine, his father, Henry, suddenly died of a lung ailment. Since Nelson defined himself by his father, his death changed his life in myriad ways. Acting paramount chief Jongintaba took Nelson in as his own son, treating him just like one of his own children.

But Nelson still lived up to his former namesake "troublemaker." His first display of trouble was to challenge boxers in the boxing ring at the Missionary College of Fort Hare, a prestigious residential school for black South Africans. There Nelson also became involved in student protests against the white colonial rule at the institution. This was the beginning of his long walk to personal and national liberation.

Nelson further bucked the establishment by running away from an arranged marriage and instead, joined a law firm in Johannesburg. He was exposed daily to the horrors and injustices of Apartheid.

Revolutionizing the system would prove an uphill battle. The oppressed masses had been humbled into submission. The geographic expanse of the nation hampered communication and mobility. Race-war prospects were unrealistic and horrific. Nonviolence became Nelson's weapon of choice.

He signed up for the Youth League of the African National Congress (ANC) and joined programs of passive resistance against the laws that forced blacks to carry passes and live in a position of permanent servility. The government banned all resistance movements and Nelson was arrested and imprisoned on Robben Island for five years because of his leadership role in the ANC In prison, a guard tried to force Nelson to jog. Nelson refused and told the guard that if he laid a finger on him, he would take the guard to the highest court in the land and the result would be poverty. The guard backed down.

Also in prison, Nelson refused to play the victim and educated himself by reading every book he could get his hands on. Five years turned into twenty-seven, but international pressure eventually led to Nelson's release. On February 2, 1990, President F. W. de Klerk lifted the ban on the ANC and demanded Mandela be given his freedom.

Through patience, wisdom, and vision, Nelson went on to turn the tables on Apartheid as the first black South African president voted into office by democratic elections.

An ordinary man who stirred up trouble and challenged a system that oppressed an entire race of people, Nelson Mandela became a chief architect of a whole new nation, a president of royal blood and uncommon abilities in extraordinary circumstances. Through naming his son "troublemaker" and performing his royal duties, Henry laid a foundation and map for his son to follow. Decades later, Nelson Mandela dedicated *A Long Walk to Freedom* to his six children, twenty-one grandchildren, and three great-grandchildren—the legacy of his father, Henry, and the future hope of South Africa.

A Father of Influence encourages his children to challenge unjust systems.

John Milton Sr.

1560–1647

John Milton. Despite his blindness, John Milton
authored one of the greatest works in the English
language, *Paradise Lost*, a feat he probably would not have
accomplished if it were not for his father's support
in time and finances.

Though John Milton was raised a Puritan, he was far from the
typical stereotype—never sour, hypocritical, or prudish. He led
a full life, attending the theater, playing his own portable
organ and stringed instruments, reading stimulating books, posing for
a portrait by a respectable continental artist, and watching young
ladies in London parks. In 1638, young Milton admitted he was
driven into a kind of ecstasy while listening to popular operatic singer
Leonora Baroni, and he wrote poems in Latin celebrating her talent
and artistry. No doubt, he would attend the Shakespearean theater,
the Blackfriars, in which his father was a shareholder.

When John Milton Sr. wasn't composing music for Queen
Elizabeth or church music for the emerging Protestant church, he
worked as a scrivener—a legal secretary—preparing and notarizing
legal documents on real-estate transactions and money-lending. Such
a position afforded John Sr. the prosperity to use private tutors to educate his children, including John Jr., in classical languages. The elder
Milton then gave his son John a formal education at St. Paul's School.
There, young John developed an interest in the ministry, but as he
grew older, his independent spirit led him to give this up for broader,
scholarly pursuits.

John Jr. went on to attend Christ's College at Cambridge University. He was a hardworking student, but his argumentative spirit led to a dispute with a tutor, causing him to be suspended. John was disliked by many students, and his life at Cambridge remained difficult as he struggled with the demands and peculiarities of the curriculum. Perhaps this loneliness drove him to consider the fellowship of the divine because it was at Cambridge that he first dabbled with writing poems of Christ and penned *On the Morning of Christ's Nativity*.

Following his schooling at Cambridge, where he graduated cum laude, John Jr. undertook six years of self-directed private study in both the ancient and modern disciplines of theology, philosophy, history, politics, literature, and science. John Sr. allowed his son to base his studies in the family home in Hammersmith, a London suburb. About three years later the Miltons moved to Horton in Buckinghamshire, and young John continued to live with them there. Throughout this time, John Jr. had determined that his prospective career lay in poetical writing. It is because of this particular intensive study that John Milton Jr. is considered to be among the most learned of all English poets.

Following these years of private study at his father's home, John Jr. left for a tour of Europe, which lasted about fifteen months, all at his father's expense. While in Italy, Milton confirmed his resolution to become famous as a poet.

In a Latin poem, *Ad Patrem*, composed in 1638, Milton thanked his father for his continuing support, answered his father's anxieties about his choice of careers, and celebrated his father's talents as a musician and poet. In an English translation, a portion of the poem reads, "But as for you, dear father, since it is not granted me to make a just return for your deserts, nor to recompense your gifts with my deeds, let it suffice that I remember, and with gratitude count over, your repeated gifts, and treasure them in a faithful mind. You too, my youthful verses, my pastime, if only you dare hope for endless years— dare think to survive your master's pyre and look upon the light—and if dark oblivion does not drag you down to crowded Orcus, perchance you will treasure these praises and a father's name rehearsed in song as an example to a distant age."

It wasn't until his fifties that John Milton began writing his epic poem, *Paradise Lost.* Remarkably, it was inked entirely by scribes because by this time Milton was too blind to write anything legible. He would compose verses at night in his head and then dictate them from memory to his aides in the morning. The unparalleled scope of the work beautifully depicts the creation of the universe, earth, and humanity; conveys the origin of sin, death, and evil; imagines events in hell, the kingdom of heaven, the garden of Eden, and the sacred history of Israel; engages with political ideas of tyranny, liberty, and justice; and defends theological positions on predestination, free will, and salvation. The book was met with instant success and acclaim.

Throughout their years together, John Milton Jr.'s relationship with his father remained positive and nonconfrontational. For all his father's care and financial gifts, John Jr. would take in his father when he was old and infirm. The allowances, financial and otherwise, the senior Milton bestowed on his son afforded him the opportunity to become one of the greatest authors in the history of the English language, still inspiring and challenging his readers in classrooms everywhere. A monument to Milton's greatness still stands in Poet's Corner in Westminster Abbey in London today.

> *Encourage each other.*
>
> **1 THESSALONIANS 4:18 NLT**

A Father of Influence gives his children time and financial backing to develop their talents.

Increase Mather

1639–1723

Cotton Mather. The son of Richard Mather and the father of Cotton Mather, Increase Mather gave his son a family name aimed at influencing him to become an important colonial leader, author, clergyman, and scholar.

The Mather name in seventeenth- and eighteenth-century New England was synonymous with extraordinary spiritual and civic leadership. Cotton Mather had a noble heritage and an impressive pedigree. He was headed for greatness. His father, Increase Mather, was an accomplished preacher and respected scholar, deeply religious, and very intelligent. He received the very first doctorate of divinity degree granted in America. Increase's father, Richard, was also a preacher in the New World and the author of the first book printed in America. On giving birth to a son, Richard named him Increase because of the great increase in freedom and good fortune he had experienced in America. Cotton Mather's maternal grandfather, John Cotton, helped establish the Puritan Church of New England and headed the Church of Boston. Together, the devout nonconformist Puritans believed that each person should seek God personally without the need for a priest. As such, many Puritans were arrested and put into prison by nervous leaders of the Church of England.

So when Increase Mather and Maria Cotton, daughter of John Cotton, had a son, they named him after the two families: Cotton Mather. For all his life, Cotton Mather would feel the weight of that heritage and his responsibility to live up to it, a charge he accomplished admirably.

Growing up, Cotton lived in the home where his mother was born, the original home of John Cotton. Cotton read books authored by both grandfathers. Home life was filled with love, gentleness, books, prayers, study, and lots of family history. Cotton often saw his father spend up to sixteen hours a day in his study preparing sermons, which he preached with power and persuasion. Cotton also listened to his father and other Puritan ministers discuss and settle governmental issues of the colony.

> *Don't forget anything of what you've seen.... Teach what you've seen and heard to your children and grandchildren.*
>
> **DEUTERONOMY 4:9 MSG**

By the time he was twelve years old, Cotton could already read the New Testament in Greek. That same year, he enrolled at Harvard College. Thinking he wanted to be a physician, he chose classes in science and medicine. Cotton was only fifteen years old when he graduated from Harvard. Almost presciently, Harvard President Urian Oakes singled out Cotton and predicted his greatness and contributions to society.

Two years after graduation, he preached in what was once his maternal grandfather's church. The following week, he preached in Boston's Second Church, or North Church, Increase's congregation. Later that year, he also preached at First Church, in the pulpit of Richard Mather, his paternal grandfather. Cotton did all this preaching despite the fact that he had only recently overcome his stuttering problem.

Though he was offered a position at a church in New Haven, Connecticut, Cotton decided to accept a position as an assistant at his father's church. For many years the two enjoyed a close working relationship. Later, Cotton preached and pursued a master's degree at Harvard, while his father, Increase, accepted an invitation to become president of Harvard.

When Increase Mather went to England with New England governor Sir William Phips, Cotton confidently preached at his father's church of close to fifteen hundred people. When Increase returned, he and his son faced the problem of charges of witchcraft in Salem, some fourteen miles away from Boston. In Salem, a few girls showed symptoms of being bewitched, and the Mather family was brought in to assess the situation. Though Puritans and preachers, Cotton and Richard were both men of science. They had studied natural phenomena and knew the strange occurrences could stem from causes other than witchcraft. Their judgments helped dampen the hysteria. Increase wrote, "Many innocent persons have been put to death under the notions of witchcraft, whereby much innocent blood hath been shed." Cotton fully agreed, and warned against "spectral evidence," the taking of one person's testimony as fact. Cotton encouraged the judges not to use the death penalty, but instead, scatter the so-called witches. Cotton even offered to take them into his home for "treatment." Governor Phips eventually ordered the courts to disband and set the remaining condemned persons free.

In an article titled "A Father's Resolutions," Cotton wrote, "Let me daily pray for my children with constancy, with fervency, with agony. Yea, by name let me mention each one of them every day before the Lord. I will importunately beg for all suitable blessings to be bestowed upon them: that God would give them grace, and give them glory, and withhold no good thing from them."

Cotton would continue to echo his family legacy by authoring numerous enduring scientific and religious works that would even go on to shape and influence many Americans, including many of America's founding fathers. In understanding and living up to a good name, Cotton showed the difference a nominal label could make on the life of a child.

**A Father of Influence passes on a
rich heritage to his children.**

Jimmy Russell Warren

Unknown

Rick Warren. Pioneering Jimmy Warren gave his son, Rick, an example of relevant, everyday Christian living, a model that would shape his son's philosophy in creating Saddleback Church and writing *The Purpose-Driven Life*.

Jimmy Warren Sr. never cared for titles or positions. He simply wanted to do the Lord's work. Originally a resident of the southeastern United States, he moved in the early 1950s to California to help Golden Gate Baptist Theological Seminary in any capacity he could.

While accomplishing this mission, Jimmy worked the Northern California area as a traveling pastor. He looked forward to reaching out to those who otherwise would not have heard the gospel. He didn't mind driving through fog or over mountain roads to reach the outlying parishes.

Over the years, Jimmy Warren became well known in the Sonoma County and greater San Francisco areas. The California Southern Baptist Convention appointed him as the director of missions for Yokayo Association. His job was to help pastors shepherd and serve their congregations more effectively.

At this time, the family moved to Ukiah, California, in the Redwood Valley of Medocino County. Here, Rick, his brother, Jimmy Jr., and sister, Chaundel, would grow up and experience their most impressionable years. Since this was a rural area with only a few vineyards and sawmills, families had to be self-reliant. Yet neighbors learned to help each other whenever needed. Ukiah had open spaces, helpful, safe neighborhoods, and good churches—a perfect place to raise a family.

In the turbulent 1960s, Jimmy Warren began a youth ministry movement, while his son Rick began a peer ministry at Ukiah High School. Rick's ministry was called The Fishers of Men Club. With it, he produced a Christian musical, sponsored after-school rock concerts, and developed a Christian newspaper. Meanwhile, Jimmy Sr. was locating and hiring youth pastors for the various churches under his care. He also developed youth programs that created a sense of community among disparate young people.

In the early 1970s, Jimmy Warren Sr. started three churches in the Mendocino area—one in the living room of their own home. As the congregation expanded, they moved to a larger room upstairs, and then to other accommodations. Eventually, the church, now known as First Baptist Church of Redwood Valley, broke ground for its own facility. In later years, Rick would grow his congregation in similar fashion, moving from facility to facility before settling the church's ten thousand members into the current Saddleback Church location.

In addition to congregations and buildings, the Warrens also built leaders, especially youth leaders. Through Jimmy Warren's ministry, at least twenty-five members of the Yokayo Association youth program went on to become successful pastors of their own churches. Today, Rick Warren focuses his ministry efforts more on developing new leaders than any other activity. Both father and son learned to develop leaders more quickly by removing some of the obstacles that hinder church growth. For example, the Warrens made sure that pastors under their care didn't have to worry about tasks like starting congregations and building or maintaining church buildings.

Finally, Jimmy Warren taught his son the importance of having a good wife and partner in ministry. Jimmy's wife, Rick's mother, Dot, knew the Bible and understood it. She worked hard to make her home a welcoming, friendly place, where nobody felt like a stranger. Shortly after Rick graduated from high school, he married his high school sweetheart, Kay, a woman who shares his mother's ideals and believes in her husband's ministry goals.

In building Saddleback's ministry to what it is today, Rick had to utilize many of the same strategies and methods he has seen his father practicing through the years. He had to study, establish relationships, build leaders, empower others, create excitement, and continually find new, creative ways to improve ministry so that it met people's needs directly, while remaining true to biblical principles. And throughout it all was a deep heart for evangelism, reaching the lost with the good news of Jesus Christ. In the book *A Life of Purpose*, University of Southern California's Dr. Miller says, "Saddleback attends to consumer demand by fine-tuning their worship and organizational style to today's culture, not the cultures of the past."

> *[God] creates each of us by Christ Jesus to join him in the work he does, the good work he has gotten ready for us to do, work we had better be doing.*
>
> EPHESIANS 2:9 MSG

The best-selling *The Purpose-Driven Life* by Rick Warren was born out of Rick's desire to reach beyond the religious community to "the unchurched." Witnessing the abundant amount of "self-help" books in Southern California, Rick wanted to create the ultimate "anti-self-help book." The very first words in *The Purpose-Driven Life* are "It's not about you." The central idea of the book is the idea that once a person allows God to take control of his or her life, life becomes full and rewarding. In easy-to-read, forty-day installments, *The Purpose-Driven Life* has been read by the congregants of more than twenty-eight hundred churches of all denominations across the country, a clear answer to Rick's prayer and hope.

Today, both Dot and Jimmy Sr. have graduated to heaven, but their legacy lives on in the lives of one of our country's most influential and respected Christian leaders. On his deathbed, Jimmy kept repeating, "Got to save one more for Jesus. Got to save one more for Jesus." Rick says this scene is still vivid in his mind, and his father's words motivate him every day.

A Father of Influence encourages his children to encourage, inspire, and motivate the Christian community.

John Eareckson

Unknown

Joni Eareckson Tada. Despite quadriplegia due to a diving accident in 1967, Joni Eareckson Tada was able to find joy and purpose, largely due to the example she found in her father, Johnny.

Named after her father but spelled with a feminine o-n-i, Joni Eareckson never intended to become an advocate for Christ to the disabled community. Yet on July 30, 1967, her life took a drastic and unexpected turn. On a swim outing to Chesapeake Bay with her sister, she dived into shallow water and sustained a near-fatal break to her spinal column. Joni suddenly found herself thrust unceremoniously into a difficult and frightening world.

During the first critical months after her accident, her family stayed close to her side. Her father read to her as she lay in the striker frame, and then when she decided she'd like to read on her own, he built a small stool to fit under the frame, where she could read and turn pages with a mouthstick.

The first book Joni asked her father to bring was the Bible. She was desperate to understand why this had happened to her, and how her life could have meaning under these circumstances.

During the long hours, she also spent time remembering the happy days before her accident. She especially thought about her father who had overcome his own disability. He had been a National AAU wrestling champion and a five-time winner of national YMCA championship wrestling honors. He even earned a berth on the U.S. Olympic team of 1932. During one match, his opponent grabbed and twisted his leg in a manner that made Johnny walk with a limp for the rest of his life. But this injury never slowed him down or discouraged him from marriage, work, family life, and church activities.

Joni also knew her father, Johnny Eareckson, to be an incurable romantic and creative artist. Still she knew he was the type of person who kept up with technological advances. He wasn't afraid of unusual or hard work, and often sought it out for what it could teach him. Johnny also loved horses, sculpture, painting, and home construction. (Joni would also develop a love of horses and art.) During his life Johnny was a sailor and even owned and managed his own rodeo. He valued personal character, individual happiness, and spiritual development. He was a man who loved life.

Johnny loved his family so much; he built them a home and started his own flooring business so he could spend more time with them. He liked to take them horseback riding and on trips to the ocean. His children came to expect a lesson on geography, geology, and animals as they visited new places.

Joni could not remember her father losing his temper. He was always amiable. Nothing and no one ever seemed to rattle him. Growing up, the Eareckson children based their behavior on "not hurting Daddy." They wouldn't do certain things not because it was simply questionable or wrong, but because of what it would do to Daddy.

Even with such a person at her side, though, Joni struggled with the harsh realities of her condition. A few months after her accident, she had surgery to fuse her spinal column. Perhaps it was then that she began to realize the permanent nature of her injury. Soon after she asked a friend to hold up a mirror and for the first time since her accident, she saw the devastating effect her injury had brought upon her body. She saw two darkened, glassy eyes. She saw her thin frame, once weighing 125 pounds, now only 80 pounds. She saw her yellow, jaundiced skin and shaved head. Finally, she saw her teeth, black from the

> *I praise you because I am fearfully and wonderfully made; your works are wonderful, I know that full well.*
>
> **PSALM 139:14**

effects of medication. She felt like vomiting. She wanted to die. She even begged friends to help her commit suicide. But they didn't. They couldn't.

Johnny gave his daughter hope when he insisted she come home from the hospital for Christmas. Then he sent her to Rancho Los Amigos, a rehabilitation center in Los Angeles with remarkable advancements in therapy. Joni was excited. She felt at last she might be able to make some improvement. She did learn to move her shoulders and upper arms, allowing her to feed herself, but she never regained use of her hands or legs.

With each forward step came harsh setbacks. But Johnny continually told his daughter with sparkling eyes and a face radiating with love that he'd do anything at all to help. He then told her that his legacy wasn't the things he did with his hands, the house and the furniture he made, but his family—especially his daughter. He reminded her that God knows what He is doing. Slowly, over time, she gained the strength and encouragement to go on.

Joni did find joy in living, and purpose, too. She realized she could help people who were going through the same difficulties she had faced. In 1979, Joni formed the ministry *Joni and Friends* to communicate the gospel and equip Christ-honoring churches worldwide to evangelize and disciple people affected by disabilities. Over the years, she has taken a stand for life and abundant living, speaking up and giving a Christian response to controversial issues that affect the disabled. Not only did Johnny Eareckson's love and encouragement help his daughter to take control of her life, but it also touched the lives of countless others who would be helped through her ministry.

A Father of Influence gives his children a sense of value and purpose that can carry them through adversity and even the darkest trials.

Wendell Ball Colson

1899–1974

Charles W. Colson. Wendell Colson had only one child, his son, Chuck, but he taught him to work hard and distinguish right from wrong, traits that helped him recover from the darkest period of his life to write more than twenty books while leading Prison Fellowship, a ministry to inmates and their families.

When Chuck Colson was a boy, his Massachusetts-based family temporarily moved into a renovated barn with a high roof. The eaves were populated with bats. Chuck and his father positioned themselves in the rafters, turned the lights out, and opened fire with .22-caliber shotguns. They hit plenty of bats, but some of them fell through the beams down to the rooms on the ground floor, alarming the lodging guests staying below. After writing an essay about it for a class assignment, the professor gave him an A and said he should become a writer. Chuck Colson would not write a book until he was a prisoner, thirty years later.

Author, former presidential aide to Richard Nixon, Christian thinker, and founder of Prison Fellowship, Chuck Colson loved and valued his father, whom he called his best friend and the greatest influence in his life. Chuck would go on to credit his father with instilling in him a strong work ethic and a godly sense of right and wrong.

When Chuck Colson was born in 1931, the Great Depression was just gripping America. The Colsons never went hungry, however, because Wendell held down a steady job in the food industry throughout the decade. In the early part of the 1940s, during World War II, Wendell became an air-raid warden, responsible for going house to house at night, reminding residents in the neighborhood to draw blackout curtains over their windows so enemy planes could not see light on the ground. Charlie himself went house to house to collect money to buy a jeep for the U.S. Army.

Chuck, as his father preferred to call him, has said he took all his core values from his father and held him as a role model of diligence, dedication to work, and patriotic duty. In the book, *Charles W. Colson: A Life Redeemed*, a contemporary called Wendell "the straightest of straight arrows ... a loveable, kind old bear of a man with a wonderfully calm and easygoing tolerance."

Wendell also had a keen sense of humor. He loved to play practical jokes on the family. Chuck inherited this tendency and got into trouble as a youth letting off stink bombs in movie theaters and hiding snowballs in the caps of train drivers.

Chuck also marveled at his father's academic achievement. Initially, Wendell had dropped out of high school to support his widowed mother. But later he attended night school to become a CPA. It took him twelve years to get his credentials. When Chuck was eight years old, he watched his father, wearing a gown and mortarboard, accept a degree from Northeastern Law School. Wendell eventually sent his son to Browne & Nicols, a well-known private school in Cambridge, Massachusetts.

Though accepted to Harvard, Chuck chose to attend Brown University instead, obtaining his JD from George Washington University, and then served in the United States Marine Corps. In the late 1960s, he became a valued aide to President Richard Nixon—loyal even to a fault. With fierce allegiance to the president, he would say and do anything to protect his chief executive.

Colson was Nixon's go-to man, and when the administration began to slide into paranoia and questionable tactics, he went along. Soon he was spending time alone with Nixon, plotting the scheming. Colson found himself morally compromised.

Eventually, Colson admitted not only to ordering the Watergate break-in, but also to devising a smear campaign against Daniel Ellsburg, the hero of the antiwar movement. The mounting political and personal pressure on the Colson family aggravated his father's heart condition. Chuck visited the ailing Wendell in the hospital and told him he would lick the indictments, but it was not to be. Chuck Colson went to prison in July of 1974, and the pressure proved too much for the elder Colson. Wendell Ball Colson died while Charles was serving his sentence.

> *If you reprove the wise, they will be all the wiser.*
> PROVERBS 19:25 NLT

Just prior to his imprisonment, Chuck Colson gave his life to Christ at the prompting of his friend Tom Phillips, who had given him a copy of C. S. Lewis's *Mere Christianity*. Colson's conversion was genuine, but he had hurt so many people that even Christian Republicans doubted his sincerity.

In prison, Colson saw the humanity and brotherhood of his fellow prisoners. He felt the lock-'em-up-and-throw-away-the-key philosophy wasn't Christlike. He felt the goal should instead be rehabilitation.

In 1976, after serving eight months of his one- to three-year sentence, Colson founded Prison Fellowship. Today the organization extends to six hundred prisons in eighty-eight countries. The Washington-based ministry also provides scholarships to ex-felons, reaches out to the families of inmates through the Angel Tree project, and honors socially active Christians through the annual Wilberforce Award.

A friend to ex-drug dealers, murderers, sex offenders, presidents, senators, and more because of his ministry and humanitarian work, Colson has earned the respect of Christians and non-Christians alike, taking the values he learned from his father to improve the lives of prisoners everywhere.

Because many people in Washington doubted Chuck Colson's conversion to Christianity, he wrote his testimony and the story of his imprisonment in his book *Born Again*. The book's dedication reads, "To my Dad—whose ideals for my life I have tried, not always successfully, to fulfill—and whose strength and support is with me today." Since that first book, he has produced more than twenty others with worldwide sales of more than ten million copies in circulation—encouraging those held captive through imprisonment or sin.

**A Father of Influence teaches his children
right from wrong.**

Gene E. Peretti

Unknown

Frank E. Peretti. Although author Frank Peretti
continually faced bullying and persecution from his
classmates, his father, Gene, gave him refuge from his fears
and instilled in him the confidence to become a best-selling
author of Christian fiction.

Known for his dramatic thrillers with a Christian worldview,
Frank Peretti's entrance into the world was as exciting as his
fictional writings. Frank was born in Canada to a pastor in
mid-January, 1951. His mother, Joan, began to have labor pains at
eleven that night. Outside, the snow flew and blew. The thermome-
ter read 30 degrees below zero. The young Peretti couple had no
telephone, so they couldn't call their doctor to let him know they
were coming. Even so, around one in the morning, they piled into
their 1940 Ford and headed out for the thirty-five-mile trip to Galt
Hospital in Lethbridge, Alberta.

Their first stop was to drop off their toddler son at the home of a
minister friend. Mission accomplished, they were on their way again.
Suddenly, the car lurched sideways with the sound of metal grating
against metal. Coming to a stop, Gene stepped outside and discovered
the front left tire had virtually disappeared! Complicating matters, on
a thorough search of the trunk, he realized there was no jack with
which to install the spare. Yet, ingeniously, using his toolbox as a ful-
crum, he took a metal post to create a lever to lift the car so he could
attach the spare. Then, doing the unthinkable, he asked his now pain-
wracked wife to use her own weight to provide the necessary leverage

to perform the move. Knowing this was the only way to make the car operational for the drive to the hospital, she agreed.

The couple and the doctor arrived just in time for Frank Edward Peretti's birth. But something was wrong. The baby's head wouldn't lie naturally. His neck seemed strangely crooked. The doctor said nothing was wrong, but clearly something was. After testing, other professionals called it cystic hygroma, a lesion caused by a mass of dilated lymphatic tissue, but the medical delivery crew didn't have a clue. Baby and mother were released, but the small lump on the side of the child's throat got bigger not smaller. The family packed up and moved to Seattle to be near Gene's parents and the Children's Orthopedic Hospital there. Barely two months old, young Frank had his neck cut open and operated on. Then, Frank's tongue began to swell and ooze a black fluid. By the time he was four, Frank had endured seven rounds of surgery. Furthermore, Frank's ailment left him small for his age, but doctors said he would grow in time. Gene took a job at the Boeing Company, and protected his infirm son as best he could. Life was bearable for Frank—until he had to attend school.

Kindergarten started out all right for Frank, but as the year went on the teasing began. By first grade, the teasing was so intense that Frank would wait until his mother dropped him off at school, then turn around and walk back home. Frank's parents would complain to the teachers and the principal, and the teasing would stop—for a while. But it would always begin again. The only relief the young Peretti found was at home and in church. Through it all, Frank's parents provided protection and encouraged healthy, creative distractions. One time, Gene let his son borrow tools and scrap lumber to build a twenty-foot model of the *Titanic* in their backyard. Then Frank's dad let him and his brothers build model airplanes in the garage. Not once did Mr. Peretti tell his boys that their ideas wouldn't work or were dumb.

The creativity Frank Peretti enjoyed and used as a refuge from tormentors in his youth has now been channeled into his best-selling books. His first, released in 1986, was a runaway best seller about demons and angels called *This Present Darkness*. Its sequel in 1988,

Piercing the Darkness, was also well received. His biblically based characters provided millions of Christians with a better understanding of the spiritual world we do not see but the Bible assures us is present all around us. After writing one more book on the spirit realm, *Prophet* in 1992, he explored dark forces in a fictional logging town with *The Oath*. Peretti penned a few other offerings, and then wrote a biographical story of his troubled childhood called *The Wounded Spirit*, which he dedicated "To Mom and Dad, whose love and encouragement never wavered."

> *God chose the foolish things of the world to shame the wise; God chose the weak things of the world to shame the strong.*
>
> **1 CORINTHIANS 1:27**

A Father of Influence teaches his children to turn adversity into strength.

John Wesley Rice III

1923–2000

Condoleezza Rice. Raised with the idea that the best
defense against racism is achievement and education,
John Wesley Rice gave his daughter every advantage for
success in life. Condi would go on to become the only black
woman secretary of state in the history of
the United States.

amed for an Italian musical term, *con dolcecezza*, meaning
"with sweetness," Condoleezza Rice seemed groomed for
success and achievement from an early age. Her parents
signed their only child up for piano lessons at age three and filled
her childhood with ballet, figure skating, tutoring in French and
Spanish, football, and a constant flow of books at her bedside table.
When she was ten years old, in 1964, her parents took her on an
educational field trip to Washington DC. With museums, memorials,
and historic places everywhere, young Condi (as her father called
her) was thrilled and inspired. On Pennsylvania Avenue, Condi
peered through the front gate of the White House, looked at the pil-
lars, and told her father, as reported in *Condi: The Condoleezza Rice
Story*, "Daddy, I'm barred out of there now because of the color of my
skin. But one day, I'll be in that house." Twenty-five years later, she
was working fourteen-hour days as President George H. W. Bush's top
advisor on the Soviet Union.

Achievement has been in the Rice family for decades. In pre–Civil
War days, the Rice family served as house slaves, not field slaves,

which meant they could read and write. Her grandfather, "Grandaddy Rice," attended Stillman College. After finishing the program, he was ordained as a Presbyterian minister. (Her family has been Presbyterian and well educated ever since.) Condi's father was encouraged to excel and also received a seminary education. He went on to receive a graduate degree and hold several university posts. He would become a powerful force in Birmingham's black community, encouraging black youth to rise above the limitations that segregation and racism placed on them.

I can do all things through Him who strengthens me.

PHILIPPIANS 4:13 NASB

John Rice encouraged his daughter with the same philosophy of life he received. She emulated his devotion to causes, his strength of character, and his faith. She considers herself to be a very religious person who was put on this earth to be an eternal optimist. Humble about her accomplishments, she thinks she is merely above average in intelligence, and while being both a professor and provost at Stanford University, she says she recognizes real genius even though she doesn't fit the bill herself.

After a brief stint as dean of students at Stillman College, John Rice moved his family to Colorado, where he obtained a master of arts in education at the University of Denver. Then he was offered a position as assistant director of admissions and began teaching as well. He taught a class called "Black Experience in America" and invited national-level speakers such as Howard Robinson, executive director of the Congressional Black Caucus, and Reverend Channing Phillips, the first black person to be nominated for the presidency of the United States. Condi often sat in, listening to her father and special speakers. In 1974, after five years of teaching, John Rice upgraded from instructor to adjunct history professor.

This same year, Condi graduated cum laude from the University of Denver. The next year, she obtained a masters degree in government from Notre Dame University. By 1981, at age twenty-seven, she had received her PhD in international studies and was an assistant professor of political science at Stanford University.

Condi first came to the attention of top-level politicians when

Gerald Ford's national security advisor, Brent Scowcroft, heard her give a speech in 1987 on the Soviet ideology. He was so impressed with her that she was one of the first people he called when he was looking for a national security advisor in the first Bush administration. There she gained the respect of her colleagues and became a personal friend of the Bush family.

When George W. Bush campaigned for president in 2000, he asked Condi to help him as a foreign policy advisor. She took a one-year leave of absence from Stanford, but when Bush was elected, he asked her for much more. He invited her to become a member of his cabinet, the first woman to hold the post of national security advisor. After the events of September 11, 2001, her expertise became even more important. When Bush was elected to a second term as president, Secretary of State Colin Powell stepped down and Bush appointed her to take his place. After a rigorous swearing-in procedure, the Senate confirmed her to the post, making her the first African American woman to hold that seat.

As Condi grew up, her father was a football coach. He gave her a love of the game and all sports. When titles and positions in the top levels of government came calling, Condi kept herself humble by telling others that her dream job was not political—she wanted to be the commissioner of the National Football League. She and President Bush enjoy musing on football's place as an American institution, and she remains fascinated with the comparisons between military and football history.

John Rice gave her nearly as much instruction at home as she received in the classroom. Condi Rice's father made sure she not only fit into modern culture but also became a major player in it. An intellectual father who knew no limits, he taught his daughter that she could achieve anything she set her mind on doing.

A Father of Influence tells his children they can achieve anything they set their minds to.

Étienne Pascal

1588–1651

Blaise Pascal. Home schooled by his father, Étienne,

Blaise Pascal was one of the world's greatest

mathematicians, who late in life became a Christian and a

renowned religious scholar.

Born at Clermont-Ferrand in the Auvergne region of France, Blaise Pascal and his brother and two sisters lost their mother, Antoinette Begon, when Blaise was only three years old. Étienne Pascal at the time was a local judge and member of the *petite noblesse*. Also a scientist and a mathematician, Étienne contributed substantially to those disciplines by deciding, while serving on an official scientific committee, whether Jean-Baptiste Morin's scheme for determining longitude from the moon's motion was practical.

When Blaise was eight, Étienne moved the family to Paris. There, the elder Pascal decided that he would educate his son, who by that time had shown extraordinary intellectual abilities. Like his father, the young Pascal showed a great aptitude for mathematics and science. After all, the youth witnessed his father's regular conversations with leading geometricians of Paris such as Roberval, Desargues, Gassendi, and Descartes.

When Blaise was eleven, he wrote a short treatise on the sounds of vibrating bodies. Rather than encourage his son, Étienne responded by forbidding him to further pursue mathematics until the age of fifteen, so that he could focus his study on Latin and Greek, subjects considered more essential to a fundamental education. Nevertheless, Blaise would not squelch his interests and a year later, Étienne caught him writing an independent proof—the sum of the angles of a triangle is equal to two right angles—on a wall with a piece of coal. Aware that he couldn't and shouldn't control his son's natural educational inclinations, Étienne let Blaise study Euclid, the father of geometry.

Blaise dove right into the discipline and found the work of Desargues particularly intriguing. At age sixteen, Pascal wrote an essay on conics, out of which came Pascal's theorem, still studied by math scholars today. The work was so astute that Descartes, when shown the manuscript, refused to believe that the work was not created by Étienne rather than his son.

When Blaise was nineteen, Étienne worked as a tax commissioner. So grateful and appreciative was he of the education his father had provided that he decided to construct a mechanical calculator—now called Pascal's calculator or the Pascaline—capable of addition and subtraction. The initial prototype had five dials. When turned to the appropriate numbers, the device figured answers that appeared in boxes in the top of the calculator. Blaise made improvements to his design through the next decade and built a total of fifty machines.

In 1645, when Blaise was twenty-two, Étienne suffered a wound to the thigh and a Jansenist physician looked after him. Jansenism was a form of Catholicism, which emphasized original sin, human depravity, and the necessity of divine grace. Blaise spoke often with the doctor, and because his father was successfully treated, Blaise saw him as credible. Blaise borrowed books from the doctor by Jansenist authors and experienced his "first conversion" to Christ.

However, Blaise did not immediately show a lasting change in his life and fell away from this initial religious engagement. During this time, Étienne died, and Blaise gained control of his inheritance, spending lavishly and living a life of conspicuous consumption.

Jacqueline, Blaise's sister, reproached him for his libertine attitudes and prayed for his reform. After that he did show some contempt for the ways of the world but did not return to God until late 1654, when he was involved in an accident at the Neuilly bridge. Horses pulling his coach plunged over the parapet. Fortunately, the reigns broke, leaving the coach hanging halfway over the edge. Though his life was spared, Blaise was so terrified by the experience that he fainted and remained unconscious for fifteen days. On his awakening, Blaise had an intense vision. He wrote out the details, which included images of fire and words referring to the God of Abraham, Isaac, and Jacob. He concluded by quoting a psalm on not forgetting God's Word. (Later, after his death, it was discovered that he had sewn the record of the vision to the inside of his coat.)

> *Listen, my sons, to a father's instruction; pay attention and gain understanding.*
>
> **PROVERBS 4:1**

His religious faith revitalized, Blaise turned to writing. His first major literary work on religion, the *Provincial Letters*, was written as a series of letters to a friend. The work criticized situational ethics based on lofty arguments. King Louis XIV was incensed and ordered the books shredded and burned. But the author's use of humor and satire in his arguments gladdened the public and influenced other later French writers such as Voltaire and Jean-Jacques Rousseau.

Blaise Pascal wasn't able to finish his most influential theological work, the *Pensées* (meaning "thoughts"), before his death. (The original title was *Apologie de la religion Chrétienne*, or "Defense of the Christian Religion.") The finished project was just a compilation of numerous scraps of paper with isolated thoughts on different subjects. But, on publication, it became a classic, a landmark of French prose. He touched on topics such as infinity, faith, reason, soul, and matter, yet offered no definitive conclusions but the grace of God.

These works and the lasting legacy of Blaise Pascal—one of the greatest minds of the Western world—were due, in no small part, to his father's influence in fostering his education. He exposed Blaise to some of the greatest pieces of scientific and mathematical thought of his time and introduced him to some of the keenest minds in contemporary society.

A Father of Influence knows that education begins at home.

Bobby Bowden

Unknown

Terry and Tommy Bowden. The beloved head coach

of the Florida State football program encouraged his sons,

Terry and Tommy, to pursue their own

college coaching aspirations.

Coach Bobby Bowden knows how to win. His team record with Florida State University is 286-75-4. He has won 2 national championships—1993 and 1999—and 12 conference championships. In 30 years as head coach of Florida State, he has had only 1 losing season, his first in 1976. He is the only coach in Division I-A football history to have 14 straight 10-win seasons. One of the most successful bowl game winners, he has a .672 bowl winning percentage with a 19-8-1 record. His 359 total coaching victories rank first among all-time Division I-A head coaches, current or former. With a record like that, his sons might find it scary to walk in his footsteps. In fact, one did.

Bobby's son Terry grew up admiring his father and wanted to be just like him. Achievement itself wasn't difficult. Like his father, Terry excelled in sports and academics. Terry attended West Virginia University where he played running back on the football team in 1977–78. He also was a member of Phi Kappa Psi fraternity and graduated magna cum laude with a degree in accounting. Then, he did post-graduate work at Oxford University in England and received his Juris Doctor degree from Florida State University School of Law.

Terry's fears came when he was offered the chance to coach

football at the collegiate level. In 1993, Auburn University needed a new head coach. A huge, tradition-filled program, this school was in the top ranks of Division I-A football. Terry had not coached any school higher than Division I-AA. Terry sold himself as the right man and he believed it—initially. Then doubts began to creep in.

> *He mocks at fear and is not dismayed or terrified; neither does he turn back [in battle] from the sword.*
>
> **JOB 39:22 AB**

In the book *Winning Isn't Everything* by Bobby, Terry, and Tommy Bowden and the Bowden family, Terry writes of his fears at that time: "Am I really ready for this? Is there something people know at this level that I don't understand? Is this Little League stuff I've been doing going to work at the majors?"

It was at this moment Bobby stepped in and alleviated his son's fears. Having been a successful coach for so many years, he knew what it took and he knew his son had the goods. He bombarded his son with encouragement and affirmation, reviewed his program, and approved his style.

Bobby further encouraged Terry by telling him that coaching is like playing golf. Even if you have a great average over a lifetime, you can't go out on the course and expect to play a low-stroke game every time. Some days you'll have a higher score; some days you'll have low numbers. Bobby told him that one year he might land the great head coaching job, and a few years later, he might be nothing more than the assistant. Highs and lows, wins and losses are all part of the game.

Terry's brother, Tommy, filled him in on the complexities of a school as large as Auburn. He went over the politics, explaining who was likely to be in his corner and who might not be. He went over the peculiarities of building a team, who to work with and who to cut. Terry took it all in.

That very first season in 1993 at Auburn, Terry coached the Tigers to a perfect 11-0 season. Unfortunately, the team was ineligible for post-season play including bowl games because of infractions caused by the previous coaching staff. Terry Bowden would go on to lead the team in a string of undefeated games until the final game of the 1994 season against their biggest rival, Alabama. Auburn finished the first two seasons with a 20-1-1 record, the longest win streak in AU football history.

In 1998, Tommy took over as head coach at Clemson University in South Carolina. From his arrival through the 2005 season, Tommy has never lost more games than he has won, season to season. Twice he has been honored with the ACC Coach of the Year. In 2004, he became the first coach in NCAA history to defeat two coaches, who have each racked up two hundred or more career wins, within a one-month span. One coach was Lou Holtz, who helmed South Carolina University. The other coach was his father, Bobby Bowden of Florida State University. Furthermore, Tommy Bowden broke forty-six school records with his team the very first year of coaching. Tommy thanks his father for his great encouragement and leadership throughout the years.

Bobby Bowden continues to coach at Florida State, racking up wins and encouraging his family and team. Because he has been such a great example on and off the field, the Fellowship of Christian Athletes created the National Bobby Bowden Award in 2004. Given annually, it honors one college football player for his achievements on the field, in the classroom, and in the world as an example of upstanding Christian character. In addition to his sons, Terry and Tommy, Bobby also encourages as many as he can by coauthoring books on leadership, wisdom, and courage.

A Father of Influence alleviates his children's fears.

Tim Russert Sr.

Unknown

Tim Russert Jr. Veteran journalist and host of NBC's *Meet the Press*, Tim Russert was so impressed by his father that he penned two books on paternal wisdom and lessons.

TV political correspondent Tim Russert Jr. and his father always shared a close bond, but they didn't always openly display affection. Several years ago, all that changed with an NBC series called Going Home. The program was about the network's new anchors and their return to their home communities to talk about the experiences and people who had helped shape their lives. Tim Jr. traveled to the American Legion Post 721 in south Buffalo, and there attended a luncheon with his father and his father's war buddies. They talked about family life and World War II. With the cameras rolling, Tim Jr. spontaneously put his hand on his father's shoulders and told him how much he meant to him. The audience was so moved that it flooded NBC with letters and phone calls. People wanted to talk about their fathers. As Tim Jr. read the letters and fielded the calls, his relationship with his father became even stronger.

A parachute packer during the war, Tim Russert Sr. almost didn't father any children. In October of 1944, near Insdale, England, the bomber plane he was flying in crashed. They had been circling, preparing to land, the rain pouring down and the wind howling. Anxious to get the plane down, the pilot flew too low, tipping the wing, and contacting the ground. The plane tumbled end over end and caught on fire. Several men were thrown clear including Tim. Eight others were killed instantly and three died the next day.

Tim Sr. eventually settled in south Buffalo, New York, in a primarily Irish-Catholic neighborhood. He and his wife were the parents of three girls and one boy—Tim Jr. was the second born. Since the two males in the family had the same name, people would distinguish father and son as Tim and Timmy. But when Timmy turned ten, people started calling them Big Tim and Little Tim. Then, when Little Tim grew to six foot two in high school, it was Big Russ and Tim.

Little Tim was a boy who looked for adventure and was tempted by mischief. When things went wrong, though, Big Tim was always there to teach his son a lesson—like how not to use a hula-hoop, the proper thing to do when you break a neighbor's window with your baseball, and how to properly dispose of broken glass.

Big Tim also taught his son how to shoot rats and safely handle fireworks. He insisted his son address grown-ups properly—never by their first names. He taught his son how to give a firm handshake when meeting people and the importance of good manners. In addition, Big Tim made sure that his son developed an appreciation for veterans, not only on Memorial Day but the whole year through.

The elder Russert worked two jobs and expected his children to work hard too. They did their homework every night and generally got good grades. When they made the honor roll, which Tim Jr. usually did, Big Tim would tell him not to gloat or brag.

Tim Jr. attended John Caroll University in Cleveland and law school at Cleveland-Marshall College of Law at Cleveland State University. Admitted to the bar in New York and the District of Columbia, Tim Jr. was chief of staff to Democratic Senator Daniel Patrick Moynihan from 1977 to 1982 and then counselor to New York Governor Mario Cuomo's office in 1983 and 1984.

At that time, Tim met Larry Grossman, president of NBC news, and was hired at the network. His first big assignment was to induce the pope to appear on the *Today* show. Big Tim urged his son to write a letter in Polish, the pope's native language. It worked and the pope agreed to the appearance, securing Tim's position at the network.

A good example of Tim Sr.'s influence on his son happened on election night 2000. Tim Russert Jr. sat with Tom Brokaw in the NBC studios talking about state-to-state results of the presidential contest between George W. Bush and Al Gore. As results were coming in, Tim wrote the names of the states on the back of a legal pad. Then, he held the homemade chart up to the camera and explained to the audience. Throughout it all, Tim thought about his father, because the elder Russert always used 8 1/2-by-11 yellow legal pads to keep track of budgets and figures. In the following days, NBC News got high praise from viewers who appreciated the simple way Tim used to keep track of a very complicated election.

They said, "Yes—your servant our father is quite well, very much alive." And they again bowed respectfully before him.

GENESIS 43:28 MSG

In 2004, Tim Jr. authored *Big Russ and Me*, a best-selling biography of his youth and of life with his father, Tim Russert Sr. The introduction states, "I have learned so much from Big Russ, and I feel so grateful to him that I wanted to write a book about the two of us, and also about the other important teachers in my life who have reinforced Dad's lessons and taught me a few new ones … I hope this book will encourage readers to think about the things they learned from their fathers. Whatever we achieve and whoever we are, we stand on their shoulders."

As *Big Russ and Me* circulated among the American people, Tim Jr. received more than sixty thousand letters from readers. They felt compelled to share their own stories—experiences and lessons learned from their fathers. Tim Jr. was so moved by what he read that he released a collection of some of these letters in the book *Wisdom of Our Fathers: Lessons and Letters from Daughters and Sons*. The journalist gave these voices an opportunity to express themselves publicly and in so doing, created a forum of love and respect in appreciation of the men—like Big Russ—who not only brought them into the world but also gave them the tools to live in it.

A Father of Influence teaches his children to honor their father.

Ellis Roberts

1881–Unknown

Oral Roberts. A church-planting evangelist himself,
Ellis Roberts taught his son, who was stricken with
tuberculosis as a teenager, to believe in Christ, the healer.
After a miraculous recovery from what had been deemed
to be a fatal illness, Oral preached on Christ's healing all
over the world and began a faith-based university and
medical facility.

The last of five children, Oral Roberts was born to Ellis, a Welsh
American father and Claudius, a Cherokee Indian mother, in
1918. At that time World War I was ending and a flu epidemic
was wiping out parts of America, but the flu had not reached the
Roberts home in Ada, Oklahoma.

Ellis had built a new church and a small parsonage in Ada. There,
Oral first learned about Jesus. To the Roberts family, He was not just a
historical character but a real, living person who wanted relationships
with all people. Oral and his brother, Vaden, would often wake up at
5:00 a.m. because they could hear their parents praying through the
thin walls. One morning, Oral heard his parents praying for him
specifically. He never forgot it.

Ellis Roberts had only a limited education but he had a burning
desire to preach the gospel, build churches, and win souls. He memo-
rized large portions of the King James Bible. He would spend hours
each day studying God's Word. His natural speaking ability, spiritual
anointing, and strong prayer life contributed to his powerful preaching

abilities. He was in great demand. With a legacy like that, it seemed natural that Oral would be a great speaker too. But, as a child, he had trouble talking. He stuttered.

Ellis Roberts also believed in healing. He prayed for it, and he preached it. He and his wife often conducted a tag-team ministry of healing. After Ellis spoke the Word, Claudius would lay hands on the sick and believe God would heal their bodies. If they weren't healed, Ellis would recommend they see a doctor or get medicine. To the Roberts family, both medical science and supernatural healing were God's gifts.

Jesus went through all the towns and villages, teaching in their synagogues, preaching the good news of the kingdom and healing every disease and sickness.

MATTHEW 9:35

When Oral was young, his father would build brush arbors. They cut down saplings, made them into support poles, and created a lattice of tree branches for a roof. By nightfall, they would be ready to preach in these structures. Oral always attended these brush-arbor church meetings with his siblings.

At sixteen years of age, Oral ran away from home. He was tired of the poverty he had always felt being a preacher's kid. Yet when he was out on his own, living it up in sin, he kept remembering things his father had said during sermons. Even so, Oral pushed his life hard, having fun, getting into trouble, and getting only four hours of sleep each night.

During Oral's wandering period, he contracted tuberculosis. Many of his mother's Indian relatives had succumbed to the disease, including his maternal grandfather at the age of fifty and two of his sisters in their teens. His mother had always worried that his small size and frail frame might make him vulnerable.

While playing a game of basketball, Oral passed out and his basketball coach took him home. On arrival, Ellis carried his son into the house. Oral was barely conscious and hemorrhaging from both lungs. In bed, Oral coughed up blood all night long. Ellis called the doctor, who rushed over and examined the sick young man. Then Ellis and Claudius prayed fervently for their child.

The Roberts didn't keep the truth from Oral. They explained that
he was in the final stages of the dreaded disease—his only hope the
healing power of Christ. Day after day, as Oral lay suffering, he was
reminded of a passage of Scripture he had once heard his father
preach about. It was Romans 2:4: "The goodness of God leadeth [me]
to repentance" (KJV).

One morning Ellis knelt by Oral's bed and told him he was going
to pray for him and not stop until he gave his heart to God. Oral
couldn't stand to see his father so distraught and called out to Jesus to
save him. Then Oral felt God's presence, and with it, strength returning to his body. He was getting better. With time, Oral's health was
restored—even his stuttering disappeared.

Years later, Oral would found Oral Roberts Evangelistic
Association. With this group, he conducted more than three hundred
evangelistic and healing crusades all over the world. He has also
appeared as a guest speaker for hundreds of international meetings
and conventions. In 1963, he felt God was calling him to found Oral
Roberts University. At the center of the campus, he had a prayer tower
built and to this day, a group of volunteers are praying around the
clock over thousands of prayer requests received by the university.

In his autobiography, *Expect a Miracle,* Oral writes, "Papa's solid
goodness meant a lot to me. His hatred of debt, his word as his bond,
his unswerving integrity, and his love for God and the Bible had a
more important place in my mind than I realized."

Ellis Roberts never stopped believing in his son. Continually inter-
ceding for him to God, he not only saw God heal and save his son,
but he also saw his son become God's instrument in the building of a
worldwide healing ministry and a faith-based educational institution
called Oral Roberts University.

**A Father of Influence prays for his children and
encourages them to seek the healing power of Christ.**

Walter Payton

1954–1999

Jarrett Payton. NFL great, Chicago Bears running back Walter Payton met an early demise when at age forty-five he died of a rare liver disease and cancer. In death as in life, he taught his son, Jarrett, how to behave with dignity and grace.

In 1977, Walter Payton was elected the NFL's most valuable player (MVP). An inspiration and a hero to all, his work ethic was exemplified that year by rushing more than 275 yards against the Minnesota Vikings while fighting a case of the flu. Two years later, in 1979, life seemed great for the running back until his father, Edward, suddenly died of a brain aneurism. Walter's life came crashing down. He regretted not being able to talk with his father and share some quality father-son moments. He vowed never to leave his children, Jarrett and Brittany, with the same regret.

Twenty years later, Walter developed a rare liver disease that tragically compounded into terminal cancer.

In January of 1999, Jarrett was a senior at Chicago's St. Viator High School. He had been elected the fifty-eighth best high school football player in the nation according to *Sporting News* magazine. A press conference was called for the purpose of announcing what college he intended to attend that fall. Sports journalists from every local news organization were there. So was Walter Payton. Although Jarrett announced he would be attending Miami University, the morning papers virtually ignored that fact and

instead talked about how awful Walter looked. Indeed, the for-
merly robust man had lost a lot of weight, and his face was
covered by a rash.

A month later, with Jarrett by his side for support, Walter made
an official announcement to the press that he was fighting a rare disease. A liver transplant was his only option. Walter and his family
were flooded with support. Over the following months, father and
son talked continually. They talked about setting goals and how to
achieve them. They talked about football and how to maintain a com-
petitive spirit. But mainly they talked about family and God and
about sharing the blessings of God with others.

Twelve years earlier, in 1987, Walter was a veteran football player.
He had been in the NFL for thirteen years, much longer than most
NFL careers. Though he still felt like a viable force, he wasn't as fast as
he used to be, and he knew his time was short as a professional
player. When Neal Anderson was brought into the Chicago organization and groomed as Walter's replacement, it wasn't easy to deal with,
but Walter didn't make any waves. The veteran running back took
Neal under his wing, taught him the ropes, and looked out for him.

Walter retired after that season, and six-year-old Jarrett listened to
his father give a farewell speech during the halftime of the last regular
season game. The speech was brief. Walter merely said he played football because he loved the game. It was fun. He also thanked the fans
for being there for him throughout the years.

In 1987, the Bears went 14-3, and wound up facing the
Washington Redskins in the first round of the playoffs. Neal Anderson
was injured, so Walter was able to run with the ball. He went 85 yards
on 18 carries, his best effort of the year. The 'Skins won 21-17, but the
Bears finished the game with the ball in Walter's hands.

At the end of that last game at Soldier Field, Walter Payton sat on
the bench after everyone left the field, enjoying his final moments as
a player for the Chicago Bears.

Throughout the '80s and '90s, father and son often took time to
express their mutual respect and admiration for one another. Walter
called Jarrett a tremendous joy and inspiration, while Jarrett calls his

father his biggest role model and best friend.

Walter called all children the most precious resource the country has. He compared children to a farmer's crop, needing cultivation and fertilization. He said they needed time and attention because they are more important than any crop or farm.

> *I have fought the good fight, I have finished the race, I have kept the faith.*
>
> **2 TIMOTHY 4:7**

When Walter died in November of 1999, Jarrett's first year of college football, Jarrett told this story about his father recorded in Walter's autobiography, *Never Die Easy:* "When I was a kid, my dad always had a whistle that whenever he needed me, he'd whistle. No matter where I was, in the yard, on the football field, I heard his whistle and when it came to me, I knew it was important when I heard it. It commanded my attention and it was something that I became trained to, kind of like a dog with a whistle. And that was just like him saying, 'Go out there and do a good job and represent me and do everything that I've taught you.' I remember we were playing Boston College and we were in BC and we were playing the game, and for some odd reason I was just standing on the sidelines and I heard the whistle and I turned around. Knowing that my dad was at home watching the game, I still was looking around and trying to find him and see where he was. I know I'll never forget that moment."

After an exceptional college football career, Jarrett graduated from Miami University and was drafted, as a running back, into the NFL with the Tennessee Titans.

Jarrett Payton lost his father far too soon, but he will always be able to access the heritage his father left him—facing the circumstances of life, and death, with decorum and style, the same way his father lived life on and off the football field.

A Father of Influence teaches his children to finish well.

Charles Phillip "Pa" Ingalls

1836–1902

Laura Ingalls Wilder. Charles "Pa" Ingalls taught his family, including daughter and author Laura Ingalls Wilder, to bravely and courageously embrace new adventures.

Despite the horrors of the Civil War, President Abraham Lincoln was still able to consider the hope of many Americans—a home with land of their own. In 1862, he signed into law the Homestead Act. It was a chance to claim open lands belonging to the United States government—free! Beyond the Mississippi River to the west lay millions of acres. In the prairie country, soil was black and fertile. Any American over twenty-one years of age could file a claim for government land. Five years after the Homestead Act was signed, Laura Ingalls was born in the Wisconsin woods. Her father, Charles (or "Pa" as the children called him), wanted to move his young family west to grab his own piece of the American dream.

Charles was not originally from Wisconsin. He hailed from New York and moved west with his family of eight siblings when he was nine. They first settled in Illinois and then made their way north to Wisconsin. There the Ingalls boys worked on a farm, meeting new difficulties and challenges with resolve and ingenuity. During free moments, Charles liked to tell stories and play his fiddle.

In 1868, when Laura was just a baby, Charles and his wife, Caroline, sold their house in the woods and headed for Kansas, the open plain. They traveled in a horse-drawn covered wagon, filled it with as many belongings as they could manage and Jack, their bulldog, ran alongside.

Along the way, the family encountered many difficulties. They had to make precarious river crossings, and sometimes drove for miles without seeing another human being. Other times the rains poured or the sun beat down so hot the wagon ride was miserable. But Ma made good meals on the campfire every night while Pa merrily played his fiddle.

> *The LORD had said to Abram, "Leave your country, your people and your father's household and go to the land I will show you."*
> GENESIS 12:1

Finally in Kansas, the Ingalls chose a piece of land they thought was available for settling, and Charles immediately began hauling logs from the banks of a nearby creek. The cabin was finished before they realized the land would never be theirs—it belonged to the Osage Indians. Unknowingly, they had entered three miles into the Osage Diminished Indian Reserve.

One day, an Osage Indian stopped by the Ingalls cabin. Initially, the family didn't know whether he was friend or foe. Despite the language barrier, the family courageously reached out to the Osage and found him to be a hungry curiosity seeker. Ma gave him some cornbread, and he left fed and happy. This home wouldn't be theirs for long, however. They weren't allowed to remain on Indian land, and a new development further complicated their situation. The buyer of their Wisconsin home wrote to say he wanted Charles to buy the home back. So, when Laura was four years old, the Ingalls packed up and moved back to Wisconsin—only temporarily.

After two years, Pa again wanted to go west. For a second time, he sold his Wisconsin farm and this time the family headed for western Minnesota. They bought property near Walnut Creek on Plum Creek. The first house was a dugout, a hole in the ground with thick sod walls and a willow bough roof. A real house would have to be built, but unlike the land in Wisconsin and Kansas, the Minnesota property had no trees at all.

Charles was able to buy lumber on credit, which came in via railroad, but before the family could settle into their new home, another catastrophe occurred. A thick cloud of grasshoppers descended on the prairie and ate up everything in sight. When a new settler made an offer to buy the house, Charles accepted.

The family eventually settled in De Smet, South Dakota Territory, and had many more adventures together. Laura improved her education and worked as a seamstress and teacher, but quit teaching in 1885 to marry homesteader Almanzo Wilder. Soon they had a child of their own, a daughter Rose. Though Laura would do more traveling and publish a few articles some twenty-five years later, it wouldn't be until the 1930s that she would pen her beloved Little House series.

Over the course of her life, Laura Ingalls Wilder lived in Wisconsin, Minnesota, South Dakota, Iowa, Missouri, Kansas, California, and Florida. She realized the traveling, pioneering lifestyle of her youth was unique and special. So few had seen so much country and so much change over the course of a lifetime. Realizing that the young and future generations might enjoy the historical stories of her youth, Laura, well advanced in years, penned nine novels including the beloved books *Little House in the Big Woods* and *Little House on the Prairie*. Continuing to charm and delight readers, the stories were also made into a popular television series, still airing in syndication today.

Pa Ingalls had an itchy foot and didn't like to stay in any one place for any length of time. He loved the open plains where acres of crops could grow plentifully. By uprooting his family and taking them across the country, he taught them resilience, courage, resourcefulness, and adventure. Through his recollections and fine gift of storytelling, he also encouraged his daughter to tell of this life in her subsequent historical novels.

A Father of Influence teaches his children to embrace change.

Fathers of Influence from the Bible

✤

It's the living—live men, live women—who thank you,
just as I'm doing right now.
Parents give their children
full reports on your faithful ways.

Isaiah 38:19 msg

Apostle Paul

ACTS 9:1–22 TLB

New Testament Christians. He once persecuted those who put their faith in Jesus Christ, but when confronted with the truth, he was converted. The apostle Paul planted and tended the early churches of believers. His letters to them, consisting of instruction and encouragement in the faith, now comprise two-thirds of the New Testament text.

Paul, threatening with every breath and eager to destroy every Christian, went to the High Priest in Jerusalem. He requested a letter addressed to synagogues in Damascus, requiring their cooperation in the persecution of any believers he found there, both men and women, so that he could bring them in chains to Jerusalem.

As he was nearing Damascus on this mission, suddenly a brilliant light from heaven spotted down upon him! He fell to the ground and heard a voice saying to him, "Paul! Paul! Why are you persecuting me?"

"Who is speaking, sir?" Paul asked.

And the voice replied, "I am Jesus, the one you are persecuting! Now get up and go into the city and await my further instructions."

The men with Paul stood speechless with surprise, for they heard the sound of someone's voice but saw no one! As Paul picked himself up off the ground, he found that he was blind. He had to be led into Damascus and was there three days, blind, going without food and water all that time.

Now there was in Damascus a believer named Ananias. The Lord spoke to him in a vision, calling, "Ananias!"

"Yes, Lord!" he replied.

And the Lord said, "Go over to Straight Street and find the house of a man named Judas and ask there for Paul of Tarsus. He is praying to me right now, for I have shown him a vision of a man named Ananias coming in and laying his hands on him so that he can see again!"

"But Lord," exclaimed Ananias, "I have heard about the terrible things this man has done to the believers in Jerusalem! And we hear that he has arrest warrants with him from the chief priests, authorizing him to arrest every believer in Damascus!"

But the Lord said, "Go and do what I say. For Paul is my chosen instrument to take my message to the nations and before kings, as well as to the people of Israel. And I will show him how much he must suffer for me."

So Ananias went over and found Paul and laid his hands on him and said, "Brother Paul, the Lord Jesus, who appeared to you on the road, has sent me so that you may be filled with the Holy Spirit and get your sight back."

Instantly (it was as though scales fell from his eyes) Paul could see, and was immediately baptized. Then he ate and was strengthened.

He stayed with the believers in Damascus for a few days and went at once to the synagogue to tell everyone there the Good News about Jesus—that he is indeed the Son of God!

All who heard him were amazed. "Isn't this the same man who persecuted Jesus' followers so bitterly in Jerusalem?" they asked. "And we understand that he came here to arrest them all and take them in chains to the chief priests."

Paul became more and more fervent in his preaching, and the Damascus Jews couldn't withstand his proofs that Jesus was indeed the Christ.

A Father of Influence gives his life wholeheartedly to God and diligently pursues His will.

King David

2 SAMUEL 7:1–8, 10–16; 1 KINGS 1:28–30, 48;
2:1–4, 10–12 CEV

Solomon. Because his father, David, demonstrated and instructed him in how to be a godly king, he became a fit king of Israel and accomplished his father's dream of building a temple for God.

 King David moved into his new palace, and the LORD let his kingdom be at peace. Then one day, as David was talking with Nathan the prophet, David said, "Look around! I live in a palace made of cedar, but the sacred chest has to stay in a tent."

Nathan replied, "The LORD is with you, so do what you want!"

That night, the LORD told Nathan to go to David and give him this message:

David, you are my servant, so listen to what I say. Why should you build a temple for me? I didn't live in a temple when I brought my people out of Egypt, and I don't live in one now. A tent has always been my home wherever I have gone with them. I chose leaders and told them to be like shepherds for my people Israel. But did I ever say anything to even one of them about building a cedar temple for me?

David, this is what I, the LORD All-Powerful, say to you. I brought you in from the fields where you took care of sheep, and I made you the leader of my people.

I have given my people Israel a land of their own where they can live in peace, and they won't have to tremble with fear any more. Evil nations won't bother them, as they did when I let judges rule my people. And I have kept your enemies from attacking you.

Now I promise that you and your descendants will be kings. I'll choose one of your sons to be king when you reach the end of your life and are buried in the tomb of your ancestors. I'll make him a strong ruler, and no one will be able to take his kingdom away from him. He will be the one to build a temple for me. I will be his father, and he will be my son.

When he does wrong, I'll see that he is corrected, just as children are corrected by their parents. But I will never put an end to my agreement with him, as I put an end to my agreement with Saul, who was king before you. I will make sure that one of your descendants will always be king.

David said, "Tell Bathsheba to come here." She came and stood in front of him. Then he said, "The living LORD God of Israel has kept me safe. And so today, I will keep the promise I made to you in his name: Solomon will be the next king!"

[David] prayed, "I praise you, LORD God of Israel. You have made my son Solomon king and have let me live to see it."

Not long before David died, he told Solomon:

My son, I will soon die, as everyone must. But I want you to be strong and brave. Do what the LORD your God commands and follow his teachings. Obey everything written in the Law of Moses. Then you will be a success, no matter what you do or where you go. You and your descendants must always faithfully obey the LORD. If you do, he will keep the solemn promise he made to me that someone from our family will always be king of Israel.

David was king of Israel forty years. He ruled seven years from Hebron and thirty-three years from Jerusalem. Then he died and was buried in Jerusalem. His son Solomon became king and took control of David's kingdom.

A Father of Influence teaches his children how to pursue a dream that God has given them.

Father Abraham

GENESIS 17:1–8; 21:1–5; 22:1–2, 9–18 TLB

Isaac/Jacob, and all those who place their faith in God. Abraham believed in God's promise and obeyed His commandments. Therefore, God made him the father of many nations, and he set an example of faith and relationship with God for all those who would come after.

When Abram was ninety-nine years old, God appeared to him and told him, "I am the Almighty; obey me and live as you should. I will prepare a contract between us, guaranteeing to make you into a mighty nation. In fact you shall be the father of not only one nation, but a multitude of nations!" Abram fell face downward in the dust as God talked with him.

"What's more," God told him, "I am changing your name. It is no longer 'Abram' ('Exalted Father'), but 'Abraham' ('Father of Nations')—for that is what you will be. I have declared it. I will give you millions of descendants who will form many nations! Kings shall be among your descendants! And I will continue this agreement between us generation after generation, forever, for it shall be between me and your children as well. It is a contract that I shall be your God and the God of your posterity. And I will give all this land of Canaan to you and them, forever. And I will be your God."

Then God did as he had promised, and Sarah became pregnant and gave Abraham a baby son in his old age, at the time God had said; and Abraham named him Isaac (meaning "Laughter!"). Eight days after he was born, Abraham circumcised him, as God required. (Abraham was one hundred years old at that time.)

Later on, God tested Abraham's [faith and obedience].

"Abraham!" God called.

"Yes, Lord?" he replied.

"Take with you your only son—yes, Isaac whom you love so much—and go to the land of Moriah and sacrifice him there as a burnt offering upon one of the mountains which I'll point out to you!"

When they arrived at the place where God had told Abraham to go, he built an altar and placed the wood in order, ready for the fire, and then tied Isaac and laid him on the altar over the wood. And Abraham took the knife and lifted it up to plunge it into his son, to slay him.

At that moment the Angel of God shouted to him from heaven, "Abraham! Abraham!"

"Yes, Lord!" he answered.

"Lay down the knife; don't hurt the lad in any way," the Angel said, "for I know that God is first in your life—you have not withheld even your beloved son from me."

Then Abraham noticed a ram caught by its horns in a bush. So he took the ram and sacrificed it, instead of his son, as a burnt offering on the altar. Abraham named the place "Jehovah provides"—and it still goes by that name to this day.

Then the Angel of God called again to Abraham from heaven. "I, the Lord, have sworn by myself that because you have obeyed me and have not withheld even your beloved son from me, I will bless you with incredible blessings and multiply your descendants into countless thousands and millions, like the stars above you in the sky, and like the sands along the seashore. These descendants of yours will conquer their enemies, and your offspring will be a blessing to all the nations of the earth—all because you have obeyed me."

A Father of Influence trusts God with every aspect of his life—even the care of his children.

The Forgiving Father

LUKE 15:11–32 MSG

The Prodigal Son. By demonstrating forgiveness to a son who scorned his authority, wasted his inheritance, and deserted his family, the forgiving father showed us how to return home, receive our heavenly Father's love and forgiveness, and live in harmony with Him.

Then he said, "There was once a man who had two sons. The younger said to his father, 'Father, I want right now what's coming to me.'

"So the father divided the property between them. It wasn't long before the younger son packed his bags and left for a distant country. There, undisciplined and dissipated, he wasted everything he had. After he had gone through all his money, there was a bad famine all through that country and he began to hurt. He signed on with a citizen there who assigned him to his fields to slop the pigs. He was so hungry he would have eaten the corncobs in the pig slop, but no one would give him any.

"That brought him to his senses. He said, 'All those farmhands working for my father sit down to three meals a day, and here I am starving to death. I'm going back to my father. I'll say to him, Father, I've sinned against God, I've sinned before you; I don't deserve to be called your son. Take me on as a hired hand.' He got right up and went home to his father.

"When he was still a long way off, his father saw him. His heart pounding, he ran out, embraced him, and kissed him. The son started his speech: 'Father, I've sinned against God, I've sinned before you; I don't deserve to be called your son ever again.'

"But the father wasn't listening. He was calling to the servants, 'Quick. Bring a clean set of clothes and dress him. Put the family ring on his finger and sandals on his feet. Then get a grain-fed heifer and roast it. We're going to feast! We're going to have a wonderful time! My son is here—given up for dead and now alive! Given up for lost and now found!' And they began to have a wonderful time.

"All this time his older son was out in the field. When the day's work was done he came in. As he approached the house, he heard the music and dancing. Calling over one of the houseboys, he asked what was going on. He told him, 'Your brother came home. Your father has ordered a feast—barbecued beef!—because he has him home safe and sound.'

"The older brother stalked off in an angry sulk and refused to join in. His father came out and tried to talk to him, but he wouldn't listen. The son said, 'Look how many years I've stayed here serving you, never giving you one moment of grief, but have you ever thrown a party for me and my friends? Then this son of yours who has thrown away your money on whores shows up and you go all out with a feast!'

"His father said, 'Son, you don't understand. You're with me all the time, and everything that is mine is yours—but this is a wonderful time, and we had to celebrate. This brother of yours was dead, and he's alive! He was lost, and he's found!'"

A Father of Influence demonstrates for his children the love and forgiveness of God.

Elijah

1 Kings 19:9–21 msg

Elisha. One of the great prophets of Israel, Elijah taught Elisha all he could about how to rightly deliver the Word of the Lord before passing his authority to him.

Then the word of God came to him: "So Elijah, what are you doing here?"

"I've been working my heart out for the God-of-the-Angel-Armies," said Elijah. "The people of Israel have abandoned your covenant, destroyed the places of worship, and murdered your prophets. I'm the only one left, and now they're trying to kill me."

Then he was told, "Go, stand on the mountain at attention before God. God will pass by."

A hurricane wind ripped through the mountains and shattered the rocks before God, but God wasn't to be found in the wind; after the wind an earthquake, but God wasn't in the earthquake; and after the earthquake fire, but God wasn't in the fire; and after the fire a gentle and quiet whisper.

When Elijah heard the quiet voice, he muffled his face with his great cloak, went to the mouth of the cave, and stood there. A quiet voice asked, "So Elijah, now tell me, what are you doing here?" Elijah said it again, "I've been working my heart out for God, the God-of-the-Angel-Armies, because the people of Israel have abandoned your covenant, destroyed your places of worship, and murdered your prophets. I'm the only one left, and now they're trying to kill me."

God said, "Go back the way you came through the desert to Damascus. When you get there anoint Hazael; make him king over

Aram. Then anoint Jehu son of Nimshi; make him king over Israel. Finally, anoint Elisha son of Shaphat from Abel Meholah to succeed you as prophet. Anyone who escapes death by Hazael will be killed by Jehu; and anyone who escapes death by Jehu will be killed by Elisha. Meanwhile, I'm preserving for myself seven thousand souls: the knees that haven't bowed to the god Baal, the mouths that haven't kissed his image."

Elijah went straight out and found Elisha son of Shaphat in a field where there were twelve pairs of yoked oxen at work plowing; Elisha was in charge of the twelfth pair. Elijah went up to him and threw his cloak over him.

Elisha deserted the oxen, ran after Elijah, and said, "Please! Let me kiss my father and mother good-bye—then I'll follow you."

"Go ahead," said Elijah, "but, mind you, don't forget what I've just done to you."

So Elisha left; he took his yoke of oxen and butchered them. He made a fire with the plow and tackle and then boiled the meat—a true farewell meal for the family. Then he left and followed Elijah, becoming his right-hand man.

A Father of Influence takes the time to teach his children and prepare them to take hold of their destinies.

Jairus

MARK 5:21–24, 35–43 MSG

The dying daughter. Jairus was unwilling to simply

sit and watch his precious daughter die.

He ran to Jesus, humbled himself, and asked

Him to heal his daughter.

After Jesus crossed over by boat, a large crowd met him at the seaside. One of the meeting-place leaders named Jairus came. When he saw Jesus, he fell to his knees, beside himself as he begged, "My dear daughter is at death's door. Come and lay hands on her so she will get well and live." Jesus went with him, the whole crowd tagging along, pushing and jostling him.

While he was still talking, some people came from the leader's house and told him, "Your daughter is dead. Why bother the Teacher any more?"

Jesus overheard what they were talking about and said to the leader, "Don't listen to them; just trust me."

He permitted no one to go in with him except Peter, James, and John. They entered the leader's house and pushed their way through the gossips looking for a story and neighbors bringing in casseroles. Jesus was abrupt: "Why all this busybody grief and gossip? This child isn't dead; she's sleeping." Provoked to sarcasm, they told him he didn't know what he was talking about.

But when he had sent them all out, he took the child's father and mother, along with his companions, and entered the child's room. He clasped the girl's hand and said, "Talitha koum," which means, "Little girl, get up." At that, she was up and walking around! This girl was twelve years of age. They, of course, were all beside themselves with joy. He gave them strict orders that no one was to know what had taken place in that room. Then he said, "Give her something to eat."

A Father of Influence is willing to humble himself in order to help his children.

Joseph

MATTHEW 1:18–25; 2:1–3, 7–15, 19–23 CEV

Jesus. When Jesus was in danger, Joseph protected the
helpless infant who would become the Savior of the world
from being destroyed before He could accomplish His mission.

This is how Jesus Christ was born. A young woman named
Mary was engaged to Joseph from King David's family. But
before they were married, she learned that she was going to
have a baby by God's Holy Spirit. Joseph was a good man and did
not want to embarrass Mary in front of everyone. So he decided to
quietly call off the wedding.

While Joseph was thinking about this, an angel from the Lord
came to him in a dream. The angel said, "Joseph, the baby that
Mary will have is from the Holy Spirit. Go ahead and marry her.
Then after her baby is born, name him Jesus, because he will save
his people from their sins." So the Lord's promise came true, just as
the prophet had said, "A virgin will have a baby boy, and he will be
called Immanuel," which means "God is with us."

After Joseph woke up, he and Mary were soon married, just as
the Lord's angel had told him to do. But they did not sleep together
before her baby was born. Then Joseph named him Jesus.

When Jesus was born in the village of Bethlehem in Judea,
Herod was king. During this time some wise men from the east came
to Jerusalem and said, "Where is the child born to be king of the
Jews? We saw his star in the east and have come to worship him."
When King Herod heard about this, he was worried, and so was
everyone else in Jerusalem.

Herod secretly called in the wise men and asked them when

they had first seen the star. He told them, "Go to Bethlehem and search carefully for the child. As soon as you find him, let me know. I want to go and worship him too."

The wise men listened to what the king said and then left. And the star they had seen in the east went on ahead of them until it stopped over the place where the child was. They were thrilled and excited to see the star.

When the men went into the house and saw the child with Mary, his mother, they knelt down and worshiped him. They took out their gifts of gold, frankincense, and myrrh and gave them to him. Later they were warned in a dream not to return to Herod, and they went back home by another road.

After the wise men had gone, an angel from the Lord appeared to Joseph in a dream and said, "Get up! Hurry and take the child and his mother to Egypt! Stay there until I tell you to return, because Herod is looking for the child and wants to kill him."

That night, Joseph got up and took his wife and the child to Egypt, where they stayed until Herod died. So the Lord's promise came true, just as the prophet had said, "I called my son out of Egypt."

After King Herod died, an angel from the Lord appeared in a dream to Joseph while he was still in Egypt. The angel said, "Get up and take the child and his mother back to Israel. The people who wanted to kill him are now dead."

Joseph got up and left with them for Israel. But when he heard that Herod's son Archelaus was now ruler of Judea, he was afraid to go there. Then in a dream he was told to go to Galilee, and they went to live there in the town of Nazareth. So the Lord's promise came true, just as the prophet had said, "He will be called a Nazarene."

A Father of Influence looks to God to help him protect those children he has been entrusted with.

Manoah

JUDGES 13:2–20, 22–25 NCV

Samson. Because Manoah respected the angel of God who came to him and gave him instructions about how his son should be raised, Samson was prepared to carry out the unusual destiny God had called him to.

Tthere was a man named Manoah from the tribe of Dan, who lived in the city of Zorah. He had a wife, but she could not have children. The angel of the LORD appeared to Manoah's wife and said, "You have not been able to have children, but you will become pregnant and give birth to a son. Be careful not to drink wine or beer or eat anything that is unclean, because you will become pregnant and have a son. You must never cut his hair, because he will be a Nazirite, given to God from birth. He will begin to save Israel from the power of the Philistines."

Then Manoah's wife went to him and told him what had happened. She said, "A man from God came to me. He looked like an angel from God; his appearance was frightening. I didn't ask him where he was from, and he didn't tell me his name. But he said to me, 'You will become pregnant and will have a son. Don't drink wine or beer or eat anything that is unclean, because the boy will be a Nazirite to God from his birth until the day of his death.'"

Then Manoah prayed to the LORD: "LORD, I beg you to let the man of God come to us again. Let him teach us what we should do for the boy who will be born to us." God heard Manoah's prayer, and the angel of God came to Manoah's wife again while she was sitting in the field. But her husband Manoah was not with her. So she ran to tell him, "He is here! The man who appeared to me the other day is here!" Manoah got up and followed his wife. When he came to the man, he said, "Are you the man who spoke to my wife?" The man said, "I am." So Manoah asked, "When what you say happens, what kind of life should the boy live? What should he do?" The angel of the LORD said, "Your wife must be careful to do everything I told her to do. She must not eat anything that grows on a grapevine, or drink any wine or beer, or eat anything that is unclean. She must do everything I have commanded her."

Manoah said to the angel of the LORD, "We would like you to stay awhile so we can cook a young goat for you." The angel of the LORD answered, "Even if I stay awhile, I would not eat your food. But if you want to prepare something, offer a burnt offering to the LORD." (Manoah did not understand that the man was really the angel of the LORD.) Then Manoah asked the angel of the LORD, "What is your name? Then we will honor you when what you have said really happens." The angel of the LORD said, "Why do you ask my name? It is too amazing for you to understand." So Manoah sacrificed a young goat on a rock and offered some grain as a gift to the LORD.

Then an amazing thing happened as Manoah and his wife watched. The flames went up to the sky from the altar. As the fire burned, the angel of the LORD went up to heaven in the flame. When Manoah and his wife saw that, they bowed facedown on the ground.

Manoah said, "We have seen God, so we will surely die." But his wife said to him, "If the LORD wanted to kill us, he would not have accepted our burnt offering or grain offering. He would not have shown us all these things or told us all this."

So the woman gave birth to a boy and named him Samson. He grew, and the LORD blessed him. The Spirit of the LORD began to work in Samson while he was in the city of Mahaneh Dan, between the cities of Zorah and Eshtaol.

A Father of Influence respects God's wishes concerning his children even when he doesn't understand.

Zechariah

LUKE 1:5–25, 57–80 NCV

John the Baptist. Because Zechariah honored God by naming his son John as he was instructed by the angel of the Lord, the unique call on John's life was confirmed to all.

During the time Herod ruled Judea, there was a priest named Zechariah who belonged to Abijah's group. Zechariah's wife, Elizabeth, came from the family of Aaron. Zechariah and Elizabeth truly did what God said was good. They did everything the Lord commanded and were without fault in keeping his law. But they had no children, because Elizabeth could not have a baby, and both of them were very old.

One day Zechariah was serving as a priest before God, because his group was on duty. According to the custom of the priests, he was chosen by lot to go into the Temple of the Lord and burn incense. There were a great many people outside praying at the time the incense was offered. Then an angel of the Lord appeared to Zechariah, standing on the right side of the incense table. When he saw the angel, Zechariah was startled and frightened. But the angel said to him, "Zechariah, don't be afraid. God has heard your prayer. Your wife, Elizabeth, will give birth to a son, and you will name him John. He will bring you joy and gladness, and many people will be happy because of his birth. John will be a great man for the Lord. He will never drink wine or beer, and even from birth, he will be filled with the Holy Spirit. He will help many people of Israel return to the Lord their God. He will go before the Lord in spirit and power like Elijah. He will make peace between parents and their children and will bring those who are not obeying God back to the right way of thinking, to make a people ready for the coming of the Lord."

Zechariah said to the angel, "How can I know that what you say is true? I am an old man, and my wife is old, too." The angel answered him, "I am Gabriel. I stand before God, who sent me to talk to you and to tell you this good news. Now, listen! You will not be able to speak until the day these things happen, because you did not believe what I told you. But they will really happen."

Outside, the people were still waiting for Zechariah and were surprised that he was staying so long in the Temple. When Zechariah came outside, he could not speak to them, and they knew he had seen a vision in the Temple. He could only make signs to them and remained unable to speak. When his time of service at the Temple was finished, he went home. Later, Zechariah's wife, Elizabeth, became pregnant and did not go out of her house for five months. Elizabeth said, "Look what the Lord has done for me! My people were ashamed of me, but now the Lord has taken away that shame."

When it was time for Elizabeth to give birth, she had a boy. Her neighbors and relatives heard how good the Lord was to her, and they rejoiced with her. When the baby was eight days old, they came to circumcise him. They wanted to name him Zechariah because this was his father's name, but his mother said, "No! He will be named John." The people said to Elizabeth, "But no one in your family has this name." Then they made signs to his father to find out what he would like to name him. Zechariah asked for a writing tablet and wrote, "His name is John," and everyone was surprised. Immediately Zechariah could talk again, and he began praising God. All their neighbors became alarmed, and in all the mountains of Judea people continued talking about all these things. The people who heard about them wondered, saying, "What will this child be?" because the Lord was with him.

Then Zechariah, John's father, was filled with the Holy Spirit and prophesied: "Let us praise the Lord, the God of Israel, because he has come to help his people and has given them freedom. He has given us a powerful Savior from the family of God's servant David. He said that he would do this through his holy prophets who lived long ago: He promised he would save us from our enemies and from the power of all those who hate us. He said he would give mercy to our fathers and that he would remember his holy promise. God promised Abraham, our father, that he would save us from the power of our enemies so we could serve him without fear, being holy and good before God as long as we live.

"Now you, child, will be called a prophet of the Most High God. You will go before the Lord to prepare his way. You will make his people know that they will be saved by having their sins forgiven. With the loving mercy of our God, a new day from heaven will dawn upon us. It will shine on those who live in darkness, in the shadow of death. It will guide us into the path of peace."

And so the child grew up and became strong in spirit. John lived in the desert until the time when he came out to preach to Israel.

**A Father of Influence puts God's purposes
above his own.**

Joshua

JOSHUA 1:1–9; 23:1–11, 14–16; 24:1–4, 13–18, 22–31 TLB

The leaders of Israel. Because Joshua reminded the younger leaders of Israel of all that the Lord had done for them and urged them to continue to honor and obey Him, they had success in battle with their enemies.

After the death of Moses, the Lord's disciple, God spoke to Moses' assistant, whose name was Joshua (the son of Nun), and said to him,

"Now that my disciple is dead, [you are the new leader of Israel]. Lead my people across the Jordan River into the Promised Land. I say to you what I said to Moses: 'Wherever you go will be part of the land of Israel—all the way from Negeb desert in the south to the Lebanon mountains in the north, and from the Mediterranean Sea in the west to the Euphrates River in the east, including all the land of the Hittites.' No one will be able to oppose you as long as you live, for I will be with you just as I was with Moses; I will not abandon you or fail to help you.

"Be strong and brave, for you will be a successful leader of my people; and they shall conquer all the land I promised to their ancestors. You need only to be strong and courageous and to obey to the letter every law Moses gave you, for if you are careful to obey every one of them you will be successful in everything you do. Constantly remind the people about these laws, and you yourself must think about them every day and every night so that you will be sure to obey all of them. For only then will you succeed. Yes, be bold and strong! Banish fear and doubt! For remember, the Lord your God is with you wherever you go."

Long after this, when the Lord had given success to the people of
Israel against their enemies and when Joshua was very old, he called
for the leaders of Israel—the elders, judges, and officers—and said to
them, "I am an old man now, and you have seen all that the Lord
your God has done for you during my lifetime. He has fought for you
against your enemies and has given you their land. And I have
divided to you the land of the nations yet unconquered as well as the
land of those you have already destroyed. All the land from the
Jordan River to the Mediterranean Sea shall be yours, for the Lord
your God will drive out all the people living there now, and you will
live there instead, just as he has promised you.

"But be very sure to follow all the instructions written in the book
of the laws of Moses; do not deviate from them the least little bit. Be
sure that you do not mix with the heathen people still remaining in
the land; do not even mention the names of their gods, much less
swear by them or worship them. But follow the Lord your God just as
you have until now. He has driven out great, strong nations from
before you, and no one has been able to defeat you. Each one of you
has put to flight a thousand of the enemy, for the Lord your God
fights for you, just as he has promised. So be very careful to keep on
loving him.

"Soon I will be going the way of all the earth—I am going to die.

"You know very well that God's promises to you have all come
true. But as certainly as the Lord has given you the good things he
promised, just as certainly he will bring evil upon you if you disobey
him. For if you worship other gods he will completely wipe you out
from this good land which the Lord has given you. His anger will rise
hot against you, and you will quickly perish."

Then Joshua summoned all the people of Israel to him at
Shechem, along with their leaders—the elders, officers, and judges. So
they came and presented themselves before God.

Then Joshua addressed them as follows: "The Lord God of Israel
says, 'Your ancestors, including Terah the father of Abraham and
Nahor, lived east of the Euphrates River; and they worshiped other
gods. But I took your father Abraham from that land across the river

and led him into the land of Canaan and gave him many descendants through Isaac his son. Isaac's children, whom I gave him, were Jacob and Esau. To Esau I gave the area around Mount Seir while Jacob and his children went into Egypt.

"'I gave you land you had not worked for and cities you did not build—these cities where you are now living. I gave you vineyards and olive groves for food, though you did not plant them.'

"So revere Jehovah and serve him in sincerity and truth. Put away forever the idols your ancestors worshiped when they lived beyond the Euphrates River and in Egypt. Worship the Lord alone. But if you are unwilling to obey the Lord, then decide today whom you will obey. Will it be the gods of your ancestors beyond the Euphrates or the gods of the Amorites here in this land? But as for me and my family, we will serve the Lord."

And the people replied, "We would never forsake the Lord and worship other gods! For the Lord our God is the one who rescued our fathers from their slavery in the land of Egypt. He is the God who did mighty miracles before the eyes of Israel, as we traveled through the wilderness, and preserved us from our enemies when we passed through their land. It was the Lord who drove out the Amorites and the other nations living here in the land. Yes, we choose the Lord, for he alone is our God."

"You have heard yourselves say it," Joshua said—"you have chosen to obey the Lord."

"Yes," they replied, "we are witnesses."

"All right," he said, "then you must destroy all the idols you now own, and you must obey the Lord God of Israel."

The people replied to Joshua, "Yes, we will worship and obey the Lord alone."

So Joshua made a covenant with them that day at Shechem, committing them to a permanent and binding contract between themselves and God. Joshua recorded the people's reply in the book of the laws of God, and took a huge stone as a reminder and rolled it beneath the oak tree that was beside the Tabernacle.

Then Joshua said to all the people, "This stone has heard everything the Lord said, so it will be a witness to testify against you if you go back on your word."

Then Joshua sent the people away to their own sections of the country.

Soon after this he died at the age of 110. He was buried on his own estate at Timnath-serah, in the hill country of Ephraim, on the north side of the mountains of Gaash.

Israel obeyed the Lord throughout the lifetimes of Joshua and the other old men who had personally witnessed the amazing deeds which the Lord had done for Israel.

**A Father of Influence instructs his children
to honor and serve the Lord.**

Boaz

RUTH 3:1—4:17 NIRV

Obed. Because Boaz was willing to take responsibility for his deceased kinsman's wife and marry her, he became the ancestor of King David and ultimately the ancestor of Jesus, the Savior.

One day Ruth's mother-in-law Naomi spoke to her. She said, "My daughter, shouldn't I try to find a secure place for you? Shouldn't you have peace and rest? Shouldn't I find a home where things will go well with you? You have been with the female servants of Boaz. He's a relative of ours. Tonight he'll be separating the straw from his barley on the threshing floor.

"So wash yourself. Put on some perfume. And put on your best clothes. Then go down to the threshing floor. But don't let Boaz know you are there. Wait until he has finished eating and drinking. Notice where he lies down. Then go over and uncover his feet. Lie down there. He'll tell you what to do."

"I'll do everything you say," Ruth answered. So she went down to the threshing floor. She did everything her mother-in-law had told her to do.

When Boaz had finished eating and drinking, he was in a good mood. He went over to lie down at the far end of the grain pile. Then Ruth approached quietly. She uncovered his feet and lay down there.

In the middle of the night, something surprised Boaz and woke him up. He turned and found a woman lying there at his feet.

"Who are you?" he asked.

"I'm Ruth," she said. "You are my family protector. So take good care of me by making me your wife."

"Dear woman, may the Lord bless you," he replied. "You are showing even more kindness now than you did earlier. You didn't run after the younger men, whether they were rich or poor. Dear woman, don't be afraid. I'll do for you everything you ask. All of the people of my town know that you are a noble woman.

"It's true that I'm a relative of yours. But there's a family protector who is more closely related to you than I am. So stay here for the night. In the morning if he wants to help you, good. Let him help you. But if he doesn't want to, then I'll do it. You can be sure that the Lord lives. And you can be just as sure that I'll help you. Lie down here until morning."

So she stayed at his feet until morning. But she got up before anyone could be recognized. Boaz thought, "No one must know that a woman came to the threshing floor."

He said to Ruth, "Bring me the coat you have around you. Hold it out." So she did. He poured more than fifty pounds of barley into it and helped her pick it up. Then he went back to town.

Ruth came to her mother-in-law. Naomi asked, "How did it go, my daughter?"

Then Ruth told her everything Boaz had done for her. She said, "He gave me all of this barley. He said, 'Don't go back to your mother-in-law with your hands empty.'"

Naomi said, "My daughter, sit down until you find out what happens. The man won't rest until he settles the whole matter today."

Boaz went up to the town gate and sat down there. The family protector he had talked about came by. Then Boaz said, "Come over here, my friend. Sit down." So the man went over and sat down.

Boaz brought ten of the elders of the town together. He said, "Sit down here." So they did.

Then he spoke to the family protector. He said, "Naomi has come back from Moab. She's selling the piece of land that belonged to our relative Elimelech. I thought I should bring the matter to your attention. I suggest that you buy the land while those who are sitting here and the elders of my people are looking on as witnesses.

"If you are willing to buy it back, do it. But if you aren't, tell me. Then I'll know. No one has the right to buy it back except you. And I'm next in line."

"I'll buy it," he said.

Then Boaz said, "When you buy the land from Naomi and Ruth, who is from Moab, you must get married to Ruth. She's the dead man's widow. So you must take her as your wife. His name must stay with his property."

When the family protector heard that, he said, "Then I can't buy the land. If I did, I might put my own property in danger. So you buy it. I can't do it."

In earlier times in Israel, there was a certain practice. It was used when family land was bought back and changed owners. The practice made the sale final. One person would take his sandal off and give it to the other. That was how people in Israel showed that a business matter had been settled.

So the family protector said to Boaz, "Buy it yourself." And he took his sandal off.

Then Boaz spoke to the elders and all of the people. He said, "Today you are witnesses. You have seen that I have bought land from Naomi. I have bought all of the property that had belonged to Elimelech, Kilion and Mahlon.

"I've also taken Ruth, who is from Moab, to become my wife. She is Mahlon's widow. I've decided to get married to her so the dead man's name will stay with his property. Now his name won't disappear from his family line. It won't disappear from the town records. Today you are witnesses!"

Then the elders and all who were at the gate spoke. They said, "We are witnesses. The woman is coming into your home. May the Lord make her to be like Rachel and Leah. Together they built up the nation of Israel. May you be an important person in Ephrathah. May you be famous in Bethlehem. The Lord will give you children through this young woman. May your family be like the family of Perez. He was the son Tamar had by Judah."

So Boaz got married to Ruth. She became his wife. Then he made love to her. The Lord blessed her so that she became pregnant. And she had a son.

The women said to Naomi, "We praise the Lord. Today he has provided a family protector for you. May this child become famous all over Israel! He will make your life new again. He'll take care of you when you are old. He's the son of your very own daughter-in-law. She loves you. She is better to you than seven sons."

Then Naomi put the child on her lap and took care of him. The women who were living there said, "Naomi has a son." They named him Obed. He was the father of Jesse. Jesse was the father of David.

**A Father of Influence takes responsibility
before God for his family.**

Job

JOB 1; 2; 42:7–17 MSG

The daughters of Job. Because he included his daughters in the inheritance he left to his children, he demonstrated that God has included women in the inheritance of faith and God's kingdom.

ob was a man who lived in Uz. He was honest inside and out, a man of his word, who was totally devoted to God and hated evil with a passion. He had seven sons and three daughters. He was also very wealthy—seven thousand head of sheep, three thousand camels, five hundred teams of oxen, five hundred donkeys, and a huge staff of servants—the most influential man in all the East!

His sons used to take turns hosting parties in their homes, always inviting their three sisters to join them in their merrymaking. When the parties were over, Job would get up early in the morning and sacrifice a burnt offering for each of his children, thinking, "Maybe one of them sinned by defying God inwardly." Job made a habit of this sacrificial atonement, just in case they'd sinned.

One day when the angels came to report to God, Satan, who was the Designated Accuser, came along with them. God singled out Satan and said, "What have you been up to?"

Satan answered God, "Going here and there, checking things out on earth."

God said to Satan, "Have you noticed my friend Job? There's no one quite like him—honest and true to his word, totally devoted to God and hating evil."

Satan retorted, "So do you think Job does all that out of the sheer goodness of his heart? Why, no one ever had it so good! You pamper him like a pet, make sure nothing bad ever happens to him or his family or his possessions, bless everything he does—he can't lose!

"But what do you think would happen if you reached down and took away everything that is his? He'd curse you right to your face, that's what."

God replied, "We'll see. Go ahead—do what you want with all that is his. Just don't hurt him." Then Satan left the presence of God.

Sometime later, while Job's children were having one of their parties at the home of the oldest son, a messenger came to Job and said, "The oxen were plowing and the donkeys grazing in the field next to us when Sabeans attacked. They stole the animals and killed the field hands. I'm the only one to get out alive and tell you what happened."

While he was still talking, another messenger arrived and said, "Bolts of lightning struck the sheep and the shepherds and fried them—burned them to a crisp. I'm the only one to get out alive and tell you what happened."

While he was still talking, another messenger arrived and said, "Chaldeans coming from three directions raided the camels and massacred the camel drivers. I'm the only one to get out alive and tell you what happened."

While he was still talking, another messenger arrived and said, "Your children were having a party at the home of the oldest brother when a tornado swept in off the desert and struck the house. It collapsed on the young people and they died. I'm the only one to get out alive and tell you what happened."

Job got to his feet, ripped his robe, shaved his head, then fell to the ground and worshiped:

Naked I came from my mother's womb,
naked I'll return to the womb of the earth.
God gives, God takes.
God's name be ever blessed.

Not once through all this did Job sin; not once did he blame God.

One day when the angels came to report to God, Satan also showed up. God singled out Satan, saying, "And what have you

been up to?" Satan answered God, "Oh, going here and there, checking things out." Then God said to Satan, "Have you noticed my
friend Job? There's no one quite like him, is there—honest and true
to his word, totally devoted to God and hating evil? He still has a
firm grip on his integrity! You tried to trick me into destroying him,
but it didn't work."

Satan answered, "A human would do anything to save his life. But
what do you think would happen if you reached down and took away
his health? He'd curse you to your face, that's what."

God said, "All right. Go ahead—you can do what you like with
him. But mind you, don't kill him."

Satan left God and struck Job with terrible sores. Job was ulcers
and scabs from head to foot. They itched and oozed so badly that he
took a piece of broken pottery to scrape himself, then went and sat on
a trash heap, among the ashes.

His wife said, "Still holding on to your precious integrity, are you?
Curse God and be done with it!"

He told her, "You're talking like an empty-headed fool. We take
the good days from God—why not also the bad days?"

Not once through all this did Job sin. He said nothing against
God.

Three of Job's friends heard of all the trouble that had fallen on
him. Each traveled from his own country—Eliphaz from Teman,
Bildad from Shuhah, Zophar from Naamath—and went together to
Job to keep him company and comfort him. When they first caught
sight of him, they couldn't believe what they saw—they hardly recognized him! They cried out in lament, ripped their robes, and
dumped dirt on their heads as a sign of their grief. Then they sat
with him on the ground. Seven days and nights they sat there without saying a word. They could see how rotten he felt, how deeply he
was suffering.

After GOD had finished addressing Job, he turned to Eliphaz the
Temanite and said, "I've had it with you and your two friends. I'm fed
up! You haven't been honest either with me or about me—not the
way my friend Job has. So here's what you must do. Take seven bulls

and seven rams, and go to my friend Job. Sacrifice a burnt offering on your own behalf. My friend Job will pray for you, and I will accept his prayer. He will ask me not to treat you as you deserve for talking nonsense about me, and for not being honest with me, as he has."

They did it. Eliphaz the Temanite, Bildad the Shuhite, and Zophar the Naamathite did what GOD commanded. And GOD accepted Job's prayer.

After Job had interceded for his friends, GOD restored his fortune—and then doubled it! All his brothers and sisters and friends came to his house and celebrated. They told him how sorry they were, and consoled him for all the trouble GOD had brought him. Each of them brought generous housewarming gifts.

GOD blessed Job's later life even more than his earlier life. He ended up with fourteen thousand sheep, six thousand camels, one thousand teams of oxen, and one thousand donkeys. He also had seven sons and three daughters. He named the first daughter Dove, the second, Cinnamon, and the third, Darkeyes. There was not a woman in that country as beautiful as Job's daughters. Their father treated them as equals with their brothers, providing the same inheritance.

Job lived on another 140 years, living to see his children and grandchildren—four generations of them! Then he died—an old man, a full life.

A Father of Influence deals justly with his children.

Elkanah

1 SAMUEL 1:1–28; 2:11; 3:19–21 TLB

Samuel. Because Elkanah honored his wife's vow to God,

Samuel became a great prophet of Israel.

This is the story of Elkanah, a man of the tribe of Ephraim who lived in Ramathaim-zophim, in the hills of Ephraim.

He had two wives, Hannah and Peninnah. Peninnah had some children, but Hannah didn't.

Each year Elkanah and his families journeyed to the Tabernacle at Shiloh to worship the Lord of the heavens and to sacrifice to him. (The priests on duty at that time were the two sons of Eli— Hophni and Phinehas.) On the day he presented his sacrifice, Elkanah would celebrate the happy occasion by giving presents to Peninnah and her children; but although he loved Hannah very much, he could give her only one present, for the Lord had sealed her womb; so she had no children to give presents to. Peninnah made matters worse by taunting Hannah because of her barrenness. Every year it was the same—Peninnah scoffing and laughing at her as they went to Shiloh, making her cry so much she couldn't eat.

"What's the matter, Hannah?" Elkanah would exclaim. "Why aren't you eating? Why make such a fuss over having no children? Isn't having me better than having ten sons?"

One evening after supper, when they were at Shiloh, Hannah went over to the Tabernacle. Eli the priest was sitting at his customary place beside the entrance. She was in deep anguish and was crying bitterly as she prayed to the Lord.

And she made this vow: "O Lord of heaven, if you will look down upon my sorrow and answer my prayer and give me a son, then I will give him back to you, and he'll be yours for his entire lifetime, and his hair shall never be cut."

Eli noticed her mouth moving as she was praying silently and, hearing no sound, thought she had been drinking.

"Must you come here drunk?" he demanded. "Throw away your bottle."

"Oh, no, sir!" she replied, "I'm not drunk! But I am very sad and I was pouring out my heart to the Lord. Please don't think that I am just some drunken bum!"

"In that case," Eli said, "cheer up! May the Lord of Israel grant you your petition, whatever it is!"

"Oh, thank you, sir!" she exclaimed, and went happily back, and began to take her meals again.

The entire family was up early the next morning and went to the Tabernacle to worship the Lord once more. Then they returned home to Ramah, and when Elkanah slept with Hannah, the Lord remembered her petition; in the process of time, a baby boy was born to her. She named him Samuel (meaning "asked of God") because, as she said, "I asked the Lord for him."

The next year Elkanah and Peninnah and her children went on the annual trip to the Tabernacle without Hannah, for she told her husband, "Wait until the baby is weaned, and then I will take him to the Tabernacle and leave him there."

"Well, whatever you think best," Elkanah agreed. "May the Lord's will be done."

So she stayed home until the baby was weaned. Then, though he was still so small, they took him to the Tabernacle in Shiloh, along with a three-year-old bull for the sacrifice, and a bushel of flour and some wine. After the sacrifice they took the child to Eli.

"Sir, do you remember me?" Hannah asked him. "I am the woman who stood here that time praying to the Lord! I asked him to give me this child, and he has given me my request; and now I am giving him to the Lord for as long as he lives." So she left him there at the Tabernacle for the Lord to use.

So they returned home to Ramah without Samuel; and the child became the Lord's helper, for he assisted Eli the priest.

As Samuel grew, the Lord was with him and people listened carefully to his advice. And all Israel from [one end of the land to the other] knew that Samuel was going to be a prophet of the Lord. Then the Lord began to give messages to him there at the Tabernacle in Shiloh, and he passed them on to the people of Israel.

A Father of Influence honors God's call on his children's lives.

Jesse

1 SAMUEL 16; 2 SAMUEL 2:1–4; 5:1–5 NIRV

King David. Because his father taught his sons to fight for

their country, David became a great warrior king.

The Lord said to Samuel, "How long will you be filled with sorrow because of Saul? I have refused to have him as king over Israel. Fill your animal horn with olive oil and go on your way. I am sending you to Jesse in Bethlehem. I have chosen one of his sons to be king."

But Samuel said, "How can I go? Saul will hear about it. Then he'll kill me."

The Lord said, "Take a young cow with you. Tell the elders of Bethlehem, 'I've come to offer a sacrifice to the Lord.' Invite Jesse to the sacrifice. Then I will show you what to do. You must anoint for me the one I point out to you."

Samuel did what the Lord said. He arrived at Bethlehem. The elders of the town met him. They were trembling with fear. They asked, "Have you come in peace?"

Samuel replied, "Yes, I've come in peace. I've come to offer a sacrifice to the Lord. Set yourselves apart to him and come to the sacrifice with me."

Then he set Jesse and his sons apart to the Lord. He invited them to the sacrifice.

When they arrived, Samuel saw Eliab. He thought, "This has to be the one the Lord wants me to anoint for him."

But the Lord said to Samuel, "Do not consider how handsome or tall he is. I have not chosen him. I do not look at the things people look at. Man looks at how someone appears on the outside. But I look at what is in the heart."

Then Jesse called for Abinadab. He had him walk in front of Samuel. But Samuel said, "The Lord hasn't chosen him either."

Then Jesse had Shammah walk by. But Samuel said, "The Lord hasn't chosen him either."

Jesse had seven of his sons walk in front of Samuel. But Samuel said to him, "The Lord hasn't chosen any of them." So he asked Jesse, "Are these the only sons you have?"

"No," Jesse answered. "My youngest son is taking care of the sheep."

Samuel said, "Send for him. We won't sit down to eat until he arrives."

So Jesse sent for his son and had him brought in. His skin was tanned. He had a fine appearance and handsome features.

Then the Lord said, "Get up and anoint him. He is the one."

So Samuel got the animal horn that was filled with olive oil. He anointed David in front of his brothers. From that day on, the Spirit of the Lord came on David with power. Samuel went back to Ramah.

The Spirit of the Lord had left Saul. And an evil spirit that was sent by the Lord terrified him.

Saul's attendants said to him, "An evil spirit that was sent by God is terrifying you. Give us an order to look for someone who can play the harp. He will play it when the evil spirit that was sent by God comes on you. Then you will feel better."

So Saul said to his attendants, "Find someone who plays the harp well. Bring him to me."

One of the servants said, "I've seen someone who knows how to play the harp. He is a son of Jesse from Bethlehem. He's a brave man. He would make a good soldier. He's a good speaker. He's very handsome. And the Lord is with him."

Then Saul sent messengers to Jesse. He said, "Send me your son David, the one who takes care of your sheep."

So Jesse got some bread and a bottle of wine. The bottle was made out of animal skin. He also got a young goat. He loaded everything on the back of a donkey. He sent all of it to Saul with his son David.

David went to Saul and began to serve him. Saul liked him very much. David became one of the men who carried Saul's armor.

Saul sent a message to Jesse. It said, "Let David stay here. I want him to serve me. I'm pleased with him."

When the evil spirit that was sent by God would come on Saul, David would get his harp and play it. That would help Saul. He would feel better, and the evil spirit would leave him.

After Saul and Jonathan [Saul's son] died, David asked the LORD for advice. "Should I go up to one of the towns of Judah?" he asked.

The LORD said, "Go up."

David asked, "Where should I go?"

"To Hebron," the LORD answered.

So David went up there with his two wives. Their names were Ahinoam from Jezreel and Abigail from Carmel. Abigail was Nabal's widow. David also took his men and their families with him. They settled down in Hebron and its towns.

Then the men of Judah came to Hebron. There they anointed David to be king over the people of Judah.

All of the tribes of Israel came to see David at Hebron. They said, "We are your own flesh and blood. In the past, Saul was our king. But you led the men of Israel on their military campaigns. And the LORD said to you, 'You will be the shepherd over my people Israel. You will become their ruler.'"

All of the elders of Israel came to see King David at Hebron. There the king made a covenant with them in the sight of the LORD. They anointed David as king over Israel.

David was 30 years old when he became king. He ruled for 40 years. In Hebron he ruled over Judah for seven and a half years. In Jerusalem he ruled over all of Israel and Judah for 33 years.

**A Father of Influence teaches his children
to fight for their country.**

List of Sources

Aitken, Jonathan. *Charles W. Colson: A Life Redeemed*. Colorado Springs: Waterbrook Press, 2005.

Anderson, William. *Laura Ingalls Wilder: A Biography*. New York: Harper Trophy, 1992.

Assayas, Michka. *Bono: In Conversations with Michka Assayas*. New York: Riverhead Books, 2005.

Ben-Artzi Pelosoff, Noa. *In the Name of Sorrow and Hope*. New York: Schocken, 1997.

Benge, Janet, and Geoff Benge. *Eric Liddell: Something Greater than Gold*. Seattle: YWAM Publishing, 1998.

Bernstein, Jeremy. *Albert Einstein and the Frontiers of Physics*. Oxford, England: Oxford University Press, 1996.

Bowden, Bobby, and Terry Bowden. *Winning's Only Part of the Game: Lessons of Life and Football*. New York: Warner Books, 1996.

Bush, George W. *George W. Bush on God and Country: The President Speaks Out About Faith, Principle, and Patriotism*. Grand Rapids: Allegiance Press, 2004.

Buss, Dale. *Family Man: The Biography of James Dobson*. Carol Stream, IL: Tyndale, 2006.

Brough, James. *The Ford Dynasty: An American Story*. New York: Doubleday, 1977.

Cash, Johnny, and Patrick Carr. *Cash: The Autobiography*. San Francisco: Harper, 1997.

Churchill, Winston, and William Manchester. *My Early Life: 1874-1904*. New York: Scribner, 1996.

Colson, Charles W. *Born Again*. Grand Rapids: Chosen, 2004.

Cunningham, Loren, and Janice Rogers. *Is That Really You, God?* Seattle: YWAM Publishing, 1984.

DeMille, Cecil B. *The Autobiography of Cecil B. DeMille*. London: Taylor & Francis, 1984.

Dewey, Donald. *James Stewart: A Biography*. Atlanta: Turner Publishing, 1996.

Dobson, Ryan and Jefferson Scott. *Be Intolerant: Because Some Things Are Just Stupid*. Sisters, OR: Multnomah, 2003.

Eareckson Tada, Joni. *Joni*. Grand Rapids: Zondervan, 2001.

Felix, Antonia. *Condi: The Condoleezza Rice Story*. London: Pocket, 2004.

Flannagan, Roy. *John Milton: A Short Introduction*. Oxford, England: Blackwell Publishing, 2002.

Finch, Christopher. *Jim Henson: The Works: The Art, the Magic, the Imagination*. New York: Random House, 1993.

Freedman, Russell, and Orville and Wilbur Wright. *The Wright Brothers: How They Invented the Airplane*. New York: Holiday House, 1994.

Gherman, Beverly. *Jimmy Carter*. Minneapolis: Lerner Publications, 2004.

Goldenstern, Joyce. *Albert Einstein: Physicist and Genius*. Berkley Heights, NJ: Enslow Publishers, 1995.

Graham, Billy. *Just As I Am: The Autobiography of Billy Graham*. San Francisco: Harper, 1997.

Graham, Franklin. *Rebel With a Cause*. Nashville: Nelson Books, 1997.

Hearn, Marcus, and Ron Howard. *The Cinema of George Lucas*. New York: Harry N. Abrams, 2005.

Heaton, Patricia. *Motherhood & Hollywood: How to Get a Job Like Mine*. New York: Villard, 2002.

Henson, Jim. *It's Not Easy Being Green: And Other Things to Consider*. New York: Hyperion, 2005.

Hill, Anne. *Denzel Washington*. Philadelphia: Chelsea House Publishers, 1999.

Husband, Evelyn, and Donna Vanliere. *High Calling: The Courageous Life and Faith of Space Shuttle Columbia Commander Rick Husband*. Nashville: Nelson Books, 2004.

January, Brendan. *George Washington: America's First President*. New York: Children's Press Scholastic, 2003.

Jordan, Michael, and Mark Vancil. *Driven From Within*. New York: Atria Books, 2005.

———. For the Love of the Game: My Story. New York: Crown, 1998.

Kent, Deborah. Jimmy Carter. New York: Children's Press Scholastic, 2005.

King Jr., Martin Luther, and James M. Washington. A Testament of Hope: The Essential Writings and Speeches of Martin Luther King Jr. San Francisco: Harper, 1990.

King Jr., Martin Luther, and Clayborne Carson. The Autobiography of Martin Luther King Jr. New York: Warner Books, 2001.

Lynch, Doris. J. R. R. Tolkien: Creator of Languages and Legends. New York: Franklin Watts Scholastic, 2003.

Mair, George. A Life with Purpose: Reverend Rick Warren. New York: Berkley Books, 2005.

Mandela, Nelson. A Long Walk to Freedom. London: Abacus, 1995.

Mangalwadi, Vishal, and Ruth Mangalwadi. The Legacy of William Carey. Wheaton, IL: Crossway Books, 1999.

Mansfield, Stephen. The Faith of George W. Bush. Los Angeles: Tarcher, 2003.

Mara, Wil. Henry Ford (Rookie Biographies). New York: Children's Press Scholastic, 2004.

McFeely, William. Frederick Douglass. New York: W. W. Norton & Company, 1995.

McMurry, Linda O. George Washington Carver: Scientist and Symbol. Oxford, England: Oxford University Press, 1982.

McNeer, May, and Lynd War. Martin Luther. New York: Abingdon-Cokesbury Press, 1953.

McPherson, Joyce. A Piece of the Mountain: The Story of Blaise Pascal. Sheffield, England: Greenleaf Press, 1997.

Meyers, Jeffrey. Gary Cooper: American Hero. New York: William Morris, 1998.

Miler, Douglas T. Frederick Douglass and the Fight for Freedom. New York: Facts on File Publication, 1988.

Milne, Christopher. The Enchanted Places. New York: E.P. Dutton & Co., 1974.

Osteen, Joel. Your Best Life Now: 7 Steps to Living at Your Full Potential. New York: Warner Faith, 2004.

Otfinoski, Steven. Abraham Lincoln: America's 16th President. New York: Children's Press Scholastic, 2004.

Otfinoski, Steven. Harry S. Truman. New York: Children's Press Scholastic, 2005.

Parish, James Robert. Jim Henson: Puppeteer and Filmmaker. New York: Ferguson Publishing Company, 2006.

Payton, Walter, and Don Yaeger. Never Die Easy. New York: Villard, 2000.

Petty, Richard. King Richard I. New York: Macmilland & Co., 1986.

Pollock, Dale. Skywalking: The Life and Films of George Lucas. Cambridge, MA: Da Capo Press, 1999.

Reynolds, Quintin. The Wright Brothers. New York: Random House, 1981.

Richardson, Michael. Amazing Faith: The Authorized Biography of Bill Bright. Colorado Springs: Waterbrook Press, 2001.

Roberts, Jeremy. George Washington. Minneapolis: Lerner Publications, 2004.

———. Abraham Lincoln. Minneapolis: Lerner Publications, 2004.

Roberts, Oral. Expect a Miracle: My Life and Ministry. Nashville: Nelson Books, 1998.

Rogers, Judith. Winston Churchill. New York: Chelsea House Publishers, 1986.

Russell, Sharman Apt. Frederick Douglass: Abolitionist Editor. New York: Chelsea House Publishers, 1988.

Russert, Tim. Big Russ and Me: Father and Son-Lessons of Life. New York: Miramax Books, 2004.

———. Wisdom of Our Fathers: Lessons and Letters from Daughters and Sons. New York: Random House, 2006.

Saint, Steve. End of the Spear: A True Story. Carol Stream, IL: SaltRiver, 2005.

Shippey, T. A. J. R. R. Tolkien: Author of the Century. Boston: Houghton Mifflin Co., 2001.

Silverman, Kenneth. The Life and Times of Cotton Mather. New York: Welcome Rain, 2001.

Stewart, Mark, and Mike Kennedy. *Hammering Hank: How the Media Made Henry Aaron*. Guilford, NC: The Lyons Press, 2006.

Swindell, Larry. *The Last Hero: A Biography of Gary Cooper*. New York: Doubleday, 1980.

Ten Boom, Corrie. *Tramp for the Lord*. Fort Washington, PA: Christian Literature Crusade, 1974.

Ten Boom, Corrie, and John and Elizabeth Sherill. *The Hiding Place*. Old Tappan, NJ: Spire Books, 1971.

Thwaite, Ann. *A. A. Milne: The Man Behind Winnie-the-Pooh*. New York: Random House, 1990.

Trimble, Vance H. *Sam Walton: Founder of Wal-Mart*. New York: A Dutton Book, 1990.

Truman, Margaret. *Harry S. Truman*. New York: William Morrow & Company, Inc., 1973.

Turner, Steve. *The Man Called Cash*. Nashville: W Publishing Group, 2005.

Walton, Sam, and John Huey. *Sam Walton: Made in America*. New York: Doubleday, 1992.

Warren, Rick. *The Purpose-Driven Life: What on Earth Am I Here For?* Grand Rapids: Zondervan, 2002.

Wight, Jim. *The Real James Herriot*. New York: Penguin Books, 2000.

Wooden, John. *They Call Me Coach*. New York: McGraw-Hill, 2003.

Also available from Honor Books:

Mothers of Influence

If you have enjoyed this book or
if it has had an impact on your life,
we would like to hear from you.

Please contact us at

Honor Books
Dept. 201
4050 Lee Vance View
Colorado Springs, CO 80918

Or visit our Web site
www.cookministries.com

Inspiration and Motivation for the Seasons of Life